Industrialization of China and India

Their impacts on the world economy

Edited by Nobuharu Yokokawa, Jayati Ghosh and Robert Rowthorn

Routledge
Taylor & Francis Group
LONDON AND NEW YORK

First published 2013
by Routledge
2 Park Square, Milton Park, Abingdon, Oxon OX14 4RN

Simultaneously published in the USA and Canada
by Routledge
711 Third Avenue, New York, NY 10017

Routledge is an imprint of the Taylor & Francis Group, an informa business

British Library Cataloguing in Publication Data
A catalogue record for this book is available from the British Library

Library of Congress Cataloging in Publication Data
Industrialization of China and India : their impacts on the world economy / edited by Nobuharu Yokokawa, Jayati Ghosh, and Robert Rowthorn.
p. cm.
Includes bibliographical references and index.
1. Industrialization–China. 2. industries–China. 3. Industrialization–India. 4. Industries–India. I. Yokokawa, Nobuharu, 1950– II. Ghosh, Jayati. III. Rowthorn, Bob.
HC427.6.I53 2013
338.951–dc23 2012043530

ISBN: 978-0-415-69947-1 (hbk)
ISBN: 978-0-203-51748-2 (ebk)

Typeset in Times New Roman
by Wearset Ltd, Boldon, Tyne and Wear

Contents

Illustrations

Figures

Tables

Contributors

C. P. Chandrasekhar is Professor at the Centre for Economic Studies and Planning, Jawaharlal Nehru University, New Delhi. His areas of interest include the role of finance and industry in development and the experience with fiscal, financial and industrial policy reform in developing countries. He is the co-author of *Crisis as Conquest: Learning from East Asi*a (Orient Longman), *The Market That Failed: Neo-liberal Economic Reforms in India* (Leftword Books) and *Promoting ICT for Human Development: India* (Elsevier). He is a founding Executive Committee Member of International Development Economics Associates and plays an important role in managing its outreach activities. He is a regular columnist for *Frontline* (titled Economic Perspectives) and *Business Line* (titled Macroscan).

Hideki Esho is Professor of Development Economics, Faculty of Economics, Hosei University, Tokyo. He was Dean of the Faculty of Economics from 2005 to 2007 and President of the Japan Society for International Development from 2002 to 2005. He won the 1988 Development Studies Award for his work *India's Economic Development* and the 1998 International Development Studies Okita Award for his work *Political Economy of Development*.

Jayati Ghosh is Professor of Economics at the Centre for Economic Studies and Planning, School of Social Sciences, Jawaharlal Nehru University, New Delhi. She was educated at Delhi University, Jawaharlal Nehru University and the University of Cambridge, England, where she obtained her PhD in 1983. Since 2002, she has been Executive Secretary of International Development Economics Associates (IDEAs), an international network of heterodox development economists (www.networkideas.org). She is Founding Trustee of the Economic Research Foundation (www.macroscan.org). She received the NordSud Prize for Social Sciences 2010 of the Fondazione Pescarabruzzo, Italy, and was awarded the ILO Decent Work Research Prize for 2010.

Hiroshi Itagaki is Professor of International Business at the Faculty of Economics, Musashi University. His books and articles include *The Japanese Production System: Hybrid Factories in East Asia* (Macmillan, 1997), 'Competitiveness, localization and Japanese companies in China: realities and alternate approaches', *Asia Pacific Business Review*, 15 (3), 2009, and *A Comparative Study of Japanese, Korean and Taiwanese Companies in China* (in Japanese; Minerva Shobo, 2010). He has received an award from the Trade Promotion Foundation.

Makoto Itoh was Professor of Political Economy at the University of Tokyo. He has also taught widely at many universities abroad, including the New School for Social Research, New York University, Cambridge University, the University of London, Greenwich University, the University of Sydney, York University (Canada) and Shanghai University of Economics and Finance. His books include *Value and Crisis*, *The Basic Theory of Capitalism*, *The World Economic Crisis and Japanese Capitalism* and *Political Economy for Socialism*. He was granted the Marxian Economics Award by the World Association for Political Economy in 2012.

Dic Lo is Reader in Economics at the School of Oriental and African Studies (SOAS), University of London, and Co-director of the Centre of Research in Comparative Political Economy, Renmin University of China. His research focuses on China's economic transformation, globalization, and comparative studies of political economy. His recent publications include *Alternatives to Neoliberal Globalization: Studies in the Political Economy of Institutions and Late Development* (Palgrave Macmillan, 2012). He is co-editor of the quarterly journal *China Review of Political Economy*.

Tomoo Marukawa is Professor of Chinese Economy, Institute of Social Science, University of Tokyo. His work focuses on the Chinese economy and industry. His books include *Can We Live without China?* (2009), *Contemporary Chinese Industries* (2007), *Structural Changes in the Labor Market* (2002) and *The Dynamics of Market Development* (1999).

Robert Rowthorn is Emeritus Professor of Economics and Fellow of King's College, Cambridge. He is the author of a number of academic articles on economic growth, structural change, international investment and the balance of payments. His books include *De-industrialisation and Foreign Trade* (with John Wells). He has been a consultant on these topics for a variety of bodies, including the International Monetary Fund, the UN Commission on Trade and Development, the International Labour Organization and the British government.

Nobuharu Yokokawa is Professor of Economics at Musashi University, Tokyo, Japan. He was educated at Shiga University (BA), the University of Tokyo (MSc) and Cambridge University (PhD). His publications include *Value, Employment and Crisis* (in Japanese, *Shakai Hyouron Sya*). He has co-edited *Capitalism in Evolution* (Edward Elgar) and *Crises of Global Economies and the Future of Capitalism: Reviving Marxian Crisis Theory* (Routledge). Since 2007, he has been editor of the *Uno Theory Newsletter*. He is Chairman of the JSPE Committee for International Communication and Exchange.

Acknowledgements

The editors of this volume would like to thank Musashi University for financing the research project on the industrialization of China and India since 2005, and financing the international conference on the industrialization of China and India and its impact on the world economy in 2010. We are also grateful to Ocyanomizu Shobo, which published the Japanese edition of *Industrialization of China and India* in 2010 and kindly allowed us to use parts of the text for this updated and extended English edition. We thank the contributors to the Japanese edition, including Professors Zhijia Yuan, Yuko Nikaido, Sanae Ohno and Jyunko Maru. We thank Yongling Lam, our editor at Routledge, for her help.

Introduction

Nobuharu Yokokawa, Jayati Ghosh and Robert Rowthorn

Global capitalism has always been a dynamic and constantly mutating system, but even so, the dramatic changes witnessed in its geographical spread during the past two decades may be the most significant that have occurred over the previous century. After a long period during which the early-twentieth-century division of labour was cemented and reinforced, a new international division of labour is being established with the emergence of populous and potentially large developing economies as major players on the world scene. While several emerging economies in different parts of the world are increasingly important, the rise and economic diversification of China and India is of special significance because of their sheer size and future potential in terms of directing the course of global economic affairs. In this context, certain questions become very pressing. How sustainable is the economic rise of China and India? What problems and prospects does the current industrialization process in these countries generate? How will it impact on the developed world, in Asia (countries like Japan) and Europe and North America? Does a continued improvement in the material conditions of the majority of people in China and India, and more equitable sharing of the gains, require a change in their growth strategies?

This book provides a fresh set of perspectives on some of these central questions. Contributions from eminent economists from Japan, China, India and Europe shed light on the answers to all of these questions and more. While based on solid research, the chapters of this volume are written in an accessible style so as to appeal to wider audiences. Before we provide an overview of the contributions, we need to consider what makes this book distinctive. Given the recent explosion of literature on this subject, why do we provide yet another book on China and India? What does this book have to say that hasn't already been said elsewhere?

For obvious reasons, the questions outlined above have already been addressed in the burgeoning literature. Indeed, books describing the industrialization of China and India have proliferated in number and approach over the past decade. Nonetheless, this book makes a unique contribution because of the particular political economy perspective that is brought to bear on the subject by the various authors who analyse the issues from both global and regional angles.

Within the extant literature, Winters and Yusuf's book (2007) is among the substantial works published on the industrialization of China and India and the impact on the world economy. It contains a great deal of data pertaining to the period up to 2005, together with simulations and projections. However, this book was published before the recent economic crisis, and much of its analysis has been overtaken by subsequent global events. Minqi Li (2008) offers a rare attempt to study the systemic impact of the rise of China on the capitalist world economy. There are other books that deal with accumulation and growth processes within China and India, and the patterns of integration of these economies with the global economy. However, a dominant theme in many of them is the somewhat simplistic idea that trade and investment openness and consequent income growth will solve most of China's or India's economic problems. Such analysis tends to underplay the association of the recent economic boom with a significant increase in inequalities, the slow and halting nature of the improvement in conditions of life for the bulk of the population as well as the difficulties of sustaining this particular pattern of output growth.

This book provides new perspectives on recent Asian dynamism that go beyond the mainstream views by attempting to situate the recent economic expansion within a broader analysis of capitalist accumulation and the various processes that it generates both within and across economies. The contributions include analyses of recent growth patterns in both China and India; assessments of the sustainability of such growth and potential constraints and pitfalls; the role of international finance in affecting both national and international growth and employment patterns; the factors determining particular accumulation strategies; and the results of these strategies. These forces within the two economies of China and India are situated within a broader assessment of the impacts on the world economy that identifies the broader tendencies in international capitalism and changing patterns of uneven development. Specific issues emerging within the Asian region are pinpointed, including not just the relations between the three large Asian economies but also the wider geopolitical implications as well as the political economy of these changes. Some of the arguments are briefly summarized in what follows

This book is the outcome of a project on China and India that started in 2005 in Japan. A book based on seminars and public lectures held at Musashi University from 2005 to 2008 was published in 2010 in Japanese. Thereafter, an international conference was held at Musashi University in November 2010. This book contains revised and updated versions of papers presented at the conference.

In addition to contributions from distinguished experts from other countries, Japanese political economists are well represented in this book. Japan has been an important laboratory for developing and debating ideas about capitalism and its dynamics. There are diverse approaches to political economy as well as several distinct strands of Marxian political economy in Japan, foremost among which is the Uno School, whose influence is also evident in this volume. Therefore, this volume also makes high-quality Japanese studies on China and India available to an English-language readership.

The first part of the book considers the re-emergence of China and India and its impact on advanced economies. Robert Rowthorn presents projections of the future economic growth of China and India, and considers what the development of these countries implies for today's advanced economies. China's huge trade surplus may be a serious problem in the short term, but other issues will become more important over the longer term. Over time, the international terms of trade are likely to shift against the advanced economies. China will gradually cease to be an exporter of cheap, labour-intensive goods, so the advanced countries will have to find alternative, perhaps more expensive sources of supply. World commodity prices may rise because of increased demand from China and India for energy, minerals and the like. Future commodity prices are hard to predict, but the loss to the global North in this form is potentially much greater than the loss of cheap imports from China. In aggregate terms, it is uncertain how far the growth of China and India will damage the existing advanced economies, but it is bound to provoke structural changes that are harmful to particular subgroups of people. Economists tend to regard such effects as temporary adjustment costs, but the modern experience of deindustrialization indicates that the effects of structural change may last for generations and be very painful to the communities involved. Dealing with these structural changes in a humane fashion may be one of the greatest economic challenges posed by the rise of China and India.

Nobuharu Yokokawa builds a dynamic theory of comparative advantage. He starts by examining Ricardo's theory of comparative advantage, which explains comparative advantage if there is no productivity growth. In the real world, countries that specialize in dynamic industries with increasing returns make gains, and those which specialize in decreasing returns lose. In dynamic industries, value added per unit of labour (VAL) increases with the increase in productivity and then eventually decreases, since the volume of product increases with productivity growth, but value added per product will eventually decrease with diffusion of technology and the falling relative price of the product. Dynamic comparative advantage does not last for ever, because of the eventual decrease of VAL and increases in wages. Countries have to make their industrial structures more sophisticated, and move to new dynamic industries to keep their international status. Yokokawa investigates various historical experiences using this framework, including the reindustrialization of Europe and Japan to catch up with US productivity in the golden age, and the 'flying geese' pattern of development in East Asia from the mid-1970s to the mid-1980s, current account surplus reversals in East Asia, and compressed and quasi-Lewis-type industrialization in China. Finally, he considers the possibility of a global flying geese pattern of industrialization, with China as the engine of growth.

C. P. Chandrasekhar investigates the rapid growth of exports of hi-tech manufactured products from China and software and IT-enabled services from India. Such growth has given rise to the perception that 'knowledge capital' plays a crucial role in the increasing global presence of these countries. However, Chandrasekhar argues that it is necessary to distinguish between the generation and control of knowledge and the production of goods and services. He shows that transnational corporations from the advanced countries, through their control over knowledge, are able to exploit the opportunities offered by the knowledge economy, whereas the talents of countries like China and India are being used to strengthen the control over knowledge of these transnational firms. He concludes that there is a new international division of labour emerging, in which knowledge is controlled by firms in the developed countries even while the production of knowledge-based industries and services moves to countries such as India and China.

Hiroshi Itagaki focuses on the industrialization of China and India, and its impact on Japanese manufacturing companies. Their industrialization has common as well as distinct features. The commonality is their unprecedentedly rapid absorption of technologies. However, the types of technology absorption are different from each other. Chinese companies emphasize the importance of taking advantage of new business opportunities strategically by copying superficial features of products from advanced countries. In contrast, some Indian companies, represented by automobile or motorcycle manufacturers, have absorbed and accumulated technologies from key components to finished products step by step. The rapid industrialization of China and India poses not only threats but also a new business frontier for Japanese companies. The implications of this frontier vary, however, depending on the characteristics of technology absorption of two countries. Japanese companies may exploit a division of labour with Chinese firms that behave in a different manner from Japanese ones. On the other hand, Japanese companies can expect partnership with Indian firms, whose approach to technology shows some similarities.

The contributions in the second part of the book focus on China. Dic Lo examines the interaction between China and the world economy since the turn of the century, which, he argues, has been of great importance in shaping the direction of globalization. He focuses on scholarly debates on the structural dynamics behind this interaction. The neo-liberal theory of 'China causing global imbalances' asserts that China's mode of integration into the world market has been of detriment to the economies of the advanced countries. In contrast, left-wing critical scholars tend to argue that China is facing internal and external dependence, which is damaging the economic development of China itself, together with that of many developing economies. Lo disagrees with both of the two theories. He concludes his chapter by presenting an alternative policy approach that is better suited to the needs of the social and economic development of China and the rest of the developing world.

Tomoo Marukawa argues that although the Chinese economy is often characterized in terms of the strong involvement of the state in the market, an examination of China's total industrial output shows that the private sector's share is steadily increasing and the state-owned sector's share is consistently declining. He sheds light on the dynamic side of the Chinese economy: the private sector, especially 'mass capitalism', in which even ordinary people with only a limited amount of money and human capital can become firm owners. He argues that the 'mass capitalistic' side of the Chinese economy deserves as much attention as its 'state capitalistic' side. He then investigates the present status of the private sector in the Chinese economy: the rise of mass capitalism in Wenzhou and the spread of mass capitalism from Wenzhou to other parts of the country, along with migration of the residents of Wenzhou; the rise of the 'guerrilla handset' industry in Shenzhen; and the spread of mass capitalism to other industries.

Makoto Itoh considers the theoretical possibilities for constructing a socialist market economy in China. He argues that the forms of market economy have a historical nature much broader and older than the capitalist relations of production and that market economies have existed even in communal societies. He points out that public ownership and state-led industrial policy have facilitated organizational and technological innovation. He then investigates the possibility of a socialist labour market which would enable the flexible and efficient movement of workers across workplaces, and at the same time provide solid social security and stability of economic life for workers as masters of society. He is optimistic that such a strategy will become more prevalent in China, as he observes signs of political endeavour to alter the increased economic inequalities and attempts to create a much more egalitarian society in four respects: increasing government revenues, developing the backward western inland area, enhancing levels of public spending on education and social welfare, and putting in place fiscal policies to encourage domestic demand. According to him, three theoretical and practical problems still require resolution: revising the Chinese tax system for more egalitarian income distribution; dealing with issues arising from appropriation of differential rent in a socialist manner; and enabling unions' and workers' mobilization of more democratic forms of economic liberalization.

The chapters in the third part of this volume are devoted to analysing the Indian economy. Jayati Ghosh argues that it is too optimistic to believe that the Indian economy is now capable of rapid expansion under its own steam within the current growth trajectory, or that it can become an alternative growth pole in the global economy. She points out that the recent phase of rapid economic growth in India was based on a relatively fragile pattern of external dependence that may be hard to sustain over the medium term – and indeed there is already evidence that this trajectory has run its course. The economic boom in India was related to financial deregulation and capital inflows that sparked a retail credit boom and combined with fiscal concessions to spur consumption among the richest sections of the population. There was a substantial rise in profit shares in the economy and a proliferation of financial activities. However, this was not related to stable expansion of employment or much improvement in living standards for the bulk of the population. Ghosh identifies the social underpinnings of the growth process, which relied on various forms of social discrimination and exclusion such as caste, gender, community and location to segment labour markets and maximize surplus extraction. Partly in consequence, economic growth was associated with little improvement in basic social and human development indicators or even in material conditions for a large part of the population. Agrarian crises and social and political instability are already emerging as constraints to this pattern of growth. She concludes that, given the continuing uncertainties in the global economy, a sustainable trajectory in the future will require a significant reorientation of the Indian economy in the direction of domestic wage-led growth.

Hideki Esho investigates the trajectory of Indian economic management since independence to find out whether it provides a new model of economic development. Following Rostow and Lewis, he argues that the turning point of Indian economic development was the 1980s, when India's economy changed from being supply constrained to being demand led. He focuses on the service-sector-led economic growth of India since 1991 and emphasizes that the dynamo of India's economic growth has been IT-related services and that the value added of manufacturing industry has stagnated as a share of GDP. He questions whether such a leapfrogging pattern of economic growth is sustainable and investigates the conditions for such a development trajectory to be successful.

Taken together, these chapters provide a distinct and different approach as compared with the mainstream literature to the analysis of how China and India are likely to grow in future and what this will mean for the rest of the world, particularly developed countries in Europe and Asia. On the one hand, the assessments of the future economic trajectories of both China and India are more balanced and therefore less optimistic than much of the recent mainstream literature. The focus not just on external economic integration but also in its relationship with internal imbalances, inequalities and social and political factors allows for a more nuanced and careful projection for the future. For this reason, several of the chapters are able to provide some explanation for the very recent slowdown in these economies as well as the instabilities that are emerging in these societies and the continued medium-term potential for economic expansion. On the other hand, the book also provides a more comprehensive examination of the longer-run dynamics of the global capitalist system in which these economies are necessarily destined to play more significant roles in future. The complexities of this process, the challenges they throw up for advanced economies, and the implications in terms of rapidly changing geopolitics are all examined in some detail. The book's authors show that for the foreseeable future we will continue to live in interesting times, but understanding the true nature of the processes involved will be crucial in our ability to negotiate them.

References

Li, M. (2008) *The Rise of China and the Demise of the Capitalist World Economy*, London: Pluto Press.

Winters, L. A. and Yusuf, S. (eds) (2007) *Dancing with Giants: China, India, and the Global Economy*, Washington, DC: World Bank, 2007.

Part I

The renaissance of China and India

1 The impact of China and India on the advanced economies

Robert Rowthorn

This chapter is concerned with the impact of Chinese and Indian growth on today's advanced economies. It contains no discussion of the recent economic crisis, since the effects of this event, although painful, will be mostly transitory. The crisis reduced growth rates throughout the world and drove the advanced economies into negative territory (Figure 1.1). Exports from China and India fell sharply, but both economies continued to grow quite strongly. The crisis may be a visible watershed marking the impending decline of Western hegemony, but the underlying trends described in this chapter were already at work well before this crisis broke out and they will continue long after it has ended.

Growth projections[1]

For most of the past three decades, China has grown much faster than India and its per capita income is now roughly twice the Indian level. Indian growth has recently

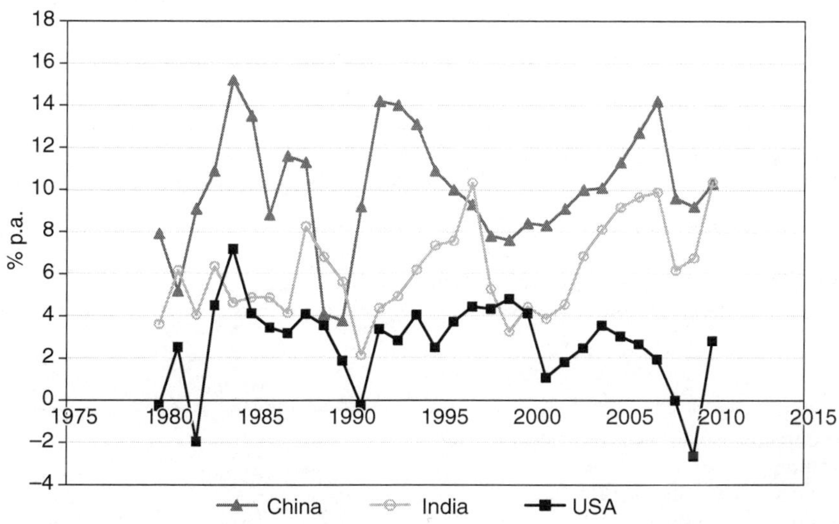

Figure 1.1 GDP per capita growth rates (source: IMF 2011b).

accelerated, although there are some major obstacles to be overcome if this is to be sustained. Infrastructure is poor in India, bureaucracy is a serious problem and there is widespread illiteracy. In 2006, almost 19 per cent of the Indian population aged 15–24 was illiterate. This compares to only 1 per cent in China.

Immediately before the crisis, over the period 2004–08, per capita income in China rose at 10.4 per cent a year as compared to 1.2 per cent in the United States. With these growth rates, starting from 2008 it would take only 26 years for China to catch up with America.[2] Over the same period, per capita income in India rose at an average rate of 7.3 per cent a year. At this rate it would take India 66 years to catch up with America. These projections are based on a mechanical extrapolation of past performance. In practice, both China and India are likely to slow down as their per capita incomes get closer to the US level. To allow for this, I have made some alternative projections that rest on a more realistic vision of the convergence process. Details are given in an appendix.

Table 1.1 shows the projected values of key variables in 2040.[3] It is projected that per capita incomes in China and India will be equal to 48 per cent and 25 per cent, respectively, of the US level by 2040. Both countries will have four times the population of the United States by the end of the period, and despite their relatively low per capita incomes they will be among the world's largest economies. If output is measured at purchasing power parity, China will overtake the United States in terms of total production by 2020 and will produce almost twice as much by 2040. India will just achieve parity with the United States by the end of the period. The picture is somewhat different if output is evaluated at market exchange rates. With this measure, the projections imply that total GDP in China will be around 150 per cent of the US level in 2040, while for India the figure is around 60 per cent.

The above projections are highly speculative and should be treated with caution. However, they are in line with the past experience of smaller countries such as South Korea and Taiwan. In 1983, Korea had a per capita income similar to China's in 2008. Over the next 25 years, per capita income in Korea rose by 322 per cent. The Taiwanese experience was much the same. If China and India follow the example of those countries, the results will be similar to those shown in Table 1.1. My projections are broadly similar to those produced by Wilson

Table 1.1 China and India in 2040: projections

	USA = 100	
	China	*India*
Per capita income at purchasing power parity (PPP)	48	25
Population	374	402
Gross domestic product at PPP	181	100
Gross domestic product at market exchange rate	147	61

Source: author's estimates – see appendix.

and Purushothaman (2003) and Maddison (2007), although projected growth rates for China and India are somewhat faster than theirs, reflecting the recent acceleration of economic growth in these countries.[4]

Ageing

A potentially important issue in the context of economic growth is that of ageing. As a result of its one child policy and longer life expectancy, the proportion of old people in China is starting to increase quite fast. India is expected to undergo a similar process, but more gradually and with some delay. To the extent that ageing reduces the fraction of the population that is productively employed, it is likely to mean a lower GDP per capita than would otherwise be the case. With a given output per worker, the smaller the ratio of workers to the population as a whole, the smaller the total volume of output. This is a matter of arithmetic. Ageing may also undermine economic dynamism. The old may be wise, but on average they are less flexible and less creative than the young. This was a traditional concern of French demographers worried by their country's low birth rate. Alfred Sauvy famously complained of the need to preserve a younger, more productive population and to avoid a state where 'old men lived in old buildings thinking old ideas' (cited in Chesnais 2001).

The UN Population Division produces long-range projections of the evolution of population and age structure under various assumptions. These projections should put concerns about Chinese ageing into perspective. A common indicator of age structure is the 'old age dependency ratio', or 'dependency ratio' for short. This is the number of people aged 65-plus expressed as a fraction of the number aged 15–64. The UN projects that the Chinese dependency ratio will rise from 0.11 in 2010 to 0.38 in 2050.[5] This is a large increase, but by the end of the period the dependency ratio in China is still be well below the projected figure for Europe (0.47) and Japan (0.74), and is similar to the US figure (0.35). The projected dependency ratio for India is 0.20. These comparisons suggest that ageing should not seriously inhibit China's capacity to compete against today's advanced economies, while India may derive some benefit from the youth of its population.

Economic structure

Manufacturing industry has played a central role in Chinese development and the country now accounts for around 15 per cent of world exports of manufactured goods. However, India has been on an unusual growth path, with a greater role for services and a smaller role for manufacturing than is normal for a country at its stage of development (Das 2006; Dasgupta and Singh, 2005). Over the past quarter-century, the output of services has grown faster than manufacturing output (Figure 1.2), and services have emerged as a high-productivity sector. In 2004, services employed only 22 per cent of the Indian workforce but accounted for more than 50 per cent of value added (Rowthorn 2008). India also has large and rapidly growing exports in IT-related areas such as software and call centres (Table 1.2). However, the balance between manufacturing and services may now be shifting. India's service exports were badly hit by the global financial crisis and have recovered less rapidly than manufactured exports. Between 2008 and 2011, Indian manufactured exports increased by 66 per cent as compared to an increase of 28 per cent for commercial services over the same period (WTO database).

Exports from China and India are growing rapidly and their shares in GDP have been rising. In 2008, immediately before the crisis, Chinese exports of goods and services made up 35 per cent of GDP, and for India the figure was 22 per cent.[6] China's figure is inflated by the fact that on average its manufacturing exports have high import content (Akyuz 2010). What will happen to these shares in the future? In the case of India, at least, the export ratio is likely to increase for a time, but in neither country is this ratio likely to reach anything like the level of a small, open economy such as Korea, whose exports of goods and services made up 53 per cent of GDP in 2008. In the long run, the trade ratios of China and India should eventually converge to levels similar to those observed in other very large economies, such as the United States and the European Union. If we exclude internal trade within the European Union, total exports of goods and services in these economies are around 12–15 per cent of GDP.

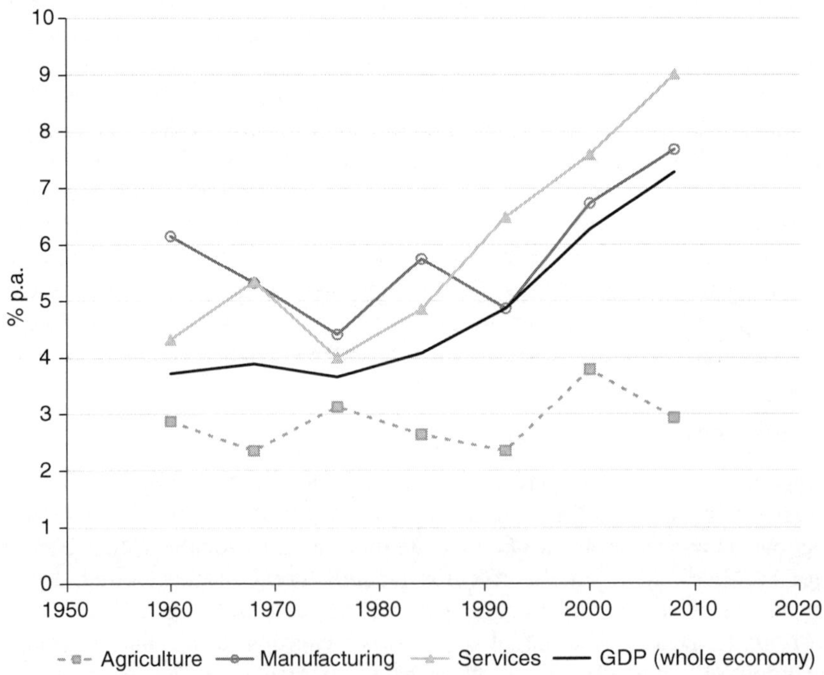

Figure 1.2 Indian growth rates by sector (eight-year averages ending in years shown) (source: *Handbook of Statistics of the Indian Economy*, Reserve Bank of India, 2008–09).

Table 1.2 Indian exports of goods and services

	Billions of US dollars		
	2000–01	*2007–08*	*Change (%)*
Chemicals	6	21	260
Engineering	7	37	448
Other goods	33	108	229
Software	6	40	536
Other services	10	50	401
Total	**62**	**256**	**315**

Source: *Handbook of Statistics of the Indian Economy*, Reserve Bank of India, 2008–09.

Economic impacts

The following is a brief outline of some of the main ways in which the advanced economies may be affected by the rise of China and India.

Comparative advantage[7]

The theory of comparative advantage, as first articulated by David Ricardo, implies that countries should specialize in producing those items for which their own costs of production are *comparatively* low. A country may be good at everything, but it should specialize in those activities that it is especially good at, or in activities that utilize its abundant factors of production. Thus, a country that has a large endowment of uneducated labour but only a small endowment of highly educated labour should specialize in the production of 'labour-intensive' goods and services that require a relatively large input of uneducated labour. Conversely, a country that is well endowed with highly educated labour should specialize in the production of 'knowledge-intensive' items that require a relatively large input of highly educated labour. In Ricardo's original formulation, the theory of comparative advantage was static and made no allowance for the fact that a country's endowments and capabilities change over the course of time. The 'flying geese' theory of Akamatsu (Ozawa 2005) takes a more dynamic approach and explains why comparative advantage is likely to shift in the course of time.

As an initially poor country develops, it will get better at producing knowledge-intensive goods and services; the supply of highly educated workers needed to produce these items will also become more plentiful. As a result, knowledge-intensive products will become relatively cheap, while in relative terms labour-intensive products will become more expensive. Such changes in the internal cost structure will be reflected in the country's trading relations with the outside world. Knowledge-intensive items will increase their share of exports, while the share, and ultimately the volume, of labour-intensive exports will decline. In the course of this transition, the terms of international trade will alter. Labour-intensive exports from the developing country will become more expensive and the rich importing countries will have to exchange more of their own output to purchase them. The rich countries will thereby suffer a loss of real income. This issue has been investigated theoretically by Paul Samuelson (2004). His analysis has been extended by Rowthorn (2006, 2008). The rich countries may also reduce their imports of such products and seek domestic substitutes instead (Sirkin *et al.* 2011).

The above logic applies most clearly to China. At present, Chinese exports of clothing and other labour-intensive items are many times greater than imports. As China develops, such exports will eventually decline, and their production will be relocated to other countries where costs are lower. This has not yet happened on a large scale despite the fact that wages in China are now higher than in India or Indonesia, and are similar to wages in the Philippines and Thailand (Yang *et al.* 2010). However, it is only a matter of time before underlying forces assert themselves and lower-cost producers replace China as suppliers of labour-intensive manufactures. The situation is more complex in the case of India. Despite its low per capita income and large surplus of labour, India is not at present a major exporter of labour-intensive manufactures. The theory of comparative advantage implies that such exports would grow rapidly if India's labour surplus could be mobilized and obstacles to international trade eliminated (Mayer and Wood 2001). However, the picture is complicated by the fact that India is already a significant and growing exporter of knowledge-intensive services and sophisticated manufactures. It seems unlikely that exports of labour-intensive manufactures will ever enjoy the same importance for India as they have for China.

If China continues to grow rapidly and its energies are increasingly directed towards the production of knowledge-intensive items, it will eventually provide a huge market for the labour-intensive manufactured exports of poorer countries. This will be of great benefit to a continent like Africa, which will never grow rich on agriculture, minerals and tourism alone. Recent attention has focused on China as a market for African natural resources, but it could eventually become an important market for clothing and other labour-intensive manufactures produced in Africa. As labour becomes more expensive in China, it is possible that Chinese firms will relocate some of their labour-intensive activities to Africa, producing goods for global markets that are currently served from China. In accordance with the 'flying geese' theory, China will stimulate economic growth well beyond its own borders. The same will also be true of India one day, but that will take much longer.

Scarce resources

World demand for natural resources is increasing because of economic development and population growth. China is a major contributor to this process, although Indian demand for natural resources is also increasing. The consumption of oil by China has been rising at about 6 per cent p.a. and at this rate it will overtake the United States around 2020. The Indian demand for oil is much lower and is increasing more slowly. Even so, India will soon overtake Japan as a consumer of this fuel. The additional demand from China and India is arriving at a time when experts are becoming seriously worried about future oil supplies. Many experts believe that conventional oil production will peak before 2030 (Sorrell *et al.* 2010). Unconventional production from oil sands, oil shale and the like may eventually fill the gap but this may take some decades to come on full stream (Aguilera *et al.* 2009; Sorrell *et al.* 2010). A combination of rising world demand for oil and a shrinking, or only slowly growing, supply could lead to a large and permanent rise in oil prices, thereby damaging countries that are heavily dependent on imports of this fuel. The same could be true of grain and certain minerals.[8] There is already some evidence of this happening. After a long period of decline, real commodity prices have been on an upward trend since around 2000.

There is great uncertainty about the future behaviour of commodity prices. In the early 1980s, economic modellers commonly assumed that the real price of oil would increase at 3 per cent p.a. In the event, the price of oil soon collapsed and it was another 25 years before it recovered to the 1980 level. The IMF (2011a) has investigated the behaviour of oil prices under various demand and supply scenarios. In its baseline simulation, world oil production increases at 0.8 per cent p.a. over a 20-year period, and this increase is accompanied by a cumulative increase of almost 200 per cent in the price of oil. Under a more optimistic scenario, the cumulative price increase is 100 per cent. There is also a simulation

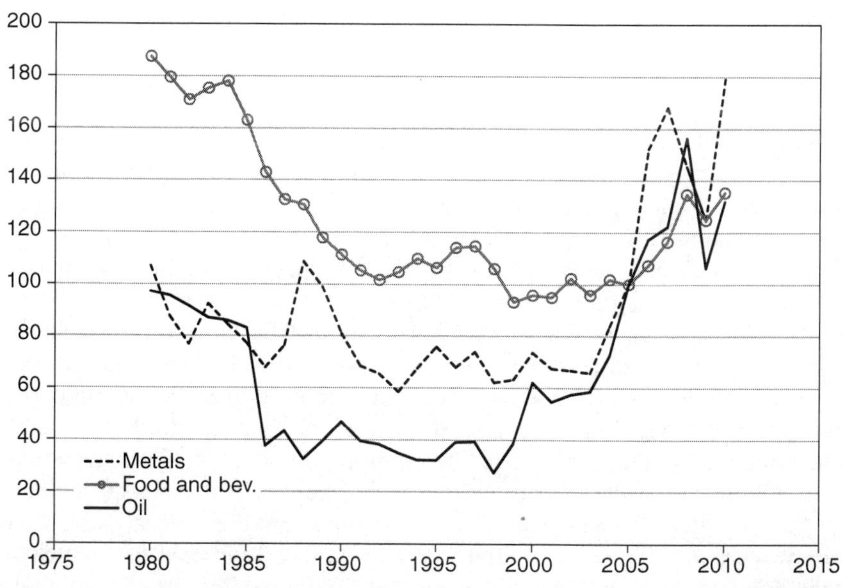

Figure 1.3 Real commodity prices (2005 = 100) (deflated by prices of manufactured exports of advanced economies) (source: IMF 2011b).

in which world oil production falls at 2.0 per cent p.a. and the price of oil eventually increases by 800 per cent. Earlier simulations by the World Bank (Shalizi 2007) were more optimistic. In their business-as-usual scenario, the real price of oil rises from $25 per barrel in 2001 to $133 in 2050 (in 2001 prices). This is equivalent to 3.4 per cent p.a. as compared to 5.6 per cent p.a. in the IMF baseline simulation. These simulations indicate the huge range of uncertainty surrounding future oil prices and, by extension, commodity prices in general.

If the economic growth of China and India does lead to serious shortages, the advanced economies will experience a loss of real income as their imports become more expensive, and they may also experience serious dislocation as they seek to adjust to the new scarcities.

Global warming

It is widely agreed by scientists that the rising concentration of carbon dioxide in the atmosphere is a major factor behind global warming and will have serious economic and environmental consequences unless it is soon checked. It is unlikely that it will be. The recent economic growth of China and India has been accompanied by a strong upward trend in CO_2 emissions which looks set to continue. Their per capita emissions are unlikely to reach anything like the present US level, but with their huge populations they are becoming major polluters. China has overtaken the United States as an emitter of CO_2, and India is catching up fast. Indian emissions of CO_2 are rising at an average of 5 per cent annually, and at this rate India will reach the present US level of emissions within 25 years or so.

Terms of trade loss

Economic growth in developing countries such as China and India may lead to an increase in the amount that advanced countries pay for certain types of imports, such as commodities or labour-intensive manufactures. The following simple calculations illustrate the potential scale of the resulting loss. In 2007, a year of fairly high commodity prices, the amount spent by the main advanced economies on net imports (=imports−exports) of commodities, such as food, fuels and mining products, was around 3 per cent of GDP for the United States and the European Union (external trade only) and 6 per cent for Japan. In the same year, clothing imports into the advanced economies were in the region of 0.5–0.6 per cent of GDP. Certain other manufactured items in addition to clothing, including many electronic goods, have an important labour-intensive component. Taking these other items into account, suppose that the total amount spent on imported labour-intensive manufactures by the typical advanced economy is around 2 per cent of GDP. Adding another 3 per cent for commodities yields a total figure equal to 5 per cent of GDP for net imports of food, fuel, minerals and labour-intensive manufactures into the United States and the European Union. For Japan, the figure is 8 per cent. These figures indicate the direct losses that the advanced economies would suffer if all such items were to double in price because of Chinese and Indian growth. These are, of course, only illustrative calculations. The actual losses could be larger or smaller.

A loss equal to 5 per cent of GDP is potentially serious, but it should be seen in perspective. If the loss occurred overnight, it could be very disruptive. However, spread out gradually in a growing economy, such a loss would be manageable. For example, in the decade 2001–11, GDP growth in the G7 countries averaged around 1.3 per cent a year. If growth continues at this rate in the future, GDP will increase by 39 per cent over the next 25 years. A terms of trade loss equal to 5 per cent of GDP would reduce the increase in real disposable income over this period to 32 per cent.

The above calculations are concerned only with the direct balance of payments cost of higher import prices. They make no allowance for the economic disruption caused by higher prices and a scarcity of basic commodities. IMF (2011a) simulations imply that in the case of oil, the losses arising from such disruption could be substantial. Nor do these calculations allow for the benefits that will accrue to the advanced economies from the future expansion of trade with China and India in knowledge-intensive services and sophisticated manufacturing. They also ignore the increase in productivity that will occur in today's advanced economies through the importation of new technologies from China and India. When benefits as well as costs are taken into account, it is conceivable that the rise of China and India could on balance lead to an increase in average living standards in the advanced economies. However, the opposite could also be the case. World Bank economists have explored this issue using a computable general equilibrium model to quantify the impact of Chinese and India development on the rest of the world. After perturbing their baseline simulation, the authors conclude that faster growth in China and India would have only a minor impact on welfare in the advanced economies (Dimaranan *et al.* 2007: table 3.6). However, as the authors concede, this finding is subject to great uncertainty.

Contribution to global knowledge

In the coming decades, China and India will spend an increasing amount on research and development. Much of the knowledge thereby generated will diffuse into the rest of the world and become available for use by others. China and India are importing technology on a large scale from more advanced economies today, but in the future they are likely to become major exporters of technology in their own right. This will be of benefit to the rest of the world, including today's advanced economies. In particular, China and India will contribute to the development of technologies that are more environmentally friendly and which serve to mitigate the otherwise harmful effects of economic growth.

The Royal Society has published a report on global scientific collaboration. It points out that China has already overtaken the United Kingdom as the second leading producer of research publications, but sometime before 2020 it is expected to surpass the United States. Commenting on China and India, the report has this to say:

> China's rise up the rankings has been especially striking. China has heavily increased its investment in R&D, with spending growing by 20% per year since 1999 to reach over US$100 billion a year today (or 1.44% of GDP in 2007), in pursuit of its goal of spending 2.5% of GDP on R&D in 2020. China is also turning out huge numbers of science and engineering graduates, with 1.5 million leaving its universities in 2006.... India produces roughly 2.5 million science and engineering graduates each year. In 2008, India, the world's second most populous country, succeeded in sending its first unmanned flight to the moon, becoming only the fourth country to land a craft on the lunar surface.
>
> (2011: 19)

Chris Llewellyn Smith, who chaired the group which produced the report, has welcomed the internationalization of science with these words:

> Global issues, such as climate change, potential pandemics, bio-diversity, and food, water and energy security, need global approaches. These challenges are interdependent and interrelated, with complicated dynamics that are often overlooked by policies and programmes put in place to address them.... Science has a very important role in addressing global challenges and collaboration is necessary so that everybody can agree on global solutions. The more countries are involved in science, the more innovations we will have and the better off we will be.[9]

Structural change

The entry of China and India onto the world stage will provoke structural changes that are painful for particular subgroups of people in today's advanced economies. As China and India develop, their exports will become increasingly sophisticated and they will become powerful competitors in areas where the existing advanced economies now enjoy a near-monopoly. Those areas will include not just manufactured goods but also IT-related services, where India already has a strong presence. Many firms in the advanced economies will go out of business or be forced to shed labour in the face of this new competition. Other firms will prosper as they exploit the new export markets in China and India. As always in the case of structural change, there will be winners and losers. The mass importation of cheap clothing and the like from China has been beneficial to consumers in the advanced economies, but it has destroyed the livelihoods of millions who used to produce them (Rowthorn and Coutts 2004). The offshoring of services to India could have a similar effect in the future (Blinder 2006).

The real exchange rate

According to Ricardo's theory of comparative advantage a country will specialize in producing those items for which its costs of production are *comparatively* low. A country may be good at everything, but it will specialize in those activities it is especially good at. A country cannot have a comparative advantage in everything. Ricardo's point is frequently ignored by commentators who claim that China will soon outcompete the advanced economies in everything, from labour-intensive clothing to the most sophisticated, knowledge-intensive goods and services. Western firms will be no match for Chinese producers with their low wages, rising productivity and increasing mastery of modern technology. This claim is misleading because it ignores what happens to the real exchange rate. The potential significance of the exchange rate can be seen from the following example.

Consider a country that experiences a large increase in productivity affecting all sectors of the economy, which is accompanied by a much smaller increase in wages. The result will be a substantial reduction in unit costs affecting all types of production. What happens to foreign trade will depend on the real exchange rate. If the real exchange rate is fixed, a large and universal reduction in unit costs will make exports of all kinds super-competitive in international markets. This will cause a massive growth in exports and will also restrain the growth of imports, resulting eventually in a huge balance of payments surplus such as we have recently observed in China (Figure 1.4). A payments surplus on this scale is not sustainable and some form of adjustment must eventually occur. For example, domestic wage inflation or a formal revaluation of the national currency may cause the real exchange rate to rise, thereby undermining the competitive position of locally produced goods and services and eliminating or greatly reducing the trade surplus. If the real exchange rate is flexible, it is not possible for a country to outcompete the rest of the world across the whole spectrum of products. The real exchange rate will adjust so as to preserve external balance and keep total exports roughly in line with total imports.

Profits and investment

The preceding discussion suggests that wage restraint in China will not result in an ever-growing trade surplus. Sooner or later the real exchange rate will adjust, or something else will happen, to bring exports into line with imports. However, there is also another issue to consider. If wages lag behind productivity growth in China or other developing countries (the South), this will increase the rate of profit in these countries, thereby increasing their attraction as locations for production by firms from developed countries (the North). Northern firms may respond by relocating their existing production facilities to the South or else use the threat of relocation as a bargaining counter to extract concessions from their existing workforce. They may even offer to repatriate some activities that are currently offshore. For example, it is reported that the Ford Motor Company is bringing up to 2,000 jobs back to the United States from China in the wake of a favourable agreement with the United Auto Workers union that allows the company to hire new workers at $14 an hour (Sirkin *et al.* 2011). This example illustrates how globalization has affected labour relations in the advanced economies. As Richard Freeman (2005a, b) has pointed out, the integration of low-wage countries like China and India into the global labour market has undermined the bargaining power of workers in the advanced economies. This effect comes partly through competition from low-wage imports and partly through the impact of globalization on the location and investment possibilities of transnational firms.

Surveys of international business opinion have found that China and India are the two most attractive countries in the world in which to invest (Table 1.3), and they should become even more attractive as Chinese and Indian markets expand and these countries become more familiar to outside firms. Indeed, the prospect of locating in large and fast-growing markets is likely to be one of the main reasons for outside firms to invest in China and India in the coming decades. It is possible that rising investment in these countries will choke off investment in the advanced economies. This could happen because of higher interest rates caused by a future global shortage of savings, or perhaps because of managerial overstretch. Transnational firms may decide that they lack the managerial capacity to invest simultaneously on a large scale in many different economies at once. Faced with a choice between China, India and the advanced economies in the future, they may give priority to China or India and cut back on the advanced economies so as to avoid overstretch. These are theoretical possibilities, but how important they will be in practice remains to be seen.

The locus of international investment is shifting towards China and other developing countries, but many firms still find it profitable to invest in the

Table 1.3 UNCTAD survey, 2008–10: the most attractive locations for FDI in the next three years. (Responses and comparison with the 2007–09 survey responses)

Economies	*2007–08 survey*	*Economies*	*2008–10 survey*
China	56	China	55
India	45	India	41
United States	38	United States	33
Russian Federation	23	Russian Federation	28
Brazil	14	Brazil	22
Vietnam	13	Vietnam	12
United Kingdom	10	Germany	9
Australia	10	Indonesia	8
Germany	7	Australia	7
Mexico	7	Canada	6
Poland	7	Mexico	6
		United Kingdom	6

Source: UNCTAD *World Investment Report 2008*, table 1.20.

advanced economies. The *World Investment Report* estimates that in 2009 the advanced economies attracted 51 per cent of global direct investment inflows, which is four times as much as China and India combined (UNCTAD 2010: annex table 1). The share of China in new direct investment has been rising, and its share excluding Hong Kong, in the world stock of inward direct investment has risen from 1.0 per cent in 1990 to 2.6 per cent in 2009 (ibid.: annex table 2). There has been a recent upsurge of investment in India, but in 2009 its share in the world foreign direct investment (FDI) inflow was still only 3.1 per cent and its share of the FDI stock was still only 0.5 per cent.

International investment is a two-way affair. As China and India develop, it is inevitable that their firms will start to internationalize their activities on a large scale, taking over or merging with foreign companies and setting up new establishments of their own. In the case of China this is already happening, although by global standards the overseas activities of Chinese transnational companies (TNCs) are still relatively small. In the case of India, overseas expansion has hardly started and the operations of Indian firms remain overwhelmingly domestic. Of the top 100 non-financial TNCs ranked by foreign assets in 2008, there were two firms from China, including Hong Kong, and none from India (UNCTAD 2011: web table 29). There was no Chinese or Indian firm among the top 50 financial TNCs ranked by geographical spread (ibid.: web table 31). Of the top 100 TNCs with investments in infrastructure (transport, electricity, telecoms, etc.) in 2006, there were six from China, mostly Hong Kong, but none from India (UNCTAD 2008: annex table A.111.4).

Wages

The attractions of China and India as locations for investment depend on many different factors, including the productivity of labour and the level of wages. Measured in US dollars, wage rates in these countries are extremely low, and even in urban areas, Chinese manufacturing workers earned on average only 7 per cent of what their US counterparts earned in 2008 (Table 1.4). The gap is smaller if an allowance is made for differences in the cost of living. Prices in China are on average about 40 per cent below the US level, so in real terms Chinese workers are somewhat better off than a crude comparison of dollar wage rates would suggest. But this is a minor qualification and, on any measure, wages are still much lower in China and India than in the advanced economies.

The situation described above will not last. Real wages in China, for example, have been increasing rapidly, and this growth should continue in the future (Yang *et al.* 2010). Moreover, through a combination of domestic price inflation and future currency revaluation, the Chinese cost of living, measured in dollars, is likely to increase relatively fast.[10] Thus, any given increase in real wages will be associated with an even larger increase in dollar wages to compensate for the rising cost of living. This point is illustrated in the simple numerical example shown in Table 1.5. In this example, consumer prices measured in dollars

Table 1.4 International wage comparison (at market exchange rates),[a] USA = 100

India 2005	
All employees	3.1
Production workers	2.6
China 2008	
Urban and TVEs[b]	4.1
Urban	7.1
TVE	2.4

Sources: Indian figures are from Sincavage *et al.* (2010) and Chinese figures are from Banister and Cook (2011).

Notes
a Refers to hourly labour compensation in manufacturing.
b TVE = town and village enterprises.

increase by 1 per cent a year faster in China than in the United States. It is also assumed that real wages are rising at 5 per cent a year faster in China. For this to happen, dollar wage rates in China must grow about 6 per cent a year faster than American wages.

Measured in dollars, the hourly compensation of the average urban manufacturing worker in China in 2009 was only 7.1 per cent of the US average (Table 1.4). With the growth rates assumed in the above example, the dollar wage rate of such a worker in 2030 would be 26 per cent of the American level, and by 2040 it would reach 46 per cent. Although hypothetical, this example is not unrealistic. It illustrates how quickly economic development, through its effect on real wages and the cost of living, may undermine the competitive advantage that China derives from low wages.

The Chinese surplus

In 2001, China had a small current account surplus equal to 1.4 per cent of GDP. Over the next few years, exports surged ahead of imports and the surplus increased dramatically, peaking at 10.6 per cent of GDP in 2008 (Figure 1.4). In dollar terms, the Chinese current account surplus in that year was greater than the combined surpluses of Germany and Japan. Since then, the Chinese surplus

Table 1.5 Real wages and dollar wages: a numerical example of percentage annual growth rates

	China	*USA*	*China – USA*
(1) Cost of living in dollars	3	2	1
(2) Real wage rate	6	1	5
(3) Wage rate in dollars [= (1) + (2)]	9	3	6

has fallen back somewhat, but in absolute terms it remains very large. This situation has been the cause of tension with some of China's trading partners, especially the United States. Throughout this century, Chinese merchandise exports to the United States have been four to five times as large as imports (Figure 1.5). China has a small deficit on its trade in services with the United States, but this is of trivial importance compared to its huge merchandise surplus.[11]

China is not the first country to have a large current account surplus and to run afoul of its major trading partners. The same has happened at various times to Germany, Japan, Korea and Taiwan, among others. In each case, there has been pressure to reduce the offending surplus. Researchers at the IMF (2010) have analysed the methods used by countries to reduce or eliminate an unwanted surplus. After examining 28 distinct historical episodes, they conclude that the main policy instrument for achieving this objective is a currency appreciation. A stronger currency makes it more difficult for local producers to compete on world markets, thereby encouraging imports and discouraging exports. The IMF researchers find that, provided it is accompanied by appropriate monetary and fiscal policies, a currency appreciation does not in general reduce the rate of economic growth, although it may cause a structural change in the economy by shifting resources from exporting towards the home market. However, as the example of Japan illustrates, it is not always easy to choose appropriate macro policies. Following the Plaza Accord in 1985, a huge appreciation of the Japanese yen was engineered and Japanese exports fell sharply. To stimulate the domestic economy and offset lost export demand, the government responded with an expansionary fiscal and monetary policy. However, this policy overshot the mark and was continued for too long, giving rise to an unsustainable asset

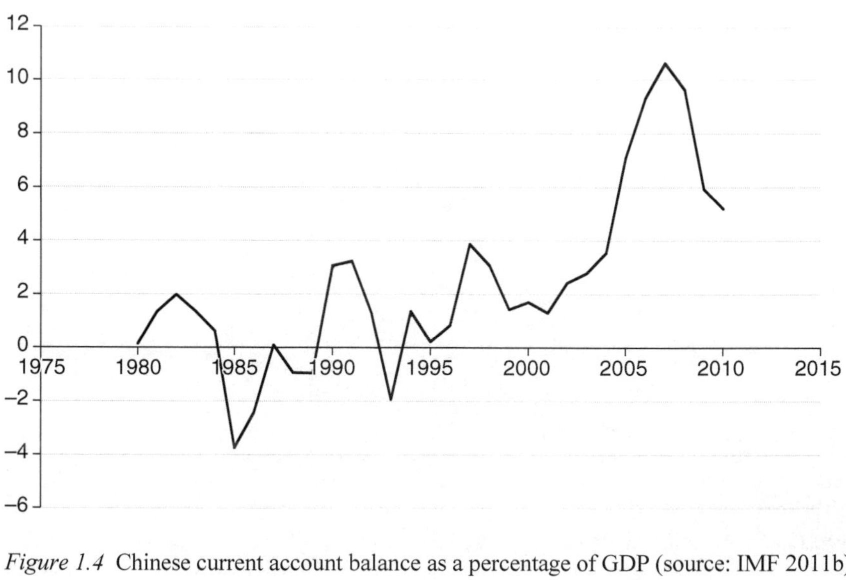

Figure 1.4 Chinese current account balance as a percentage of GDP (source: IMF 2011b).

price bubble. When this bubble eventually burst, it ushered in years of near-stagnation. The Chinese do not wish to replicate the Japanese experience.

Better role models for China are, perhaps, Korea and Taiwan, which both had large current account surpluses in the mid- to late 1980s (IMF 2010). Following a policy-induced appreciation of 25 per cent of the local currency against the US dollar, the Korean surplus as a share of GDP fell by 10 percentage points in the three years after 1988. In Taiwan, there was a 54 per cent appreciation and the surplus fell by more than 13 percentage points in the three years after 1986. In each case, the local economy continued to grow strongly after currency appreciation and no special measures were required to stimulate aggregate demand. One important effect of currency appreciation was to make low-value-added, labour-intensive exports less competitive, thereby accelerating the shift to 'higher-quality' exports. The previously undervalued currencies of these countries had given an implicit subsidy to the producers of labour-intensive exports, but at the cost of delaying inevitable structural change.

An appreciation in the nominal exchange rate is not the only way to reduce a surplus. What matters for international competition is ultimately the real exchange rate, as measured by relative unit labour costs in a common currency. The producers of internationally tradable goods and services are constrained in their ability to raise prices by pressure from their foreign competitors. If money wages increase fast enough and there is no change in the nominal exchange rate, this will squeeze the profits of such producers, resulting in more imports and fewer exports than would otherwise be the case. In the case of China, the most

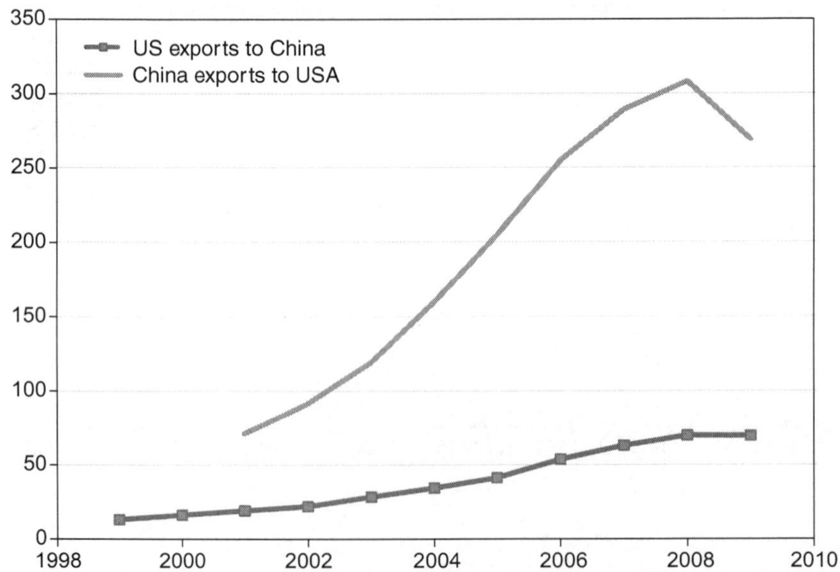

Figure 1.5 USA–China merchandise trade, 1999–2000 ($ billion) (source: WTO database, 2011, WTO database, http://stat.wto.org/Home/WSDBHome.aspx?Language=).

severely affected would be the producers of labour-intensive exports, who would be squeezed out by the combined pressure of high wages at home and low world market prices. This has already been happening to some degree, but the continued existence of a large current account surplus indicates that Chinese wages have not been increasing fast enough.

The macroeconomic effects of a large increase in the real exchange rate depend on conjunctural factors which vary with time and place. If the underlying dynamism of the economy at the time is weak, special fiscal and monetary policies may be required to stimulate aggregate demand so as to compensate for the loss of net export demand. This was the case in Japan in 1985, although in the event the application of such policies was botched. Conversely, if the underlying dynamism of the economy is strong, domestic demand will spontaneously step in to fill the gap left by the decline in net exports, as was the case in Korea and Taiwan. To the extent that higher money wages are translated into higher real wages, this will increase the purchasing power of Chinese workers at the expense of profits. If the marginal propensity to save out of wages is lower than the marginal propensity to save out of profits, the result will be to increase domestic consumption and thereby demand. Quite apart from the issue of aggregate demand, there will still be the problem of dislocation in industries that are find it hard to compete against foreign rivals because of higher labour costs. Their producers will have to innovate, switch to new markets or contract.

Concluding remarks

The rise of China and India will affect the advanced economies in a variety of ways. On the negative side, imports of commodities, such as food or oil, and of labour-intensive manufactures may become more expensive. On the positive side, as China and India develop they will invest more in research and development, thereby promoting the discovery of new technologies that can be used by the existing advanced economies. They will also provide growing markets for the exports of the advanced economies, thereby stimulating international specialization and raising global productivity. The benefits resulting from new technologies and new forms of trade specialization may be large enough to outweigh any terms of trade loss caused by the potentially higher cost of commodities and labour-intensive imports.

There is also investment to consider. As the centre of gravity of the world economy shifts towards Asia, firms may find it more profitable to invest in China and India rather than in the existing advanced economies. If this shift occurs on a large scale, which is by no means certain, it will force governments and trade unions in the advanced economies to find ways to make their economies more attractive as a location for investment.

It is uncertain how far the growth of China and India, and of other developing countries, will damage the existing advanced economies in aggregate terms. However, it is bound to provoke structural changes that are harmful to particular groups of people. The effects of structural change are often dismissed as temporary adjustment costs, but the experience of deindustrialization indicates that such effects may last for generations. Despite government efforts to revive them, many old industrial areas in the advanced economies have still not recovered from the collapse of local mining and manufacturing employment. It seems unlikely that the rise of China and India, and of other developing countries, will provoke structural changes on the huge scale that we have witnessed during the past 40 years of deindustrialization. Even so, structural change will occur, and dealing with it effectively will pose a challenge for government policy.

Appendix: projections

This appendix describes briefly how the projections shown in Table 1.1 were derived. For a full description of the method, see Rowthorn (2006) or Rowthorn (2008).

Per capita GDP was projected using convergence equations of following type

$$y(t+1) - y(t) = -\beta y(t) \quad \text{where } y = \log\left(\frac{Y}{Y_{USA}}\right) \text{and } Y = \text{ GDP per capita.}$$

The values of β were initially estimated using data on GDP per capita at purchasing power parity (PPP) for the period 2000–08. This yielded the following coefficients:

China: $\beta = .0321$; India: $\beta = .0143$.

The coefficient for India was then adjusted on the assumption that India is now on a faster growth path than previously observed. This yielded the following coefficients:

China: $\beta = .0321$; India: $\beta = .0220$.

With 2008 as base year, the above coefficients were used to project the trajectories of GDP per capita at both PPP and market prices. Total GDP was derived by multiplying projected per capita GDP by projected population (from UN, 2009).

Notes

1 Smith (2008) provides a good overview of the political and economic background to modern growth in China and India. See also Jacques (2009).

2 Measured at purchasing power parity, per capita incomes in China and India were equal to 17.7 per cent and 5.8 per cent respectively of the US level in 2008 (IMF 2009).

3 Despite the use of revised IMF data and more recent observations, the projections presented in this chapter are similar to those in Rowthorn (2006) and Rowthorn (2008). The main difference is that China grows somewhat faster than was originally assumed and India somewhat more slowly, but these differences do not alter the general picture.

4 My projections for GDP at market exchange rates in 2050, as a percentage of the US level, are as follows: China 179, India 89. The corresponding Wilson and Purushothaman figures are 126 and 79. Maddison's projections terminate in 2030. My projections for GDP per capita at PPP in 2030, as a percentage of the US level, are as follows: China 37, India 18. Maddison's projections are 34 and 15 respectively.
5 All projections cited in this paragraph refer to the 'medium variant' (see UN 2009).
6 All trade statistics cited in this paragraph come from WTO (2009).
7 The issue of comparative advantage is discussed at greater length by Rowthorn (2006, 2008).
8 Kesler (2007) provides a useful survey of mineral prospects in the twenty-first century. The IMF (2011a) considers the future behaviour of oil prices.
9 Cited in the *Guardian* (London), 28 March 2011.
10 This normally happens when countries develop. They begin with a cost of living that is low by international standards, but as they get richer, their cost of living converges towards that of more developed countries. This point is discussed by Rowthorn (2006, 2008). Its explanation relies on the 'Baumol effect' whereby the relative price of non-tradable goods and services rise because of lagging productivity growth (Baumol, 1967).
11 Consistent statistics on trade in services between the United States and China are not available. According to the WTO (2010: table 1.16a), US exports of commercial services to China in 2008 were worth $15.645 billion and imports from China were worth $9.825 billion, giving a Chinese deficit of $5.8 billion. According to the WTO (2010: table 1.16b), Chinese exports of commercial services to the United States in 2008 were worth $22.790 billion and imports from the United States were worth $23.520 billion, giving a Chinese deficit of $0.7 billion. Thus, depending on how it is measured, the Chinese deficit with the United States in commercial services was between $0.7 billion and $5.8 billion. Either way, it was tiny in comparison with the Chinese bilateral trade surplus with the United States in merchandise (agricultural products, minerals, fuels, manufactures, etc.).

References

Aguilera, R. F., Eggert, R. G., Lagos C. C. G. and Tilton, J. E. (2009) 'Depletion and the future availability of petroleum resources', *Energy Journal*, 30 (1): 141–175.

Akyuz, Y. (2011) 'Export dependence and sustainability of growth in China and the East Asian production network', South Centre, Research Paper 27, April.

Banister, J. and Cook, G. (2011) 'China's employment and compensation costs in manufacturing through 2008', *Monthly Labor Review*, March: 29–52.

Baumol, W. J. (1967) 'Macroeconomics of unbalanced growth: the anatomy of urban crisis', *American Economic Review*, 57: 451–426.

Blinder, A. S. (2006) 'Offshoring: the next industrial revolution?', *Foreign Affairs*, 85 (2): 113–128.

Chesnais, J. C. (ed.) (2001) *Alfred Sauvy: la vieillesse des nations. Textes choisis, présentés et annotés par Jean-Claude Chesnais*, Paris: Gallimard.

Das, G. (2006) 'The India model', *Foreign Affairs*, July–August.

Dasgupta, S. and Singh, A. (2005) 'Will services be the new engine of Indian economic growth?', *Development and Change*, 36 (6): 1035–1057.

Dimaranan, B., Ianchovichina, E. and Martin, W. (2007) 'Competing with giants: who wins, who loses?', in L. A. Winters and S. Yusuf (eds) *Dancing with Giants: China, India; and the Global Economy*, Washington, DC: World Bank, pp. 67–100.

Freeman, R. (2005a) 'Does globalization of the scientific/engineering workforce threaten U.S. economic leadership?', NBER Working Paper 11457.

Freeman, R. (2005b) 'China, India and the doubling of the global labor force: who pays the price of globalization?' Online, available at: http://www.japanfocus.org/-richard-freeman/1849.

IMF (2009) *World Economic Outlook Database April 2009*. Online, available at: www.imf.org/external/pubs/ft/weo/2009/01/weodata/index.aspx.

IMF (2010) *World Economic Outlook April 2010*. Online, available at: www.imf.org/external/pubs/ft/weo/2010/01/pdf/text.pdf.

IMF (2011a) *World Economic Outlook April 2011*. Online, available at: www.imf.org/external/pubs/ft/weo/2011/01/pdf/text.pdf.

IMF (2011b) *World Economic Outlook Database April 2011*. Online, available at: www.imf.org/external/pubs/ft/weo/2011/01/weodata/index.aspx.

Jacques, M. (2009) *When China Rules the World*, London: Allen Lane.

Kesler, S. E. (2007) *Mineral Supply and Demand into the 21st Century*. Online, available at: http://pubs.usgs.gov/circ/2007/1294/reports/paper9.pdf.

Maddison, A. (2007) *Chinese Economic Performance in the Long Run, 960–2030 AD*, 2nd ed., Paris: OECD.

Mayer, J. and Wood, A. (2001) 'South Asia's export structure in a comparative perspective', *Oxford Development Studies*, 29 (1): 5–29.

Ozawa, T. (2005) *Institutions, Industrial Upgrading, and Economic Performance in Japan: The 'Flying-Geese' Paradigm of Catch-up Growth*, Northampton, MA: Edward Elgar.

Rowthorn, R. E. (2006) 'The renaissance of China and India: the implications for the advanced economies', UNCTAD Discussion Paper no. 182, Geneva: United Nations.

Rowthorn, R. E. (2008) 'The renaissance of China and India: the implications for the advanced economies', in P. Arestis and J. Eatwell (eds) *Issues in Economic Development and Globalization: Essays in Honour of Ajit Singh*, Basingstoke, UK: Palgrave Macmillan.

Rowthorn, R. E. and Coutts, K. (2004) 'De-industrialisation and the balance of payments in advanced economies', *Cambridge Journal of Economics*, 28 (5): 767–790.

Royal Society (2011) *Knowledge, Networks and Nations: Global Scientific Collaboration in the 21st Century*, London: Royal Society.

Samuelson, P. A. (2004) 'Where Ricardo and Mill rebut and confirm arguments of mainstream economists supporting globalization', *Journal of Economic Perspectives*, 18 (3): 135–146.

Shalizi, Z. (2007) 'Energy and emissions: local and global effects of the giants' rise', in L. A. Winters and S. Yusuf (eds) *Dancing with Giants: China, India and the Global Economy*, Washington, DC: World Bank.

Sincavage, J. R., Haub, C. and Sharma, O. P. (2010) 'Labor costs in India's organized manufacturing sector', *Monthly Labor Review*, May: 3–22.

Sirkin, H. L., Zinser, M. and Hohner, D. (2011) *Made in America, Again*, Boston: Boston Consulting Group.

Smith, D. (2008) *The Dragon and the Elephant: China, India and the New World Order*, London: Profile Books.

Sorrell, S., Miller, R., Bentley, R. and Speirs, J. (2010) 'Oil futures: a comparison of global supply forecasts', *Energy Policy*, 38 (9): 4990–5003.

UN (2009) *World Population Prospects: 2008 Revision, Population Database*, UN Population Division. Online, available at: http://www.un.org/esa/population/publications/wpp2008/wpp2008_highlights.pdf.

UNCTAD (2008) *World Investment Report 2008*, Geneva: United Nations.

UNCTAD (2010) *World Investment Report 2010*, Geneva: United Nations.

UNCTAD (2011) *World Investment Report 2011*, Geneva: United Nations.

Wilson, D. and Purushothaman, R. (2003) 'Dreaming with the BRICs: The path to 2050', reprinted in *The World and the BRICs Dream*, London: Goldman Sachs, 2006.

WTO (2010) *International Trade Statistics, 2010*, Geneva: World Trade Organization. Online, available at: www.wto.org/english/res_e/statis_e/its2010_e/its10_world_trade_dev_e.htm.

Yang, D. T., Chen, V. and Monarch, R. (2010) 'Rising wages: has China lost its global labor advantage?' IZA DP no. 5008, June, Bonn: Institute for the Study of Labor (IZA). Online, available at: http://ftp.iza.org/dp5008.pdf.

2 The renaissance of Asia and the emerging world system

Nobuharu Yokokawa

Introduction

In this chapter, I build a theoretical foundation for Ha-Joon Chang's historical finding (2002) that almost all of today's rich countries used East Asian-type industrial, technical and trade policies (hereafter ITT policies) and purpose-built institutions when they were themselves developing countries. I start by examining Ricardo's theory of comparative advantage. This is a static theory that explains comparative advantage if there is no productivity growth. In the real world, countries that specialize in dynamic industries with increasing returns make gains, and those which specialize in decreasing returns lose. I build a dynamic theory of comparative advantage, introducing a concept of dynamic industries and value added per unit of labour (VAL). In dynamic industries, VAL increases with the increase in productivity and then eventually decreases, since the volume of product increases with productivity growth, but value added per product will eventually decrease with diffusion of technology and the falling relative price of output. Dynamic comparative advantage depends on the difference between VAL and wages. Historically, real wages tend to increase in proportion to average productivity growth. Dynamic comparative advantage does not last for ever, because of the eventual decrease of VAL and increases in wages. Countries have to make their industrial structures more sophisticated, and move to new dynamic industries to keep their international status. Therefore, all successful countries have to rely upon interventionist ITT policies and purpose-built institutions.

Akamatsu's 'flying geese' theory is a proto-dynamic comparative advantage theory from developing countries' point of view. The dynamic comparative advantage theory complements it, and covers both linear and non-linear development. I investigate the reindustrialization of Europe and Japan to catch up with US productivity in the golden age, and the 'flying geese' pattern of development in East Asia from the mid-1970s to the mid-1980s, current account surplus reversals in East Asia and compressed quasi-Lewis-type industrialization in China. Finally, I will investigate the possibility of a global flying geese pattern of industrialization with China as the engine of growth.

The dynamic theory of comparative advantage

The East Asian miracle

According to Chang (2009), the East Asian economic 'miracle' was one of the most controversial issues in economics in the 1980s and 1990s. Mainstream economists argued that there were relatively few interventionist ITT policies in Japan, South Korea and Taiwan. Heterodox economists (including Keynesians, institutionalists and Marxians) showed a good deal of evidence that interventionist ITT policies employed in these countries were the keys to the East Asian economic success. In the face of mountains of evidence, mainstream economists then argued that these policies had worked only because the East Asian countries had exceptional historical, social and cultural conditions. It was a 'miracle' that could not be generalized to other countries. Chang, through a detailed survey of the literature, proved that 'virtually all of today's rich countries, and not just the East Asian countries, used East Asian-style trade and industrial policies when they were developing countries themselves' (ibid.). Then policies that many had thought were exceptional 'suddenly became "general" policies which almost all successful developers, starting from eighteenth-century Britain down to today's China, have used' (ibid.).

Why does strong confidence in liberalism exist within the now-developed countries (hereafter NDCs)? Chang's answer to this question is also very clear. These successfully industrialized countries supported free trade and market policies as a pulling-ahead strategy only while they successfully industrialized. They then kicked away the ladder of ITT policies they had used to become industrialized countries, and forced developing countries to adopt free trade policies.

These findings are very important. However, they require a sound theoretical foundation in order to be claimed generally. I shall investigate Ricardo's comparative advantage theory, the most important theoretical foundation of free trade, and then build a dynamic theory of comparative advantage to support Chang's argument.

Ricardo's static theory of comparative advantage

According to Ricardo's comparative advantage theory, specialization and international trade are beneficial for both of two countries as long as there is a relative difference in the degree of productivity, even if one country's productivity is superior in all industries (Ricardo, 1817). This was a good theory for Britain. According to this theory, Britain should specialize in manufacturing and the less developed country should specialize in agriculture. Since both countries specialize in what they do best, aggregate production increases.[1] However, two qualifications must be carefully noted if this is to be beneficial for both countries. First, the relative gain of a country depends on the terms of trade. Second, productivity growth in a country must be shared by other countries. I shall investigate these qualifications in detail.

There are no rules to determine terms of trade. Let us suppose that demand and supply determine terms of trade, even though advanced countries use many methods to make these terms favourable for them, and to monopolize all the benefits of specialization.

Productivity growth in an industry is shared by all the capital within a country. Is there any mechanism for sharing growth in productivity internationally? Let us suppose that in an industrial country, productivity in a dynamic industry increases ten times. If the price of the product remains the same, the same labour produces ten times more exchange value. If wages remain the same (for example, if the wage share is 50 per cent of value added at the start), the profits of the capital with this exceptional productivity become 19 times greater than before (in other words, the profit share is 95 per cent and the wage share is 5 per cent), which Marx, in *Capital*, called 'extra profits'. When a new technology spreads, the price of a product becomes cheaper, and competition between capitals for higher profits eventually reduces the profits of this industry to the average profit by reducing the price of the product. If the product is directly or indirectly wage goods, the prices of wage goods fall, and wages can be reduced, which increases the average rate of profit. Marx called this the 'production of relative surplus value'. Productivity growth in an industry is thus shared by all capital in the country.

Whether this higher profit can be shared by capital in an agricultural country depends on the terms of trade. If the terms of trade do not change, agricultural countries do not share the benefit of productivity growth in industrial countries. On the other hand, industrial countries can obtain agricultural products at much less cost because of the improvement in the productivity of industrial goods. Their prices of wage goods may fall as a result of cheap imports, which may reduce wages. This is de facto production of relative surplus value, which further increases profits in industrial countries.

If demand for agricultural products increases with the increase of productivity in the industrial country, the agricultural countries have the opportunity to enjoy the benefits of the increased productivity in the industrial country. For example, if capital accumulation in the industrial country increases with the increase of productivity, demand for raw materials and food increases. If the supply of agricultural products is limited, the relative price of the products of the agricultural countries is increased, and the terms of trade of the agricultural countries are temporarily improved. However, if the supply is not limited, the terms of trade do not improve.

Ricardo's theory of comparative advantage was most useful for Britain in the middle of the nineteenth century. It allowed Britain to accumulate capital without supply-side constraints, to prolong the period of extra profit, and then to enjoy the production of relative surplus value through both domestic productivity growth and international trade. This was not acceptable for catching-up countries such as Germany and the United States, which knew that their infant industries could not compete with British industries on a level playing field. If they opened their countries to free trade, their infant industries would be destroyed by the competition. It was even less acceptable for semi-independent and dependent countries, including Japan in the nineteenth century, which were forced to open themselves to free trade by suzerain and de facto suzerain states. In some countries, the traditional manufacturing base was destroyed and they degenerated into agricultural countries. Ricardo's theory of comparative advantage is essentially a static theory that assumes a status quo and cannot explain advantages in the long run. I shall build a dynamic theory of comparative advantage that explains the theoretical soundness of the view held by catching-up and dependent countries.

Dynamic industries and dynamic comparative advantage

A dynamic industry is an industry in which productivity growth is faster than the average. It is also a leading industry and engine of economic growth. The nature of dynamic industries has changed historically: agriculture and wool were the most dynamic industries in the seventeenth century; the cotton industry between the mid-eighteenth and mid-nineteenth centuries; heavy industry and the chemical industry from the late nineteenth to the early twentieth century; the machinery and electronics industries from the 1920s to the 1970s; and IT and knowledge-intensive industries since the 1980s (Figure 2.1).

VAL is the amount of value added that is produced by one hour's labour. It is decomposed to the number or volume of commodities produced by one hour's labour and value added per unit of product. The value added per unit of product is large when a new product is exclusively supplied by a limited number of firms. This is referred to in different ways, such as extra profits, super-profits, monopoly rents and technological rents. In dynamic industries, VAL increases

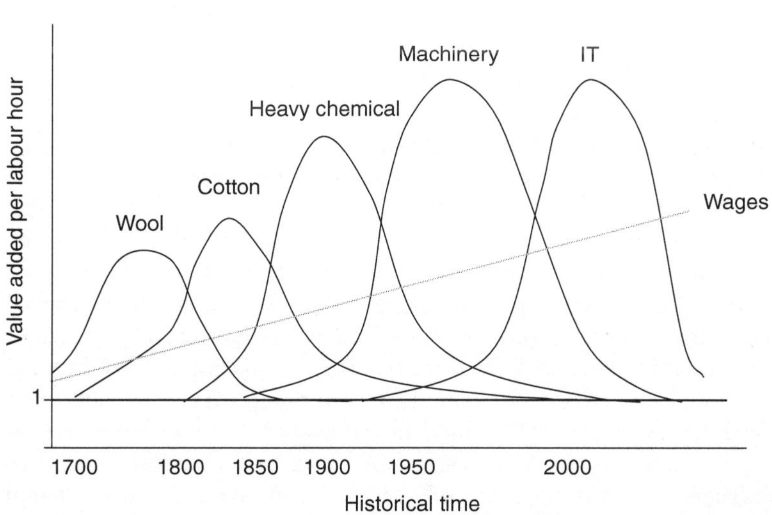

Figure 2.1 Dynamic industries and value added per unit of labour (VAL).

with the increase in productivity, and eventually decreases, since the volume of product increases with productivity growth, but value added per product will eventually decrease with diffusion of technology.[2]

Dynamic comparative advantage depends on the difference between VAL and wages. In the early phase of a new industry, wages may be higher than VAL. In such a case, capital cannot obtain profit. It requires promotion of infant industry protection for capital to invest in this dynamic industry. When a dynamic industry takes off, its VAL becomes higher than wages, and the faster growth of VAL than wages increases profits, and then the dynamic industry successfully becomes a leading industry in a country. With the spread of production, domestic and international competition reduce the price of the product, and eventually reduce VAL, while wages continue to rise. When wages become higher than VAL, capital cannot obtain profit and production in this industry decreases.

At any one time, old, current and new dynamic industries coexist. It is most profitable for advanced countries to specialize in current dynamic industries and obtain extra profits, prolong the process by kicking away the ladder of ITT policies, and import cheap products of older dynamic industries from less developed countries. The catching-up countries require low wages and ITT policies and purpose-built institutions to cover the difference in productivity. In catching-up countries, infant industry protection ensures competitiveness. Developing countries specialize (or are forced to specialize by FDI for low wages) in old dynamic industries where VAL reaches its lowest point, and to supply cheap products to advanced and catching-up countries to increase their production of relative surplus value.

Cyclical crises and structural crises

Historically, real wages increased in proportion to average productivity growth. Crises are the mechanism by which real wages increase in proportion to average productivity growth. I distinguish three types of crises: cyclical, structural and systemic crises.

Capital accumulation in mid-nineteenth-century England was dominated by the current dynamic industry, the cotton industry. When capital accumulation increased in the cotton industry, capital accumulation in other sectors also increased. With the progress of prosperity, employment increased, and some types of labour in the dynamic industries became scarce, and so wages rose more than productivity growth, which reduced the rate of profits and eventually caused a crisis. In dynamic industries, productivity continuously increased by means of a new method of production, which was introduced by replacing old fixed capital by new and more productive fixed capital in a depression. The new and more productive machinery created relative surplus population and reduced wages by less than productivity growth. It increased VAL and the dynamic comparative advantage. Then the accumulation of capital recommenced under sound conditions of exploitation and abundant surplus population. Thus, the conflict between capital and labour over the distribution of income was solved automatically through cyclical crises, and wages were kept within productivity growth. I call this a cyclical crisis, and it reinforces the self-regulating character of the capitalist economy.

With the progress of capital accumulation through business cycles, the available labour of the industrial reserve army was eventually absorbed. The creation of relative surplus population by the introduction of new and more productive machinery reduced the speed at which the industrial reserve army was absorbed, but it did not reverse this tendency. In order to secure workers, wages in lagging sectors had to be increased even though these sectors failed to match the fast productivity growth observed in dynamic sectors.[3] Large wage increases in the dynamic sectors spilled over into the lagging sectors, and were mostly passed on to consumers in the form of higher prices (see Rowthorn, Chapter 1 of this volume). This is Baumol's cost disease (Baumol, 1967). Once Baumol's cost disease starts, the ratchet effect of wage rises occurs. Rising wages in times of prosperity do not decrease in periods of depression. Unlike wage rises in dynamic sectors, they are not compensated by productivity growth.

Through the repetition of business cycles, dynamic comparative advantage eventually decreases. On the one hand, VAL decreases. First, productivity growth eventually peaks and then is reduced. Second, diffusion of technology both domestically and internationally reduces the price of the product and value added. On the other hand, wages increase. The increase is initially compensated for by productivity growth, and then wages start to grow faster than productivity growth, owing to Baumol's cost disease. With decreasing VAL and rising wages, dynamic comparative advantage starts to decline. This causes serious structural crises, like those at the end of the nineteenth century and in the 1970s, which destroyed existing capital accumulation regimes.

Structural crisis and linear and non-linear development

There are two strategies by which it is possible to escape from the reduction of dynamic comparative advantage. The first strategy is increasing sophistication of industrial structure, causing the lead to shift to new dynamic industries. The second strategy is to fix the comparative advantage by specializing in the industry where it has a current comparative advantage, and then kicking away the ladder of ITT policies so that other countries cannot catch up.

It is relatively easy for catching-up countries to adopt the first strategy if new dynamic industries have already been well developed by advanced countries and are readily available. When catching-up countries adopt this strategy, they follow a linear development path. For example, the East Asian countries did so after World War II, forming a flying geese pattern of industrialization.

It is more difficult for the most advanced country to adopt the first strategy because of the high risk and cost involved in developing a new dynamic industry. As can be seen from Figure 2.1, there is the possibility that the VAL of a new dynamic industry is lower than that of the current dynamic industry until the new dynamic industry takes off. Generally speaking, if the VAL of a new dynamic industry is lower than that of the current dynamic industry, its rate of profit will be lower than that of the current dynamic industry. Furthermore, it is possible that the VAL of the new industry is lower than wages initially. There is a conflict between social benefit and private benefit. If the choice is left to the market, less capital is invested in the new dynamic industry than would be socially preferable. It is therefore necessary to socialize risk and cost to develop new dynamic industries.

Britain (in the latter half of the nineteenth century) adopted the second strategy. In the latter half of the nineteenth century, the VAL in the cotton industry started to fall, and the VAL in the heavy and chemical industries started to increase. Britain left the choice of capital investment to the market. The result of this market selection was to choose the then current dynamic industries that had the highest rate of profit at the time, and face the uncertainty of a changing industrial structure to keep capital in a more liquid form, thereby promoting financialization. The result was insufficient fixed capital investment in the new dynamic industries. Instead, Britain increased capital investment in such countries as the United States and other British offshoots, where the rates of profit were higher than in Britain, thereby promoting the first globalization.

It may be easier for ambitious catching-up countries to develop a new dynamic industry. First, the difference between the VAL of the current and new dynamic industries is less than in the most advanced countries. Second, their wages are lower than those in the most advanced country. Third, they usually favour interventionist ITT policies to catch up with and to challenge the top countries. When catching-up countries take this strategy, they embark on a new development path. The United States and Germany took this strategy at the end of the nineteenth century, aggressively using ITT policies and creating complementary institutions such as limited liability companies and improved financial institutions to concentrate the latent money capital in society on the promotion of heavy and chemical industries. Consequently, productivity growth in these two countries became much higher in the new dynamic industries at the beginning of the twentieth century, and they replaced Britain as the leading industrial countries. Historically, there were two successful cases of new development paths: Britain in the eighteenth century, when it developed a new dynamic industry (cotton), and the United States and Germany at the end of the nineteenth century.

If Britain intended to maintain its hegemony, it had to socialize risk and cost to develop new dynamic industries through suitable ITT policies and institutions to promote investment in new dynamic industries. Ricardian liberalism was partially responsible for Britain's not choosing interventionist ITT policies at the end of the nineteenth century. Ricardo's theory of comparative advantage proved that liberalism was the most advantageous policy in the middle of the nineteenth century. It helped the industrialization of Britain, and it was still the dominant ideology when new ITT policies were needed at the end of the nineteenth century. If a country does not upgrade its industry when a dynamic comparative advantage is lost, its international status will be degraded. Therefore, applying interventionist ITT policies and building complementary institutions are necessary for all countries, including advanced, catching-up and developing countries, in order for them to maintain or improve their international status. The effectiveness of interventionist ITT policies and new institutions depends on a country's ability to socialize cost and risks to develop new dynamic industries in a changing economic and political environment.

This lesson was well learned by the United States, the next leading country in the capitalist world system. The United States became the top industrial country in the heavy and chemical industries, and also in the next most dynamic industries (automobiles and electrical machinery); however, it still adopted protectionist policies with ITT policies and by building complementary financial, legal and bureaucratic institutions even in the 1930s (Chang 2002). When the US dynamic comparative advantage was lost in the 1970s through the rapid catching-up of Germany and Japan, it changed its policy to one of neo-liberalism and kicked away the ladder of ITT policies in order to maintain the status quo, and also promoted the second phase of financialization and globalization, as Britain had done in the early twentieth century. However, it protected and promoted its IT and knowledge-intensive industries by massive military spending. IT and knowledge-intensive industries, combined with global value chains (GVCs), successfully became the next dynamic industries in the 1990s, and the United States recovered its dynamic comparative advantage.

The flying geese theory

Akamatsu's flying geese theory

Industrialization in East Asia has been studied in the framework of Akamatsu's flying geese theory, which is a proto-dynamic comparative advantage theory from developing countries' point of view and the most original framework for the analysis of East Asian industrialization.

1 The first thesis of Akamatsu's flying geese theory (introduction of a new dynamic industry) is Vernon's product cycle theory from the point of view of catching-up countries. According to Vernon (1966), (1) a new product is first produced and demand first develops for it in advanced countries; (2) as the product spreads through advanced countries, production expands to achieve economies of scale, and exports begin; (3) with the further spread of production the price falls, decreasing dynamic comparative advantage forces reductions in domestic production, and production moves to less-developed countries with lower wages; and (4) finally, the foreign-produced commodity is imported at much lower prices than it is possible to charge for domestically produced items.

According to Akamatsu (1962), catching-up countries start from the second of the above stages. (1) A new product is imported from advanced countries. (2) 'Previously imported goods' are domestically produced. (3) 'The domestic industry develops into an export industry.' (4) With the increase in wages and falling prices of the product due to international competition, the dynamic comparative advantage is reduced, and production declines. Thus, the first flying geese pattern is that importation, domestic production and exportation trace inverted V-shapes, one after another, like the flying pattern of migrating geese. In the original theory, the flying geese theory is an import substitution theory.

2 The second pattern is 'development from crude goods to elaborate goods' (ibid.): the shift to more sophisticated products or industries. Akamatsu emphasized a linear development path, and argued that latecomers should imitate the path taken by industrialized countries and shift specialization towards more capital- and skill-intensive industries when they lost existing dynamic comparative advantages, such as cheap labour.[4]

3 The third pattern is the 'development of advanced and less-advanced countries in a wild-geese-flying pattern' (ibid.). With the progress of Japanese industrialization, the Japanese dynamic industries shifted continuously, and this gave room for the Asian NIEs to industrialize. The Asian NIEs followed suit, so that their industrialization also took the form of the flying geese patterns. Thus, production and the trade structure in East Asia formed a well-ordered vertical production and trade pattern, or a flying geese pattern starting with Japanese geese, and followed by NIEs geese and then ASEAN-4 (Indonesia, Malaysia, the Philippines and Thailand) geese.

The new flying geese theory

There are two criticisms of Akamatsu's linear development theory. First, Gerschenkron's notion of the benefits of backwardness argues the possibility of non-linear development (leapfrogging). He emphasizes that developing countries can introduce the most advanced technology available in their industrialization (Gerschenkron, 1962: 9, 26). He also emphasizes the importance of an infant industry protection policy and other interventionist ITT policies, and complementary social institutions such as financial systems and the state, in order for the benefits of backwardness to be realized.

Second, the compressed development literature (Whittaker *et al.* 2010) argues that for countries like China and India which are industrializing today, most advanced technologies are available for all mature industries, and they can have the same dynamic comparative advantage in many industries. They may be able to start industrialization in all industries at once with the help of FDI and GVCs, as was done by China, or they may be able to choose the most suitable industries, such as IT, and leapfrog some industries, as India has done.

The theory of dynamic comparative advantage is complementary with the flying geese theory. It answers these criticisms, and complements Akamatsu's original theory in the following three respects.

1 According to Akamatsu, the flying geese pattern of development is on the one hand a catching-up process, where differences in productivity are

reduced by conversion, and on the other hand a diversion process, where advanced countries try to improve productivity further by upgrading their industries and introducing new production methods. In its original form, the flying geese theory does not cover non-linear development. In my theory, I emphasize path dependency and numerous varieties of capitalism, and consequent non-linear development of technology (i.e. uneven development). Changes in the hegemon of the capitalist world system, such as from Britain to the United States, are explained by the strategies adopted by the countries when they face structural crises in a capital accumulation regime.

2 In its original form, the flying geese theory was applied to industrialization in East Asia in the post-World War II period. My theory is applicable to both linear and non-linear industrialization in any country, whether an advanced, catching-up or developing country, and in any capitalist world system.

3 My theory emphasizes the importance of ITT policies and complementary institutions more systematically.

The capitalist world system

During the evolutionary process of capitalism, numerous varieties of capitalist economies have appeared. While most of them have failed to establish a new world system, the British variety in the nineteenth century and the US variety in the twentieth century were able to establish respective capitalist world systems with complementary institutions (Table 2.1).

The capitalist world system was first established when the British variety of capitalism created complementary institutions with cotton and railway industries as the dynamic industries. I call this 'market capitalism' because it was characterized by the coordination of the economy by the market, with free trade and the gold standard. Dynamic comparative advantages of cotton and railway industries were fully developed in this capital accumulation regime, with foreign demand as the engine of demand growth. This created the first golden age of capitalism, when cyclical crises reinforced the self-regulating character of the capitalist economy by solving the conflict between workers and capital over income distribution.

Table 2.1 Periodization of capitalist world systems

	Formation	*Establishment (golden age)*	*Diversification (globalization)*	*Systemic crisis*
Market capitalism	Mercantilism (1750s–1810s)	Liberalism (1820s–1870s)	Imperialism (1870s–1910s)	Interregnum (1920s–1940s)
Bureaucratic capitalism	Interregnum (1920s–1940s)	Welfare state (1950s–1970s)	Neo-liberalism (1980s–1990s)	2000–

After the structural crisis of the capital accumulation regime of liberalism in the late nineteenth century, the dynamic industries were now the heavy and chemical industries and the centres of economic growth shifted from the United Kingdom to the United States and Germany. A new capital accumulation regime, imperialism, was created with two challengers and one old hegemon. The dynamic advantage of heavy and chemical industries and the machinery industry was not fully developed in the period of imperialism and the interregnum because of the slow growth of effective demand, and the self-regulating character of the capitalist economy was lost.

The systemic crisis is the most serious crisis, the one that abolishes the current capitalist world system. Market capitalism finally collapsed through the systemic crisis of 'the Great Depression' in the 1930s and was replaced by bureaucratic capitalism after World War II.

The second capitalist world system was established when the United States created complementary institutions (such as the mass production and mass consumption systems), with the machinery industry as the dynamic industry. The dynamic comparative advantage of machinery industries was fully developed in this capital accumulation regime, with wages as the engine of demand growth. This created the second golden age of capitalism, when mild business cycles reinforced the self-regulating character of the capitalist economy by solving conflicts between workers and capital over income distribution. I call this 'bureaucratic capitalism' because it was characterized by the coordination of economies by well-structured bureaucratic systems of oligopolistic corporations and big governments and Bretton Woods international institutions.

After the structural crisis of the capital accumulation regime in the 1970s, a new capital accumulation regime, neo-liberalism, was created which destroyed the link between wages and productivity growth. The dynamic advantage of IT has not fully developed in the neo-liberalism accumulation regime, owing to the slow growth of effective demand, and the self-regulating character of the capitalist economy has been lost. Restoration of the link between wages and productivity growth is needed to solve the problem.

I shall now investigate Europe's and Japan's catching up in the golden age, the flying geese pattern of industrialization in East Asia from the mid-1970s and mid-1980s, the industrialization of China in a neo-liberal regime and, finally, the possibility of a global flying geese pattern of industrialization, with China as the engine of growth.

The rise and fall of the golden age and catching-up industrialization

Capital accumulation regime in the golden age

After World War II, competition between capitalism and socialism became systemic, and sought superiority in both economic and military power. The NDCs reindustrialized with the strong support of the United States and with well-designed international and domestic institutions.

The dynamic industries shifted from heavy and chemical industries to machine and electrical industries in the 1920s and 1930s in the United States. The US mass production system in machine and electrical industries, known as 'Fordism', was established in the early 1950s and introduced in Europe in the 1950s and 1960s. In Japan, the leading industries shifted from light industries to heavy and chemical ones in the 1950s and 1960s, and then to the machine and electronics industries in the 1970s (Figure 2.2). In the golden age, all countries, especially catching-up countries, benefited from rapidly increasing VAL.

Post-war governments had powerful institutions with which to maximize economic performance, such as fiscal and monetary policies, and ITT policies; and the sheer size of government stabilized economic fluctuations. In the new managed currency system, the central banks could create currency to meet the liquidity needs of the expanding domestic economy. Some countries, such as Japan and Germany, favoured direct government intervention and developed their ITT policies and supporting institutions in order to catch up with the United States.

The welfare state policy was the result of the requirements of bureaucratic (or oligopolistic) firms and states. First, bureaucratic firms could not rely upon foreign demand, and domestic demand had to replace it. Second, the success of socialist planned economies undermined the superiority of capitalist economies. Bureaucratic government had to achieve full employment and higher living standards. For these reasons, although there were huge surplus populations in

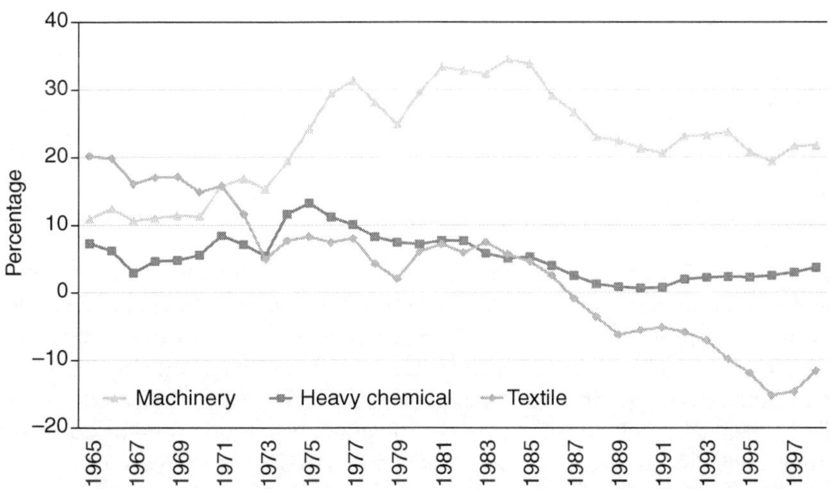

Figure 2.2 Export competitiveness of Japanese industries, 1965–98 (source: MITI 2000).

Note
Export Competitiveness = (Production/Domestic Demand) − 1.

many NDCs in the 1950s and early 1960s, wage rates increased in proportion to average productivity.

The Bretton Woods system was designed to reduce the external constraint imposed on national economies by the gold exchange standard. In order to accelerate the reindustrialization of the capitalist economies, the United States changed its trade policy from one of protectionism to one of liberalism. This US policy change to liberalism helped the reindustrialization of NDCs rather than kicking away the ladder, since it opened markets to capitalist countries and enhanced technological transfer, while tolerating catching-up countries' protectionist ITT policies. The United States also controlled supplies and prices of raw materials and fuel so that capitalist economies would not suffer from supply constraints. The smooth expansion of international trade under the multilateral trade regime (GATT), and the abundant availability of the international currency, accelerated the growth of international trade, which in turn accelerated the catching-up and GDP growth of NDCs.

Cyclical crises and the self-regulating character of capitalism

With strong support from the state and international institutions, which solved both supply-side and demand-side constraints, NDCs successfully reversed the pattern of capital accumulation from dependence on foreign demand to dependence on domestic demand, with wages as the engine of demand growth, and they established the mutually reinforcing mechanism between productivity growth and domestic economic growth, resulting in the long-lasting prosperity of the 1950s and 1960s, with occasional recessions. There were six business cycles with mild recessions in the United States (recessions in 1949, 1954, 1958, 1961, 1970 and 1973), and among catching-up countries (e.g. Japan) there were seven business cycles (recessions in 1949, 1954, 1958, 1962, 1965, 1971 and 1973). The law of value (or the self-regulating character of capitalist economy) in bureaucratic capitalism may be summarized as follows.

Prosperity

Prosperity started mainly with an increase in investment and consumption, raising both employment and the rate of profit. Accumulation of capital increased both wages and profit, and thus consumption demand and investment demand. With the progress of prosperity, firms maximized investment, utilizing credit in order to take advantage of economies of scale, which further increased profits and investment demand. At full capacity utilization, a Kaldorian profit-led accumulation mechanism came into play (Yokokawa 2012). The increase of investment raised the price level, which increased profits with sticky money wages. Labour unions tolerated higher prices because the increase in investment increased demand for labour and productivity growth, which eventually increased real wages.

Boom

Acceleration in the accumulation of capital by credit expansion and the collapse of the boom by tightening credit took different forms according to the levels of savings. Minsky's financial instability hypothesis (1982) explains boom and bust cycles in current account surplus countries in terms of financial market processes. With inflation and increased profit flows, both borrowers' and lenders' expectation become progressively more optimistic, and investment overshoots. When the monetary authority tightens credit because of inflation, the boom collapses.

In current account deficit countries, full employment was reached by expansionary monetary policy and capital inflow, which tended to cause the trade balance and the exchange rate to deteriorate. When the exchange rate dropped below the predetermined rate, the IMF fixed-rate system forced the monetary authority to tighten credit.

Recession

In all NDCs, monetary authority tightened credit before the crisis actually erupted. It reduced investment, and recession started. However, recession was a temporary problem, since economies had been cooled down before the crisis actually started. Once inflation was reduced, credit was loosened again.

Depression

In a depression period, a Kaleckian wage-led accumulation mechanism was at work (Kalecki 1954, 1971; Rowthorn 1982). Sticky money wages and a lower price level increased real wages. Increases in real wages together with automatic stabilizers increased aggregate demand. Oligopolistic firms responded to the increased demand by increasing output. In an oligopolistic market, investment increased with higher utilization rates (i.e. the acceleration principle). As a result of the acceleration principle, the increase of production more than compensated for the increase in wages, and increased both profits and the rate of utilization. Then prosperity began again.

Thus, the modest cyclical crisis automatically solved the conflicts between workers and capital over income distribution, and reinforced the self-regulating character of the capitalist economy in NDCs, with the help of complementary international and domestic institutions.

The structural crisis of bureaucratic capitalism

The long-lasting high rate of capital accumulation itself made further accumulation difficult in NDCs in the 1970s. The social institutions that supported the self-regulating character of the capitalist economy in bureaucratic capitalism declined. With the destruction of these supporting social institutions, the conflict between workers and capital over income distribution became more severe.

Uneven development and disorganizing influence on international relations

The long boom of the 1950s and 1960s was much stronger in Japan and Europe than in the United States. The rapid growth of the capital stock, encouraged by plentiful supplies of relatively cheap labour and by new technologies and management practices developed in the United States, eroded the productivity gap of European and Japanese manufacturing with the United States.

A first disorganizing influence of the uneven development on international economic relations arose because of changes in international competitiveness. Higher productivity growth and lower wage levels kept European and Japanese manufacturing goods highly competitive. This increased competition in international trade and decreased the relative strength of US trade, putting strong stress on the free trade regime under the GATT.

A second disorganizing influence was the loss of confidence in the US dollar. In spite of the decline in its current account surplus, the United States could not decrease both its capital exports and its government deficit so as to keep its dominant status in the world economy[5] and stabilize its domestic economy. The result was an increased US deficit and an increased supply of US dollars abroad, undermining confidence in the US dollar and heightening concern about the US gold reserve. As a result, the United States had to stop conversion in 1971.

A third disorganizing influence was the divergence within the fixed exchange rate system. The combination of diverging productivity growth and inflation rates generated persistent payments imbalances that undermined the fixed exchange rate system. As the result of the second and third disorganizing influences, the Bretton Woods system was abandoned.

A fourth disorganizing influence was US inability to control supplies and prices of raw materials and fuel. High demand for energy and other materials, demand topped up by speculation, raised the terms of trade and increased supply constraints.

Decelerating productivity growth and disorganizing influence on domestic economic relations

The long-lasting high rate of capital accumulation eventually reduced productivity growth. First, 'Fordism' reached the saturation stage in many NDCs by the early 1970s. Second, part of the productivity slowdown stemmed from slower output growth in industries characterized by economies of scale. Third, in Europe the scope for catching up with US productivity levels had declined. Fourth, the relative backwardness of productivity growth in the service sector forced deindustrialization (Rowthorn and Wells, 1987). Productivity growth in the service sector was difficult with available technology.

A first disorganizing influence of the decelerating productivity growth on the domestic economic relations was a reduction in VAL. Diffusion of technology increased competition both domestically and internationally, and reduced the price of products and value added. The decrease in value added per product was not compensated for by an increase in the number or volume of commodities produced by one hour's labour, because of reduced productivity growth. As a result, VAL was reduced.

A second disorganizing influence was Baumol's disease. Long-lasting capital accumulation eventually exhausted the available industrial reserve army in NDCs. Large wage increases in the dynamic sectors spilled over into the lagging sectors, and were mostly passed on to consumers in the form of higher prices, which further increased wages. Increases in wages under a declining VAL reduced the dynamic comparative advantage.

A third disorganizing influence was conflictual industrial relations in NDCs. With the over-accumulation of capital relative to available labour, labour unions became militant, and wage bargaining changed from Keynesian with sticky money wages to Marxist with sticky real wages (Epstein and Schor 1990: 130). When demand for higher real wages surpassed staggering productivity growth, wage pressure contributed to a squeeze on profitability. Thus, conflict over income distribution changed coordinated capital–labour relations into conflictual capital–labour relations.

A fourth disorganizing influence was the paralysis of Keynesian policy. Keynesian policy depended on sticky money wages. Keynes envisaged that the boost in government spending would increase demand and price levels, and prime the pump of private investment by increasing profits. Under supply constraints, government spending increased money wages and exacerbated inflation without increasing profits and investment.

Structural crisis

The 1970s started with stagflation in NDCs. Keynesian effective demand policies were ineffective for supply-side constraints and merely worsened inflation without decreasing unemployment. The new floating exchange regime increased the uncertainty of the world economy, while on the other hand it removed balance of payments fetters and enabled aggressive monetary and fiscal policies. When the economies had recovered, the first oil shock attacked, which accelerated inflation. Governments tightened both monetary and fiscal policies, and the structural crisis started in NDCs.

In this environment, neither the wage-led nor the profit-led accumulation mechanisms of the golden age worked. The Kaleckian wage-led accumulation mechanism did not work. First, slower productivity growth in wage goods industries, the high cost of raw materials and fuels, and Baumol's cost disease did not allow a reduction in the prices of wage goods in depression as much as before. Second, increased competition between capitals under staggering demand growth kept idle fixed capital to a minimum. Thus, the acceleration principle stopped working. Neither did a Kaldorian profit-led accumulation mechanism work. When firms increased investment and product prices rose, the sticky real wages soon squeezed profits, and firms lost any incentive to invest more.

With aggressive monetary and fiscal policies, the US and Japanese economies bottomed out in 1975, while those in Europe finally bottomed out in 1977. Then the second oil shock attacked OECD countries, and caused a renewed structural crisis in NDCs.

The neo-liberal accumulation regime

Without a complementary combination of industrial relations and production methods, the accumulation of capital cannot start again. There were three successful attempts to re-establish labour discipline and to recreate capital accumulation regimes in NDCs in the 1980s. Centralized bargaining in corporatist nations rehabilitated cooperative relations, and workers agreed to accept reduced wages in order to increase employment. Japanese mini-corporatism combined labour loyalty and the flexible production system. Anglo-American neo-liberal economies destroyed labour union power. In these countries, the conflict between workers and capital over income distribution was thus solved.

The neo-liberal accumulation regime

It was the Anglo-American neo-liberal accumulation regime that reshaped the capitalist world system after the structural crisis. The decisive policy shift from welfare state to neo-liberalism came in 1979. The UK government and the US Federal Reserve pushed up interest rates to unprecedented heights to cut inflation, which increased unemployment. At the same time, they demolished labour union power. This re-established a sound exploitation condition by reducing wages and creating a relative surplus population of the industrial reserve army in the United States and Britain.

Long depression and the neo-liberal policy solved supply-side constraints. However, the neo-liberal accumulation regime faced demand-side constraints, since it had destroyed the link between wages and productivity growth. Wages are both a cost of production and a source of demand. If wages do not increase in proportion to average productivity, a new source of effective demand is required. Financialization, or neo-liberal financial relaxation, solved demand constraints. It includes regulatory capture such as Wall Street's lobbying efforts to decrease regulations, regulatory relapse such as memory loss regarding the lessons of the Great Depression, and regulatory escape such as financial innovation.[6] Neo-iberal financial relaxation increased asset prices and reduced the rate of interest, which worked both on consumption demand and on investment demand. It increased consumption demand by increasing income from capital gains and the availability of many kinds of loans. At the same time, it decreased interest rates and increased investment demand.

Globalization

Facing the structural crisis, the United States (after the 1980s) adopted the second strategy to avoid the loss of dynamic comparative advantage, as Britain did in the late nineteenth century, changing its international policy to one of neo-liberalism and forcing catching-up countries to adopt this policy. The United States also promoted the second phase of globalization by increasing foreign direct investment. US companies transferred industries that had lost their dynamic comparative advantage to countries with low wages. The US globalization model also encouraged investment and the transfer of manufacturing know-how to developing countries through GVCs. The US monetary authority kept a strong dollar policy to encourage capital inflow, as Britain had done in the 1920s. Developing countries happily accepted the US model of globalization with a strong dollar policy, since it allowed them to pursue export-led industrialization policies (Palley 2010). However, the US strategy was different from the British strategy in an important respect. The United States protected and promoted IT and knowledge-intensive industries through massive military spending; these became the next dynamic industries in the 1990s.

The Bretton Woods system was effectively replaced by a market-led international financial regime. This neo-liberal international monetary regime made economies extremely vulnerable to short-term capital flows in both the advanced and the developing economies, as in the 1920s.

Boom and bust cycles in the neo-liberal accumulation regime

In the neo-liberal accumulation regime, borrowing and asset price inflation became the engines of aggregate demand growth in place of wage growth in the golden age. In prosperity, a profit-led accumulation mechanism worked. Increases in investment raised the price levels, which increased profits with constant money wages. With increasing profit flows, both borrowers' and lenders' expectations became progressively more optimistic. Financial arrangements changed from hedge finance to speculative then to Ponzi finance (Minsky 1982). When the monetary authority tightened credit, owing to inflation (or owing to an asset price bubble), the boom collapsed.

Tight monetary policy stopped investment and the crisis began. Both investment and consumption had been heavily dependent on credit; so tight monetary policy made many borrowers bankrupt. In this process, banking crises often started and developed into industrial crises. Once a depression started, economies did not recover automatically, since a wage-led accumulation mechanism did not work. Further neo-liberal financial relaxation was required in order to start prosperity again. Thus, policy-led boom and bust cycles replaced the self-regulating character of the capitalist economy.

Industrialization of East Asia

The flying geese pattern of development in East Asia

Japan was among the countries that most rapidly bottomed out from the serious structural crisis in the 1970s. As discussed, there are two strategies for avoiding a loss of dynamic comparative advantage. Japan adopted the first strategy to shift leading industries to new dynamic industries and followed a linear development path. Japan had been the most backward country among the NDCs in the golden age. When it lost dynamic comparative advantage in the heavy and chemical industries, it was able to shift towards the more sophisticated machinery industries, such as automobiles and electrical machinery, from the mid-1970s onwards (Figure 2.2, p. 41). Japan was able to recover dynamic comparative advantage, since Japanese productivity in manufacturing was about 70 per cent of the US level, while its wages were about 50 per cent of the US level in the 1970s (Glyn 2006). Once the link between productivity growth and wages was destroyed, a new source of effective demand had to be found. Japan adopted an export-led growth strategy, increasing its trade dependency from 10 per cent of GDP in the golden age to 15 per cent from the mid-1970s to mid-1985.

The upgrading of Japanese industries left room for less-developed East Asian countries to industrialize in the flying geese pattern. This is reflected in the East Asian export-led flying geese industrialization pattern as follows. Industrialization in labour-intensive sectors started in NIEs in the 1960s. US companies started to shift labour-intensive processes such as assembly lines for electrical equipment to NIEs. This was followed by Japanese FDI. The main exports from NIEs were labour-intensive products, such as clothing, textiles, groceries, and electrical and electronic equipment. Most of them were produced by subsidiaries of companies from NDCs. National strategies in NIEs promoted industrialization in heavy and chemical industries from the mid-1970s onwards. In the 1970s, Japan started to export replica factories, including know-how and skills, to East Asian countries, a process that made the introduction of heavy industries much easier and significantly increased productivity in NIEs.[7] These developments formed a well-developed flying geese pattern.

Current account surplus reversal in Japan, Korea and Taiwan, and GVC-led industrialization in ASEAN and China

In the first half of the 1980s, the US dollar was hugely overvalued. The IMF (2010) calculated that the Japanese, Korean and Taiwanese currencies were undervalued by 40 per cent, 35 per cent and 25 per cent respectively against the US dollar in the mid-1980s. Their current account surplus shares of the world's combined surplus in peak years were 42 per cent, 6 per cent and 8 per cent respectively. After the Plaza accord of 1985, these currencies appreciated rapidly. The Japanese yen had appreciated by 46 per cent against the dollar by the end of 1986, and the Taiwanese dollar appreciated by 57 per cent against the US dollar in four years (ibid.).

The current account surplus reversal triggered structural changes of accumulation regimes in these economies. They were more successful in Taiwan and Korea than in Japan (Rowthorn, Chapter 1 in this volume). First, they increased foreign direct investment initially to ASEAN and then to China to reallocate lower-value-added sections of the value chain. They reallocated domestic production towards higher-value-added sections where they still had a dynamic comparative advantage. Second, they covered the reduction of domestic production of tradables by increasing domestic production of non-tradables, such as services and construction. Third, after the current account surplus reversal, their trade dependence reduced, for example in Japan from 15 per cent to 10 per cent between 1985 and 2003. These economies had to replace foreign demand with domestic demand. Japan did not restore the link between wages and productivity growth, instead adopting neo-liberal financial relaxation to increase investment demand and consumption demand. Thus the Japanese bubble in the late 1980s and bust in the early 1990s was a typical and most serious bubble and bust in the neo-liberal accumulation regime. In contrast, political liberalization in Korea and Taiwan established the link between wages and productivity growth after 1987. They enjoyed a golden decade with wages as the engine of demand growth from 1987 to 1997 in Korea and to 2000 in Taiwan.

The Japanese share of world commodity exports peaked in 1990 and was overtaken by the East Asian NIEs in 1991 (Glyn 2006). In this period, Japan built a Pacific Rim triangle trade regime whereby Japan exported capital goods to ASEAN countries and China, and ASEAN and China exported completed products to the United States. Japanese FDI to the ASEAN-4 and China, followed by Korean and Taiwanese FDI, accelerated industrialization in the ASEAN-4 countries (Indonesia, Malaysia, the Philippines and Thailand) and China. However, their industrialization processes did not follow the original flying geese pattern:

1 These industries were transplanted for export. They thus skipped the first two processes of the first flying geese pattern, namely imports and import substitution production. Hence, the first flying geese pattern was lost.
2 The development of IT technology made it possible to separate the value chain of production, and only labour-intensive processes were transferred to countries with low wages in the 1980s. Although the most advanced technologies were imported, as Gerschenkron argued, this was only part of the aggregate production process, and it became difficult for many developing countries to upgrade industries independently of FDI. In this way, the second flying geese pattern was also lost.
3 The third flying geese pattern was also lost by Chinese compressed development, which we will see in detail in the next section.

Compressed and quasi-Lewis-type industrialization in China

The term 'compressed industrialization' is used to explain faster economic development among catching-up economies. For example, Japan achieved industrial development by following advanced countries step by step in less than 100 years, when it had taken more than 200 years in Britain, while South Korea achieved similar development in an even shorter period of 30 years. The term is now also used to describe non-linear development and the simultaneous development of industries with different levels of sophistication. China promoted industrialization in many sectors at once in this period. The international competitiveness of Chinese light industries, heavy industries and machinery were simultaneously improved.

Chinese-type compressed industrialization is an exceptional case rather than being generally adaptable to all late-industrializing countries. It was made possible by three exceptional conditions:

1 China has multiple and ample production factors. It has also become the most attractive country as a vast mass market, since it achieved 40 per cent of total East Asian growth in 1999. These enable industrialization in many sectors at once with necessary scales of production.
2 China has a number of social institutions for materializing the advantages of backwardness: an enormous population and historical economic achievement in the socialist planned economy give China production factors equivalent to those of the whole of the rest of East Asia; moreover, unlike the ASEAN countries and NIEs, China is politically integrated. These conditions give China massive bargaining power in inward foreign direct investment. China can negotiate for the transplant of entire value chains of production instead of labour-intensive production processes alone. These conditions are also beneficial to the development of the more advanced industries, such as aerospace, computer software and biotechnology. It is still possible for China to plan industrialization systematically and independently, using interventionist ITT policies and building complementary institutions.
3 It was made possible by quasi-Lewis-type industrialization. Lewis (1965) explained low wage levels in developing countries and the deflation effect of their industrialization on the world economy by his theory of 'industrialization with unlimited supply of labour'. If the supply of labour is available without limits from surplus labour in the agriculture in the industrialization of a less-developed economy, wage levels are kept at subsistence levels plus transport costs. The lack of domestic demand drives exports of products at the lowest price levels, which depresses international price levels.

At current exchange rates, Chinese wage levels were kept at 5 per cent of the US level from 1980 to 2000 (Glyn 2006). There are two reasons for this. First, Chinese agricultural employment was still 50 per cent, which gave a vast amount of relative surplus population for the reserve army. Second, Chinese wages were increasing dramatically in yuan, but the devaluation of the yuan from 1.5 yuan to a US dollar in 1980 to 8.6 yuan to a US dollar in 1994 kept Chinese wage levels at 5 per cent of US levels for the 20 years of its catching-up process (Figure 2.3). I call this 'quasi-Lewis-type industrialization', since wage increases were concealed by devaluation of the currency.

Chinese compressed and quasi-Lewis-type industrialization had the following influence on Chinese dynamic comparative advantage and on the world economy. First, in the catching-up process, increases in wages decrease the

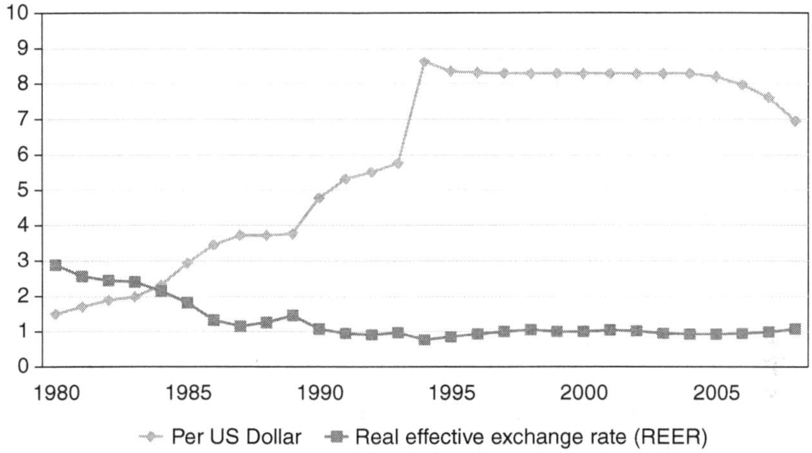

Figure 2.3 Yuan exchange rate (source: IMF IFS).

Note
REER is the real effective exchange rate, adjusted for the effects of inflation.

dynamic comparative advantages, which forces a shift from dynamic industries to more sophisticated industries. Quasi-Lewis-type industrialization kept China's dynamic comparative advantage in less sophisticated industries until the mid-1990s. Therefore, the Chinese industrial structure was not upgraded sufficiently. Second, it blocked the flying geese-type industrialization process of less-developed countries, and applied deflationary pressure on the world economy.

China-centric East Asian production network

Table 2.2 shows that Japan's influence on the Chinese economy peaked in the early 1990s. This was also the peak of the Japan-led Pacific Rim triangle trade. After China became a member of the WTO, its share of international trade skyrocketed. Chinese goods exports increased nearly fourfold, from US$394.5 billion in 2000 to US$1,512.6 billion in 2008, and its goods imports increased nearly fivefold, from US$195.2 billion in 2000 to US$982.6 billion in 2008 (RIETY-TID 2010). Japanese goods exports to China and imports from China increased dramatically, raising Japanese trade dependence to 15 per cent again between 2002 and 2007. This enabled Japan to adopt an export-led growth strategy again and to recover from the decade-long depression. However, Japan could not keep pace with China, and its share in China's international trade was reduced, both as exports and imports (Table 2 and Figure 2.4). Now China imports capital goods from Japan, Korea and Taiwan, food and raw material from less-developed countries, and exports completed products to the European Union, the United States, Asia and other areas. The cross-border division of

Table 2.2 Shares in Chinese goods trade

	Exports from China (%)					*China's imports (%)*				
	Japan	*Korea + Taiwan*	*ASEAN5*	*USA*	*EU27*	*Japan*	*Korea + Taiwan*	*ASEAN5*	*USA*	*EU27*
1991	13.1	3.4	4.8	18.5	16.7	18.1	1.7	6.1	15.6	17.5
1995	16.1	4.7	4.4	21.6	14.9	24.8	9.2	8.1	13.8	18.6
2009	9.1	6.1	6.0	22.6	23.7	14.6	17.8	11.1	8.7	14.5

Source: RIETY-TID2010, www.rieti.go.jp/jp/projects/rieti-tid/index.html.

Notes
ASEAN5 = Indonesia, Malaysia, the Philippines, Singapore and Thailand.

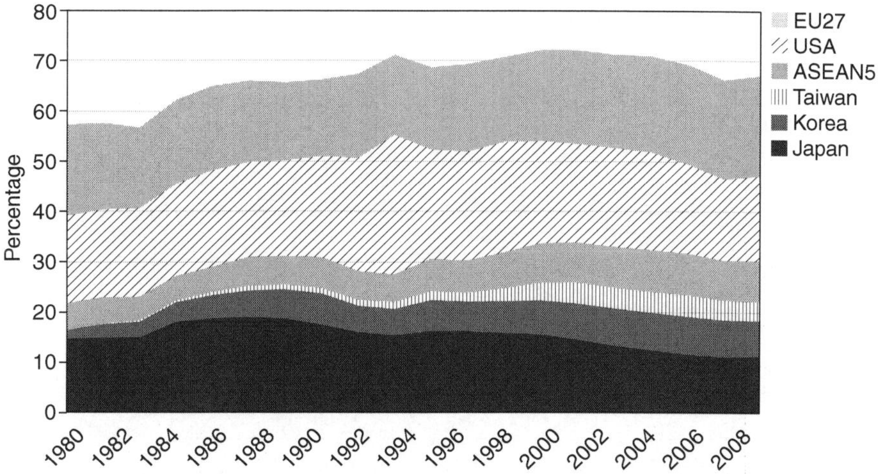

Figure 2.4 Trade shares in Chinese goods trade (export+import) (source: RIETY-TID2010, www.rieti.go.jp/jp/projects/rieti-tid/index.html).

work and trade in East Asia has been completely rebuilt by China, and the Japan-led Pacific Rim triangle trade regime has been replaced by a China-centric East Asian production network (Figure 2.4).

In this process, Chinese quasi-Lewis-type industrialization finally reached its limits. Its market exchange rate and real effective exchange rate had been stable since the mid-1990s (Figure 2.3). Its rapid rise in wages was reflected in its dynamic comparative advantage. Specialization in light industries such as textiles, toys and electrical appliances peaked in the late 1990s, and specialization in machinery such as electrical and general machinery increased rapidly from the mid-1990s onwards (Figure 2.5). Production and domestic demand in heavy and chemical industries also increased rapidly from the mid-1990s.

The fall of the neo-liberal capital accumulation regime and the structural crisis

Structural change

Just as the success of the golden age accumulation regime itself undermined the institutions that supported it and caused structural crisis, so too has the long-lasting neo-liberal accumulation regime itself undermined its complementary institutions.

1 The effect of neo-liberal financial relaxation is losing momentum. First, although aggregate demand depends on higher risk-taking by borrowers,

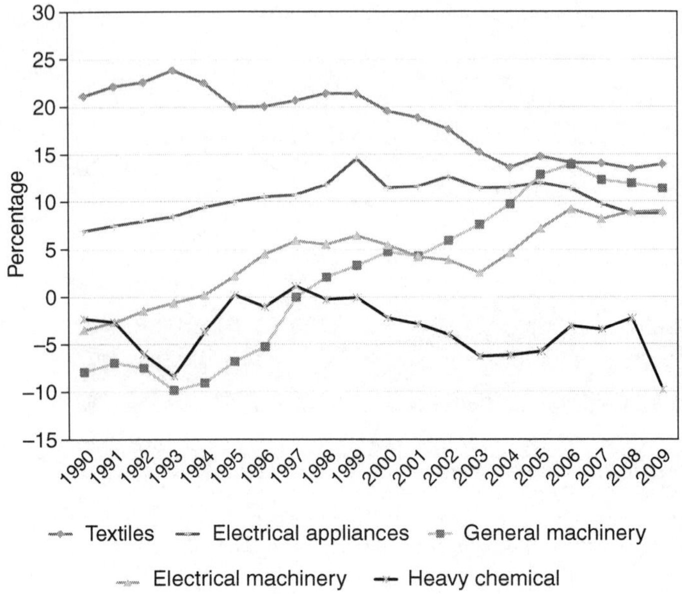

Figure 2.5 China's specialization, 1900–2009 (source: RIETI-TID2010, www.rieti-tid.com/).

Note
Specialization = (Exports − Imports)/(Total Industrial Exports + Imports).

unprecedented levels of household debt make further increases difficult. Second, neo-liberal financial liberalization destroyed the robust financial structure; so further relaxation undermines the safety of the financial system. Third, the neo-liberal monetary policy to decrease interest rates reached its limit at a zero interest rate. Further reduction is difficult. Furthermore, unprecedented levels of government debt and increasing social spending have made further tax cuts difficult. These factors have increased demand-side constraints.

2 Neo-liberal globalization shifted the centre of capital accumulation to developing economies such as China and India, whose industrialization has been very successful. However, this has increased the demand for raw materials, energy and food. Higher international commodity prices have increased supply-side constraints.
3 The engine of US demand-led growth in the neo-liberal accumulation regime has shifted from domestic financial relaxation to foreign debt since the East Asian economic crisis of 1997, increasing international imbalances. It is most significant in the Chinese and German current account surpluses, which increased significantly since 2002, surpassing Japan in 2005 and 2006 respectively. The total surplus of these three countries peaked at $837

> billion in 2007. On the other hand, the current account deficit of the United States (and Britain and southern EU countries) increased rapidly after the 2000s, and the US deficit peaked at $788 billion in 2006. Prosperity in the United States (and Britain and southern EU countries) in the early 2000s was made possible by borrowing from foreign countries. The borrowed money was spent on the consumption of imported goods and residential fixed investment, rather than on investment (i.e. on non-residential fixed investments).

With these structural changes of the accumulation regime, a serious crisis started in 2007.

Crisis of international imbalance and the future of capitalism

The sub-prime loan crisis is the most severe world crisis since the structural crisis in the 1970s. The historical process of the crisis can be summarized as follows. A housing market bubble began in the late 1990s and accelerated in the early 2000s. Banks earned large fees by securitizing mortgages and selling them to capital markets. Institutional investors all over the world bought these securities because they had higher returns than equivalently rated corporate bonds. Banks began to offer mortgages to those who could not afford them when the housing price bubble evaporated and/or interest rates rose. Home sales peaked in late 2005, and housing prices peaked in early 2006. Then the sub-prime loan crisis erupted in mid-2007. The crisis began in the United States and spread all over the world.

The question is: what kind of crisis is the sub-prime loan crisis? Is it a cyclical crisis, a structural crisis or an even more serious crisis that will abolish the present capitalist world system, as did the 1929 world crisis and the subsequent Great Depression – that is, a systemic crisis? We have three scenarios.

First scenario. This is not a structural crisis in a capital accumulation regime but a crisis of financial excess. Minskyians argue that financial excess was the only problem, and normal growth with cyclical crises will return once the finance excess has been remedied (Kregel 2008: 20). In my opinion, neo-liberal financial relaxation was introduced to solve demand constraints. It is necessary to restructure financial systems and create more robust ones. However, doing so does not solve demand constraints.

Second scenario. This is a structural crisis in the neo-liberal capital accumulation regime, but not a systemic crisis of bureaucratic capitalism. Structural Keynesians argue that the ultimate cause of the crisis is the breaking of the link between wages and productivity growth. Solving the problem requires the reversing of neo-liberalism and restoration of the link between wages and productivity growth (Palley 2010). In my opinion, this requires the reconstruction of the Bretton Woods regime internationally, and of the welfare state domestically. Without overwhelming economic power, international cooperation is required to rebuild the international monetary system. It should be more transnational and public than the US dollar standard system. Keynes's international clearing union may be rehabilitated. Reconstruction of the welfare society requires productivity growth and an egalitarian income distribution mechanism. It seems to be more possible now than it was in the 1980s, since dynamic comparative advantage has recovered, owing to the take-off of new dynamic industries, namely IT and knowledge-intensive industries combined with GVCs.

Third scenario. This is the beginning of a systemic crisis of a capitalist world system that will destroy bureaucratic capitalism. Neo-liberalism enabled the United States to enjoy prosperity in the 1990s and 2000s. Neo-liberalism is still the dominant ideology even though it faced structural crisis after 2007. If the United States wants full development of IT and knowledge-intensive industries in order to keep its economic status, it needs to solve demand constraints by rebuilding the link between productivity growth and wages, and keeping most advanced knowledge within the country by controlling transnational corporations. The neo-liberal ideology makes these policies impossible.

On the other hand, we see the possibility that the further industrialization of China may re-establish a flying geese pattern of development on a global level among developing countries, forming a new world system. Facing the collapse of the US neo-liberal capital accumulation regime, pressure to reverse the Chinese current account surplus has increased since 2008. China has changed policies at the margin from export-led industrialization to domestic demand-led industrialization, which may establish its link between wages and productivity growth. This will increase Chinese wage rates and China's real exchange rate, and reduce China's competitiveness in less sophisticated labour-intensive industries. It will allow less-developed countries to industrialize in a flying geese pattern. Furthermore, if transnational corporations choose China as their centres to promote IT and knowledge-intensive industries to maximize profit, China may embark on a new development path.

I consider that the second and third scenarios are most promising, since I believe that to build the link between wages and productivity both in advanced and in developing countries is necessary to recover from this most serious crisis of the capitalist world system, and to develop productivity of the new dynamic industry fully.

Notes

1 If surplus labour exists in the agricultural country, specialization in agriculture may further increase surplus labour in agriculture and decrease the total output of the two countries.

2 When the technology is fully diffused, one hour of labour produces one unit of value. The labour theory of value thus comes into effect in a state of equilibrium without productivity growth.

3 In dynamic sectors or dynamic regions, wages increased with industrialization in England. Hunt wrote, '[I]ndustrialization was a main cause of the relative improvement in Lancashire wages in the eighteenth century and of the wage advantage Lancastrians enjoyed throughout the following century' (1986: 961). Regional and occupational

wage variations were reduced towards the end of the nineteenth century. Hunt emphasizes the role of the trade unions: 'Rising membership and the widening of the geographical area covered by collective bargaining spread union influence beyond the existing high-wage areas and occupations, as did the post-1888 "new" unions, with their more egalitarian priorities' (ibid.: 959). It took more than 100 years for the beneficial influence of industrialization on wages to spread in England.

4 It may be noted here that for advanced economies, a reduction in VAL is a more important cause of the reduction of dynamic comparative advantage than increases in wages. For catching-up economies that import ready-made technologies, increases in wages are the main reason behind decreasing dynamic comparative advantage.

5 The massive increase in global supply of dollars came from war spending in Vietnam.

6 Financial innovation includes the shadow banking system, derivatives, options, home equity loans, and securitization and tranching of securities (Palley 2010).

7 Posco (Pohang Iron and Steel Company) in Korea is a very significant example. It is now the world's third-largest steelmaker, and Asia's most profitable.

References

Akamatsu, K. (1962) 'A historical pattern of economic growth in developing countries', *The Developing Economies* (Institute of Asian Economic Affairs), Preliminary Issue no. 1: 3–25.

Baumol, W. J. (1967) 'Macroeconomics of unbalanced growth: the anatomy of urban crisis', *American Economic Review*, 57: 451–426.

Chang, H.-J. (2002) *Kicking Away the Ladder: Development Strategy in Historical Perspective*, London: Anthem Press.

Chang, H.-J. (2009) Introduction to the Japanese edition of *Kicking Away the Ladder: Development Strategy in Historical Perspective*, Tokyo: Keizai Hyouron Sya.

Epstein, G. A. and Schor, J. B. (1990) 'Macro policy in the rise and fall of the golden age', in S. A. Marglin and J. B. Schor (eds) *The Golden Age of Capitalism: Reinterpreting the Postwar Experience*, Oxford: Oxford University Press.

Gerschenkron, A. (1962) *Economic Backwardness in Historical Perspective*, Cambridge, MA: Harvard University Press.

Glyn, A. (2006) *Capitalism Unleashed*, Oxford: Oxford University Press.

Hunt, E. H. (1986) 'Industrialization and regional inequality: wages in Britain, 1760–1914', *Journal of Economic History*, 46 (4): 935–966.

IMF (2010) *World Economic Outlook April 2010*. Online, available at: www.imf.org/external/pubs/ft/weo/2010/01/pdf/text.pdf.

Kalecki, M. (1954) *Theory of Economic Dynamics: An Essay on Cyclical and Long-Run Changes in Capitalist Economy*, London: George Allen & Unwin.

Kalecki, M. (1971) *Selected Essays on the Dynamics of the Capitalist Economy, 1933–1970*, Cambridge University Press.

Kregel, J. (2008) 'Using Minsky's cushions of safety to analyze the crisis in the U.S. subprime mortgage market', *International Journal of Political Economy*, 37: 3–23.

Lewis, A. (1965) *The Theory of Economic Growth*, London: George Allen & Unwin.

Marx, K. *Capital*. 3 vols: Vol. I. Trans. B Fowkes. Harmondsworth, UK: Penguin, 1976. Vol. II: 1981. Vol. III: Moscow: International Publisher, 1969.

Minsky, H. P. (1982) *Can 'It' Happen Again? Essays on Instability and Finance*, Armonk, NY: M. E. Sharpe.

MITI (2000) *Ajia Keizai 2000* (Asian economy 2000). Tokyo: Ministry of International Trade and Industry.

Palley, T. I. (2010) 'The limits of Minsky's financial instability hypothesis as an explanation of the crisis', *Monthly Review*, 61 (11). Online, available at: http://monthlyreview.org/2010/04/01/the-limits-of-minskys-financial-instability-hypothesis-as-an-explanation-of-the-crisis.

Ricardo, D. (1817) *On the Principles of Political Economy and Taxation*, London: John Murray.

Rowthorn, R. E. (1982) *Demand, Real Wages and Economic Growth, Studi economici no. 18*.

Rowthorn, R. E. and Wells, J. R. (1987) *De-industrialisation and Foreign Trade*, Cambridge: Cambridge University Press.

Vernon, R. (1966) 'International investment and international trade in the product cycle', *Quarterly Journal of Economics*, 80: 190–207.

Whittaker, D. H, Zhi, T., Sturgeon, T., Tsai, M. H. and Okita, T. (2010) *Studies in Comparative International Development*, 45: 439–467.

Yokokawa, N. (2012) 'Cyclical crisis, structural crisis, systemic crisis, and future of capitalism', in K. Yagi, N. Yokokawa, H. Shinjiro and G. Dymski (eds) *Crises of Global Economies and the Future of Capitalism: Reviving Marxian Crisis Theory*, New York: Routledge.

3 Knowledge and the Asian challenge

C. P. Chandrasekhar

Way back in 2005, in its 22 August issue, *Business Week* declared:

> Rarely has the economic ascent of two still relatively poor nations been watched with such a mixture of awe, opportunism, and trepidation. The postwar era witnessed economic miracles in Japan and South Korea. But neither was populous enough to power worldwide growth or change the game in a complete spectrum of industries. China and India, by contrast, possess the weight and dynamism to transform the 21st-century global economy. The closest parallel to their emergence is the saga of 19th-century America, a huge continental economy with a young, driven workforce that grabbed the lead in agriculture, apparel, and the high technologies of the era, such as steam engines, the telegraph, and electric lights. But in a way, even America's rise falls short in comparison to what's happening now. Never has the world seen the simultaneous, sustained takeoffs of two nations that together account for one-third of the planet's population.
>
> (Engardio 2005)

The growth of these two large economies is indeed daunting. Over the five years ending 2007, China continued to grow at a scorching pace of more than 10 per cent per annum. During this period, India closely followed China's performance, with GDP growing at an estimated 8.8 per cent per annum.[1] Even during 2008 and 2009, when the world was affected by the financial and economic crisis, China grew at an average rate of 9.4 per cent and India at 6.4 per cent. These figures keep alive fears of a threat from these two Asian giants to the rest of the world, including the developed countries of Europe. Though productivity and per capita income levels in these countries are still far behind those in the United States, the differential is narrowing because of their much faster rates of growth (Table 3.1).

Associated with predictions of the rise to dominance of these economies was the view that the challenge from China and India to the developed world was of particular significance because the basis of their strength was shifting from cheap labour to technology.

Table 3.1 Selected economic and productivity indicators for the United States, the EU, China and India, 1995–2010

Country	*Productivity growth (% average annual change)*			*GDP (US$)*		
	1995–2005	*2005–10*	*2010 (est.)*	*Per employee 2010*	*Per capita 2010*	*2010*
United States	2.3	1.5	1.1	100	100	100
Euro area	1.4	0.7	1.6			
China	6.7	9.8	8.7	18	24	79.5
India	4.2	5.8	5.4	12	11	28.3

Source: The Conference Board, Total Economy Database (January 2011 and September 2011), www.conference-board.org/economics (accessed 8 January 2012).

Notes

Productivity growth measured on basis of GDP per employee at 1990 purchasing power parities. GDP per capita at 1990 purchasing power parities using Geary Khamis PPPs for conversion. GDP is US dollars converted to 2010 price level, using updated Geary Khamis PPPs at 2005 purchasing power parities for conversion.

> An accelerating trend is that technical and managerial skills in both China and India are becoming more important than cheap assembly labor. China will stay dominant in mass manufacturing, and is one of the few nations building multibillion-dollar electronics and heavy industrial plants. India is a rising power in software, design, services, and precision industry.
>
> (Engardio 2005)

This focus on the production of high-technology goods and services provides an added reason as to why competition from China and India assumes relevance. The rapid pace of expansion of exports of high-tech manufactured products from China and software and IT-enabled services from India has supported the view that 'knowledge capital' plays a crucial role in the growing global presence of these countries. If these countries maintain and advance any lead they may have in these areas, the rest of the world's competition from and dependence on them will increase.

However, there are significant differences between China and India, besides the fact that the export and growth successes of the former are more dramatic than that of India. It is true that in both countries the ratio of exports of goods and services to GDP has risen quite sharply in recent years (Figure 3.1). In 1978, when China's reform began, that ratio was more or less the same in India and China, at around 6.5 per cent. Since then, the figure has risen sharply in China, to touch nearly 40 per cent in 2006, and much more slowly in India, to reach close to 21 per cent that year. However, during the crisis years 2008 and 2009, China's exports were affected far more adversely than India's. Also, while much of the expansion in exports in the Chinese case has been on account of exports of manufactured goods, export growth in India has been principally on account of services (Figure 3.2). Between 1985 and 1995, the ratio of goods exports to

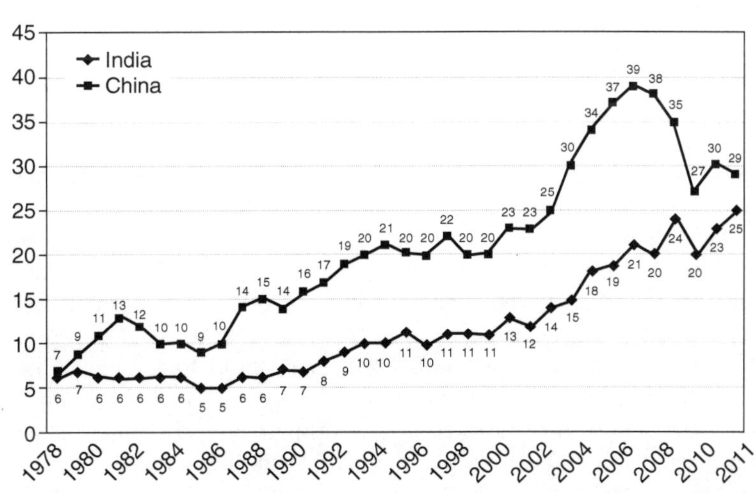

Figure 3.1 Exports of goods and services (% of GDP) (source: World Bank, *World Development Indicators Online*).

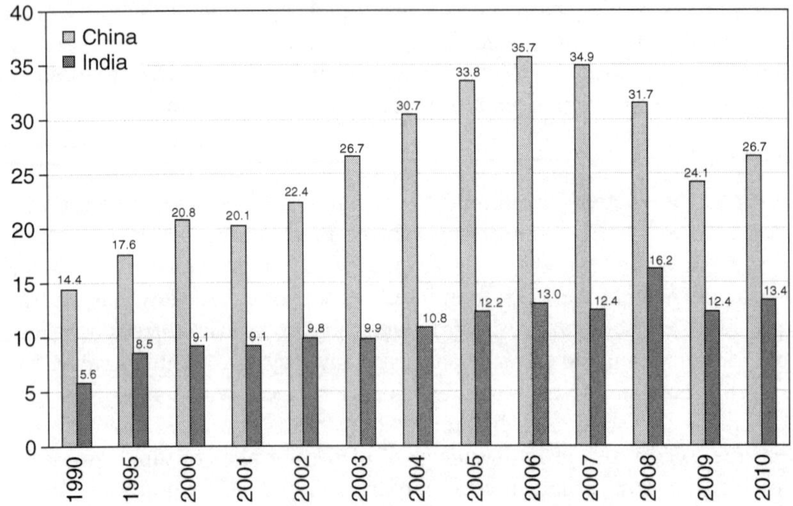

Figure 3.2 Exports of goods as a percentage of GDP (source: World Bank, *World Development Indicators Online*).

GDP rose from around 8 per cent to 18 per cent in the case of China and from 4 per cent to 9 per cent in the case of India. But after that, while the figure for China shot up to 35.7 per cent in 2006, it stood at 13 per cent in the case of India. It was only during the crisis years that India seems to have performed better, with the figure rising to 16.2 per cent in 2008, while that for China fell to 31.6 per cent. But India too was adversely affected over the next two years, though China was hit more badly in relative terms.

However, India's performance is considered noteworthy and unusual because it is the growth in services exports that explains India's more moderate trade success. Add to this the important role of private transfers, or remittances from non-resident Indians, resulting from the on-site provision of high-tech services abroad, and India's performance is indeed creditable. If net current transfers into India, consisting largely of remittances from Indian workers abroad, are treated as a form of services income, then the current account deficit reduces substantially, implying that the trade in goods and services has played a very important role in strengthening the balance of payments.

At the aggregate level, of course, it is only China that appears truly mercantilist, exporting more goods than it imports and accumulating wealth in the form of foreign reserves. In 2008, China recorded a trade surplus of $361 billion and a current account surplus of $390 billion.[2] On the other hand, India recorded a merchandise trade deficit of $92.4 billion. Even if the net surplus from services export is taken into account, the deficit stands at $76.4 billion. In sum, the role of net exports as a trigger for growth appears to be important for China, but not so for India.

Yet the rapid expansion of exports has been accompanied by high rates of growth of GDP in both these countries, enhancing their presence in the global economy. Measured in terms of prices prevailing in 2000, China's share of world exports of goods and services was 8.5 per cent in 2006 (up from 1.4 per cent in 1978), but India's share was just 1.1 per cent, though it was up from 0.4 per cent in 1978 (Table 3.2). In terms of constant price GDP, China accounted for 5.5 per cent of global GDP in 2006 and India for 1.9 per cent, both up from 0.9 per cent in 1978. (When measured in terms of 2005 purchasing power parity (PPP) dollars, China accounted for 10 per cent of global GDP and India for 4.5 per cent in 2006. This compares with 2.0 per cent and 2.3 per cent respectively in 1978. This is often cited as an indicator of the extent to which the rest of the world is benefiting from growing markets in these countries, but this would be overplaying the situation, since cross-border trade occurs in actual nominal exchange rates, not 'PPP exchange rates'.)

The role of trade in facilitating growth in the two countries explains in large part the growing perception that the two of them (especially China) threaten growth in other countries. As noted earlier, their growth is seen as threatening even the developed countries because of their perceived ability to exploit the opportunities created by the new knowledge economy.

The output of high-technology manufacturing located in China rose ninefold over the period 1995–2007 from $19 billion to $167 billion. As a result, the country's share in global output rose from 3 per cent to 14 per cent. More importantly, this growth was driven largely by exports. Thus, the manufacturing product categories that the World Bank defines as high-technology goods account for a significant share of China's exports.[3] As Figure 3.3 shows, high-tech exports from China rose rapidly after 2000, and by 2005 exceeded those from all countries, including the United States, Germany and Japan. By 2008, China was way ahead of its rivals. The result of this was a sharp increase in China's share in the global market for high-technology goods. The combined share of China and Hong Kong in exports of high-technology goods to the rest

Table 3.2 India and China relative to the world (percentage shares)

	1978	*1980*	*1985*	*1990*	*1995*	*2000*	*2005*	*2006*
GDP (constant 2000 $)								
China	0.94	1.03	1.51	1.85	2.93	3.76	5.19	5.53
India	0.93	0.89	1.01	1.12	1.28	1.44	1.77	1.86
Exports of goods and services (constant 2000 US$)								
China	1.44	1.71	1.93	1.81	2.56	3.50	7.66	8.52
India	0.43	0.45	0.39	0.46	0.67	0.76	1.07	1.05
GDP PPP (constant 2005 international $)								
China	–	1.98	2.90	3.55	5.66	7.17	9.53	10.07
India	–	2.29	2.58	2.89	3.32	3.69	4.35	4.53

Source: World Bank, *World Development Indicators Online*.

of the world rose from 6.2 per cent of the global total in 1995 to 16.6 per cent in 2005 and further to 19.8 per cent in 2008 (Table 3.3). The two major losers from this increase in China's share were Japan and the United States, with the former experiencing a 10.3 percentage point decline in share and the latter a 7.6 percentage point loss. What is noteworthy is that the European Union's exports to the rest of the world rose marginally in terms of the share in total world exports, indicating that while the European Union may not be emerging as the world's leading exporter of high-technology products, as a region it was not being displaced from global markets, as Japan and the United States were.

The five manufacturing sectors identified as high technology are Communications and semiconductors, Pharmaceuticals, Scientific instruments, the Aerospace industry, and Computers and office machinery. In the mid-1980s, the European Union ranked third after the United States and Japan in Communications and semiconductors; was almost on par with the United States at the top in Pharmaceuticals; was second after the United States in Scientific instruments; was substantially behind the United States (even if in second place) in the Aerospace industry; and stood second after the United State in Computers and office machinery.

By the mid-1990s, the ranking was more or less the same in Communications and semiconductors; the European Union had taken the lead in Pharmaceuticals and Scientific instruments; the European Union had gained relative to the United States, though the ranking remained the same, in the Aerospace industry; and Japan had taken a clear lead relative to the United States and the European Union in Computers and office machinery.

During that decade, while China had recorded an increase in the value added in all these sectors, especially in Pharmaceuticals and Communications and

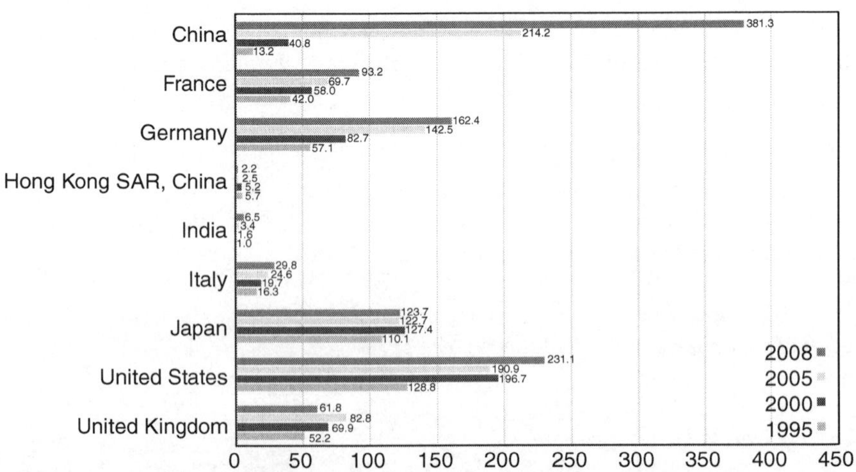

Figure 3.3 High-technology exports (% billion) (source: World Bank, *World Development Indicators Online*).

Table 3.3 Exports of high-technology goods by region/country/economy, 1995–2008

Percentages				
Region/country/economy	*1995*	*2000*	*2005*	*2008*
World excluding intra-EU and intra-China/Hong Kong	100.0	100.0	100.0	100.0
Asia-9	27.0	29.3	28.5	27.9
India	0.2	0.2	0.3	0.4
China and Hong Kong total	8.6	10.6	23.4	27.3
China and Hong Kong ROW	6.2	7.5	16.6	19.8
Intra-China/Hong Kong	2.4	3.1	6.9	7.5
EU total	38.9	37.5	39.8	37.4
EU ROW	16.3	15.6	18.1	17.4
Intra-EU	22.6	21.8	21.8	20.0
Japan	18.4	13.0	9.1	8.1
United States	21.2	21.5	14.8	13.6
All other countries	7.8	7.5	8.2	8.0

Source: National Science Board (2010).

Note
Asia-9 refers to India, Indonesia, Malaysia, the Philippines, Singapore, South Korea, Taiwan, Thailand and Vietnam.

semiconductors, it was by no means a major producer, let alone exporter, of these high-tech manufactures.

The real transformation in global shares came in the period after 1995. Between 1995 and 2007, value added in Chinese production increased 6.5 times in Communications and semiconductors, 8.3 times in Pharmaceuticals, 8 times in the case of Scientific instruments, 22 times in the case of Aerospace and 64 times in the case of Computers and office machinery. As a result, in 2007 China was the third-largest producer in Communications and semiconductors after the United States and Japan (having gone ahead of the European Union), the third-largest producer after the United States and the European Union in Pharmaceuticals, the third-largest producer after the European Union and the United States in Scientific instruments, the third largest producer after the United States and the European Union in Aerospace, and the largest producer of Computer and office machinery, followed by the United States and the European Union.

What is noteworthy is that there is only one area (Communications and semiconductors) in which the European Union, as a group of nations, has lost its position among the top three relative to 1985. What is more, it has gained in strength in the Aerospace business and Scientific instruments, and has not faced the same setback as Japan in Computers and office machinery. This ability of the European Union to retain its position in many high-tech industries was partly due to its ability to relocate production to its own hinterland. Thus, the National Science Board of the United States argues (2010: 6–19):

> Output of several Eastern European member countries – the Czech Republic, Hungary, Poland, and the Slovak Republic – grew much more rapidly in these industries than output of other member countries. This is consistent with evidence that these countries have become assembly centres for high technology industries based in more developed EU economies.
>
> (Kaminski and Ng 2001)

However, caution must be exercised in interpreting this evidence of relative 'success', whether it be in the case of the European Union, China or individual nations within the European Union. It needs to be noted that most high-tech industries are 'heterogeneous' in character, in the sense that they can be broken down into a range of processes and components involving very different levels of science and technology (S&T) intensity, and individual components can be located at different sites. Gains in terms of higher value added shares in some sub-processes or subsectors would be actual high-tech gains, whereas gains in other areas may just be a reflection of the relocation of less technology-intensive segments to cheaper locations for production. Unfortunately, sectoral data on value added shares do not permit an assessment of the geographical distribution of the value chain needed to make distinctions of this kind.

But there are studies which suggest that a breakdown of this kind has indeed been occurring. Studies of innovation in the European hinterland, especially the transition economies of Eastern Europe, have noted the lack of local appropriability of the high-tech activities driven by investment from the European core, as well as the generation of outsourcing-based low-technology activities within the supposedly high-tech areas (Kattel *et al.* 2009; Suurna and Kattel 2010; Karo and Kattel 2011). Similar tendencies can be observed in China. Output in China's Computer and office machinery industry, for example, grew at an annual rate of 45 per cent between 1995 and 2007, taking its global share from 1 per cent to 40 per cent. In Communications and semiconductors too, China's global share rose from 4 per cent to 15 per cent. Of course, not all of this expansion can be just low-end activity. Yet

> [a]necdotal evidence suggests that assembly of computers and semiconductors shifted from the United States to China and other Asian countries, contributing to China's vigorous expansion of its output in these industries. However, U.S.-based firms such as Dell and Apple continued to grow and to be highly profitable, deriving much of their profits from high-value activities such as logistics, design, and marketing that remained in the United States.
>
> (Dedrick *et al.* 2008, quoted in National Science Board 2010: 6–19)

The Indian example

In India's case, its rise as a competitor in the global arena can be traced to its success as an exporter of services. The US National Science Foundation divides the knowledge-intensive services sector into a segment that is largely location bound and substantially publicly funded (health and education), and a segment that is tradable. Globally traded commercial knowledge-intensive services consist of computer and data processing services, commercial R&D services, financial services and communications services.

Software and IT-enabled services, identified as high-tech services, account for a significant share of India's services exports. India's transition to being predominantly a service economy came about at least partly because it benefited from this increase in the global exports of services, with its share in world exports of services rising from 1.1 per cent in 2001 to 2.6 per cent in 2006 (Reserve Bank of India, 2009). As a result, India was ranked eleventh among the world's leading exporters of services. The only other developing country that contributed more than India was China. According to the Reserve Bank of India's (RBI's) balance of payments data, gross exports of software, business, financial and communication services amounted to 5.3 per cent of GDP at market prices in 2007–08, with software services exports touching 3.4 per cent of GDP. These figures compare with a merchandise exports to GDP ratio of 14.2 per cent.[4]

These trends in the production and export of high-technology goods and services are of importance because they appear to suggest that growth in India and China is concentrated in areas in which global trade, production and productivity are growing most rapidly. Overall, the transformation of these countries appears to be in keeping with the changing patterns of growth in the global economy, involving an increase in the S&T and knowledge intensity of both manufacturing and services. According to the National Science Board (2010):

> The global value-added output of knowledge-intensive service industries and high-technology manufacturing industries accounted for an estimated $15.7 trillion in 2007, of which $5.0 trillion was for the largely location-bound, publicly funded knowledge-intensive services: $2.8 trillion for health and $2.2 trillion for education. The total for tradable knowledge-intensive services and high-technology manufactures amounted to $10.7 trillion – $9.5 trillion for services and $1.2 trillion for manufacturing – out of an estimated total world economic output of $54.8 trillion.

The global market for high-technology manufactures is growing faster than that for other manufactured goods. According to the National Science Board (NSB), knowledge-intensive industries, including knowledge-intensive service and high-technology manufacturing industries, have become a major part of the global economy, contributing almost 30 per cent of global economic output in 2007. Between 1985 and 2007, gross revenue of the high-technology manufacturing sector[5] rose from $1.1 trillion to $3.5 trillion in constant dollars (National Science Board 2008, vol. 1: 6–16). Average annual growth during this 20-year period was, at 6 per cent, more than double the rate for other manufacturing industries, taking the high-technology share of all manufacturing output from 10 per cent to 18 per cent.

Knowledge-intensive services are also an area where global demand and output growth has been high. The National Science Foundation (NSF) concludes that '[m] arket-oriented knowledge-intensive services – business, financial, and communications – are driving growth in the service sector, which now accounts for nearly 70 percent of global economic activity' (National Science Board, 2008: vol. 1). The worldwide value added generated by market-oriented knowledge-intensive services more than doubled from $4.5 trillion in 1995 to $9.5 trillion in 2007. Within the services sector, business services, which includes knowledge-intensive computer and data processing and research and engineering services, is the largest segment, accounting for more than half of global value added in market-oriented knowledge services in 2007. The importance of these services for the developed countries, given the structural diversification of their economies, is obvious. The United States accounted for a little more than a third of global value added in commercial knowledge-intensive services and the European Union for about 30 per cent. Compared with that, the contributions of China and India were a modest 5 per cent each. The issue is that their shares were growing, and in India's case exports were advancing rapidly through offsite and onsite delivery.

India's high-tech lag

However, here again the tendency to club China and India together in terms of high-tech competitiveness is to ignore significant differences between the two. When it comes to high-tech manufacturing, India does not feature as a major player at all. Thus, if we take the 23-year period from 1985 to 2007, the combined share of China's and Hong Kong's high-tech manufacturing industries in global value added in the high-technology manufacturing sectors fluctuated between 2.3 per cent and 3.4 per cent over the period 1985–99 and subsequently shot up to 13.7 per cent by 2007 (Figure 3.4). On the other hand, over the 23-year period as a whole, India's share in the global high-technology manufacturing value added stagnated at below 0.4 of a percentage point right up to 2001 and then rose marginally to 0.66 per cent by 2007. Interestingly, the United States, which had seen a substantial decline in its share of global value added in high-tech areas between 1985 and 1995, managed to reverse this tendency during the second half of the 1990s, largely as a result of an expansion of the radio, television and communications sector and partly because of advances in office and computing machinery. The European Union's share was stagnant, so that China's gain was at the expense of the United States and the rest of the world outside the European Union.

The remarkable performance of China is also reflected in the relative share of the high-technology sectors in its manufacturing sector as a whole. Figure 3.5 compares the relative share of value added in the high-tech sectors in aggregate manufacturing value added in a number of countries. Across the world, that share rose from 12.5 per cent in 1985 to 15.3 per cent in 2005, before falling to 13.7 per cent in 2007. The United States performed better, with the share in its case rising from 17.0 per cent to 21.3 per cent between 1985 and 2007. The European Union's performance tracked this trend well, with the relevant share

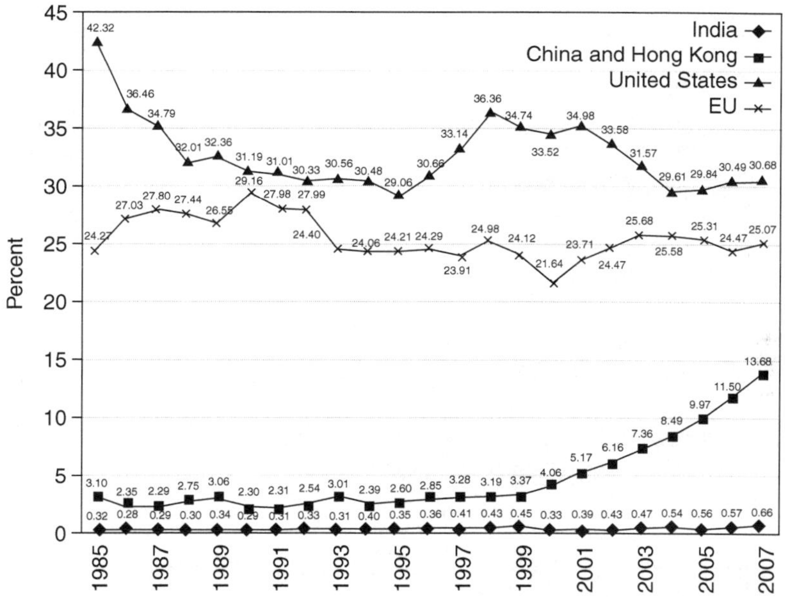

Figure 3.4 Share of world hi-tech manufacturing value added (source: National Science Board 2010: appendix tables).

rising in its case from 10.5 per cent to 12.8 per cent and then falling to 12.0 per cent. India's performance, however, is unimpressive. While the share in India rose from 2.9 per cent to 4.7 per cent, the absolute value of that share was much less than the global average. On the other hand, China and Hong Kong's performance was creditable, with the high-tech share in its case rising from 8.5 per cent to 13.2 per cent of manufacturing value added over this 23-year period.

As noted above, China's rise in the global league tables for high-tech manufacturing was the result of a rapid expansion of exports. The ratio of export sales to revenues rose from 25 per cent in 1985 to more than 75 per cent in the mid-1990s, only to moderate later as domestic consumption of high-technology products rose along with incomes. By 2005, that ratio had fallen below 60 per cent (Figure 3.6), because of a rise in domestic consumption rather than because of a decline in exports.

China's success on the export front has meant that its presence in global high-tech trade is even greater than in production, with its share in global high-tech manufacturing exports having risen from a little more than 6 per cent in 1985 to close to 20 per cent in 2008 (Figure 3.7). This rise paralleled a decline in the shares of both the United States and Japan in global trade in these products. The European Union managed to maintain and marginally increase its share. On the other hand, India has been and remains an almost non-existent player in global markets for high-technology manufacturing.

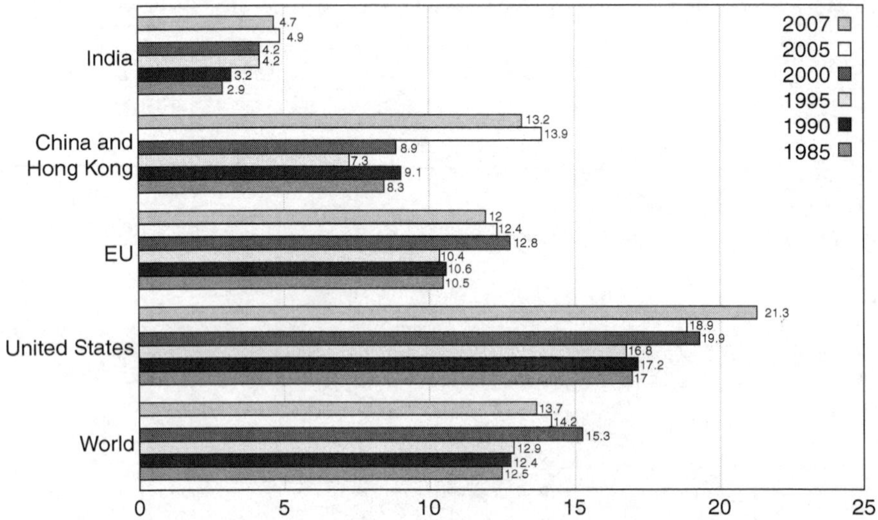

Figure 3.5 Share of hi-tech value added in manufacturing value added (%) (source: National Science Board 2008: vol. 2).

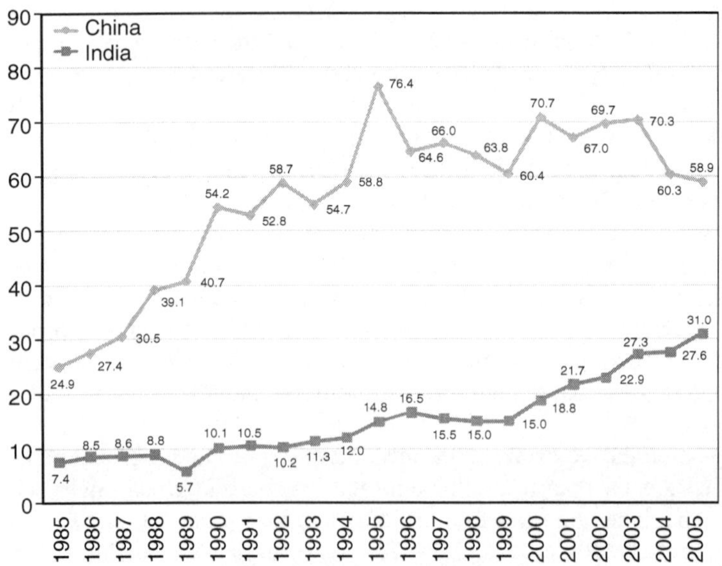

Figure 3.6 Exports in relation to the revenue of hi-tech manufacturing industries (source: National Science Board 2008: vol. 2).

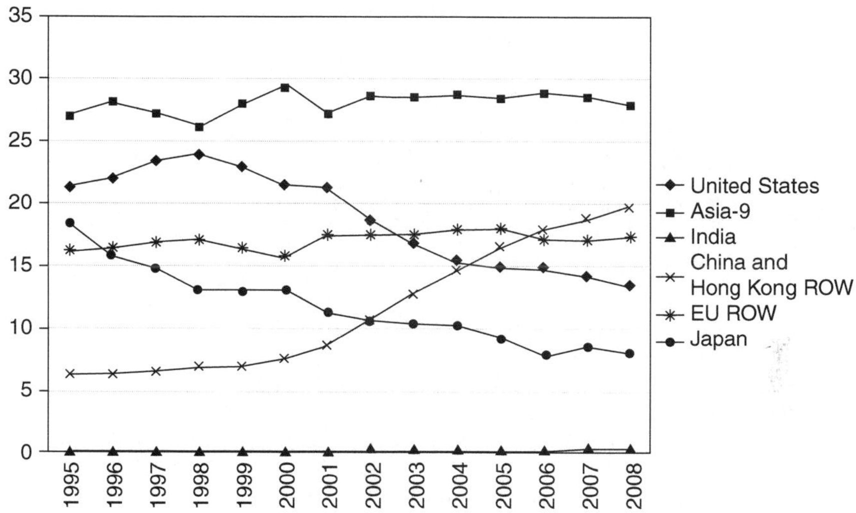

Figure 3.7 Share of world exports of high-technology goods (source: National Science Board 2010: appendix table 19).

What is of interest is the structure of the high-tech manufacturing sectors in these countries. In the case of China, the sector was completely dominated by the Communications equipment and semiconductors sector in the mid-1980s, when it accounted for two-thirds of all high-tech manufacturing value added (Figure 3.8). Since then, the production of Office and computing machinery has been rising rapidly, so that by 2007 it accounted for 26.7 per cent of high-tech value added, while that of Communications and semiconductors had fallen to 39.7 per cent. In sum, information technology hardware is central to China's high-tech success. On the other hand, though India is considered an information technology power, these two information technology sectors, which accounted for a third of high-tech value added in 1985, contributed just about 14 per cent of that value added in 2007 (Figure 3.9).

Interestingly, the industries that have come to dominate the high-tech sector in China are the same as those in the United States. In 1985, the aerospace industry accounted for close to 50 per cent of value added in high-tech manufacturing in the United States, whereas Office and computing machinery and Communications and semiconductors together contributed just 12 per cent. By 2005, the share of the latter two sectors had risen to almost 55 per cent. Thus, China's trajectory was similar to that of the global leader.

The structure of India's high-tech sector, on the other hand, was completely different. What is noteworthy is the high share of Pharmaceuticals in India's high-tech industries. That sector accounted for 53 per cent of value added in 1985 and a massive 73 per cent in 2007. It is well known that India's pharmaceutical prowess came as a result of a combination of protection for domestic

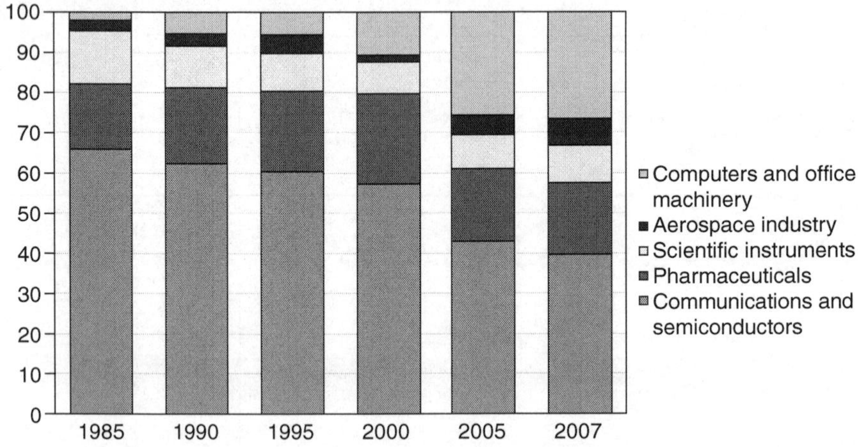

Figure 3.8 Structure of high-technology manufacturing in China and Hong Kong: share of value added (%) (source: National Science Board 2010).

production, control over the operations of foreign firms in India, and, above all, a patenting regime that recognized process patents and not product patents. These were all policies typical of the interventionist, import-substituting strategy of development adopted during the first three decades after independence. The result was the growth of a large and diverse pharmaceutical industry that could ensure the availability of good-quality drugs at prices that were among the lowest in the world. The capacities and technological capabilities built up during that time have meant that even though India has given up many

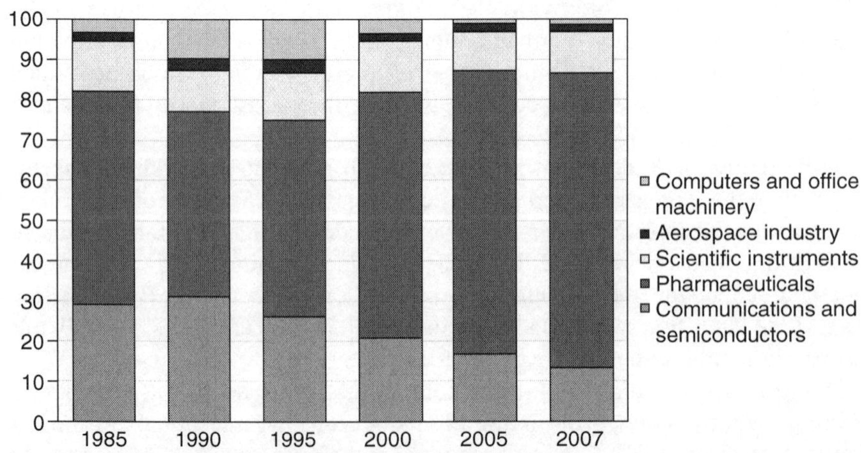

Figure 3.9 Structure of high-technology manufacturing in India: share of value added (%) (source: National Science Board 2010).

of these policies and today recognizes product patents as well, it is in a position to compete globally in many drugs that are off patent or are on the way to being so.

This competitiveness is reflected in the growing external orientation of India's high-tech sectors, possibly driven by pharmaceuticals. The ratio of exports to revenue in the high-tech industries rose from 7.5 per cent to 15 per cent between 1985 and 1999, and then doubled again to 31 per cent by 2005. The period between 2000 and 2005 was also one in which the share of pharmaceuticals in high-tech manufacturing value added in India rose from 61 per cent to 71 per cent. This suggests that pharmaceutical production and exports are the most successful components of India's otherwise dismal high-tech manufacturing performance. Office and computing machinery, with its less than 1 per cent share in 2007, and Communications and semiconductors, with its 14 per cent contribution to high-tech manufacturing value added, are conspicuous by their small presence or near-absence. India's two-decade-long liberalization and 'reform' programme has only worsened its high-tech lag. This is a feature that must be factored in when comparing the Chinese and Indian experiences.

India's services advance

Though India was a poor performer in high-tech manufacturing, its performance has been better in knowledge-intensive services. India's presence in trade in this dynamic area is now significant and rising, with a substantial share of its exports directed at the United States. During the period 1990–91 to 2007–08, India's IT and IT-enabled services exports grew at 46 per cent per annum, or doubled every 19 months.[6] IT services exports were estimated at around $40 billion in 2007–08 by the Reserve Bank of India.[7] As a result, in absolute and relative terms the size of the IT sector in India is now impressive. The National Association of Software and Services Companies (NASSCOM) estimates the size of the industry in 2007–08 at $48 billion, of which $39.5 billion consisted of revenues from software and services. Export revenues, according to NASSCOM, amounted to $31.3 billion, comprising $22.9 billion of software and services export revenues and $8.4 billion of revenues from exports of IT-enabled services and business process outsourcing (BPO).[8] The ratio of gross IT sector output to GDP rose from 0.38 per cent in 1991–92 to 1.88 per cent in 1999–2000 and 4.5 per cent in 2004–05.[9]

However, India's presence in global markets for commercial knowledge-intensive services is still small, amounting to 1.4 per cent in 2007 (Table 3.5). It is true that between 1995 and 2007 that share rose from 0.8 per cent to 1.4 per cent. Even so, India was and remains a small player in the global market, taking account of both domestic supply and exports.

But market-oriented knowledge services (consisting, according to the NSF, of Communications, Financial and Business Services) are an important presence in the Indian economy. The ratio of value added revenues from these services to

India's nominal GDP rose from 9.9 per cent in 1995 to 11.4 per cent in 2007. This does point to a significant role for these services in the national economy, especially when compared with the corresponding values for 'non-market-oriented' knowledge-intensive services (consisting of education and health services), which rose from 4.8 per cent to 5.6 per cent.

However, these figures need to be read carefully. As was noted earlier, the driver for export-led growth in India is the business services sector, which includes both software services and IT-enabled services. It is the growth of this segment that is seen as partly providing the stimulus for expansion of financial and communications services. But the contribution of business services to GDP is much smaller, having risen from 3.6 per cent to 4.3 per cent of GDP between 1995 and 2007.

What is more, unlike the case in the world as a whole and in the US economy, where the share of business services in total valued added revenues in market-oriented services was constant at around 50 per cent, or even rising, that for India fell from close to 50 per cent in 1985 to 38 per cent in 2007. Thus, if the value added figures from the NSF are reliable, the software and IT-enabled services boom is by no means the prime driver of growth in India.

Further, the NSF figures suggest that the knowledge-intensive services sectors together only accounted for 17.7 per cent of GDP in 2005. Adding on the 8 per cent contributed by railways and public administration and defence (as per the official National Accounts Statistics), the total comes to 25.7 per cent. That leaves almost half of the services sector unaccounted for, which consists substantially of unorganized services. This makes the argument that services are reflective of a new dynamism in India that much less convincing, and calls for caution when speaking of the high-tech export success of India and China in the same sentence.

The differential success of China and India in manufacturing and services trade respectively is partly reflected in their patterns of growth. Of the cumulative increase in GDP between 1990 and 2004, while 55 per cent was accounted for by manufacturing in the case of China, as much as 60 per cent was accounted for by services in the Indian case. In India, while services accounted for 43 per cent and 48 per cent respectively of the increment of GDP at current prices in the 1970s and 1980s, the figures rose to 58 per cent and 62 per cent respectively during the 1990s and the years 2000–01 to 2004–05.[10] This difference is reflected in the change in the presence of these countries in the global production of industry and services respectively (Tables 3.4 and 3.5).

Some implications

These developments in China and India raise two questions. First, are these countries successfully exploiting aspects of the changed pattern of global growth and emerging as challengers in knowledge-based sectors? Second, does this differentiate the Chinese and Indian growth miracles from those of the Asian tigers and the second-tier Asian industrializers, making the trajectory of the former robust and sustainable?

Table 3.4 Shares in world industrial value added

	1985	*1990*	*1995*	*2000*	*2005*	*2007*
All manufacturing industries						
United States	31.0	23.2	22.3	27.2	22.4	19.8
Asia-9	5.0	5.7	7.6	7.8	8.9	9.5
India	1.4	1.2	1.1	1.2	1.6	1.9
China and Hong Kong	4.6	3.3	4.6	6.9	10.2	14.3
EU	28.8	35.1	30.1	25.8	29.0	28.8
Japan	15.3	18.9	21.9	18.3	13.5	10.1
High-technology industries						
United States	42.3	31.2	29.1	34.5	29.8	30.7
Asia-9	3.1	5.2	8.9	10.0	10.9	10.3
India	0.3	0.3	0.4	0.3	0.6	0.7
China and Hong Kong	3.1	2.3	2.6	4.1	10.0	13.7
EU	24.3	29.2	24.2	21.6	25.3	25.1
Japan	18.5	23.6	26.8	21.4	15.0	10.6

Source: National Science Board 2010.

It is indeed true that aspects of the development trajectories in the two countries strengthen the idea that India and China are exploiting the benefits of the new knowledge economy. The essential feature of the latter is an improvement in the quality of human and other forms of 'intangible' resources rendered possible by the knowledge revolution. Differences in knowledge embodied in production are seen to be a crucial determinant of productivity differentials across sectors and nations. But transmission of these intangibles from the pure knowledge domain to commodities must be mediated by the application – in different stages stretching from the acquisition of knowledge, through innovation, to the different 'segments' of production – of knowledge labour of different kinds. Labour at each of these stages must acquire the necessary intangibles. Hence, any successful transition to knowledge-economy status requires investment geared to the production and dissemination of knowledge of various kinds (i.e. education, R&D, information and coordination, and in training).

Table 3.5 Shares in value added of commercial knowledge-intensive services

	1985	*1990*	*1995*	*2000*	*2005*	*2007*
World	100.0	100.0	100.0	100.0	100.0	100.0
United States	43.8	35.2	32.2	40.4	36.5	34.4
Asia-9	3.2	3.5	4.6	4.1	4.6	5.0
India	1.1	0.9	0.8	0.9	1.2	1.4
China and Hong Kong	1.9	1.8	2.3	3.2	3.9	5.0
EU	25.4	33.3	29.6	25.0	29.8	30.2
Japan	10.7	13.2	17.4	14.1	10.3	8.1

Source: National Science Board (2010).

This also implies that it is possible to distinguish between knowledge *in* the production of goods and services (or the knowledge embodied in production processes and products) and knowledge *for* the production of goods and services (which is the largely intangible knowledge itself). It need not be true that a country displaying success in knowledge-based industries and services actually controls the knowledge needed *for* such production.

The differential knowledge required at different stages can affect what has been termed the 'value capture' (or the value added excluding the cost of direct labour) associated with a particular distribution of the value chain. A study of the value chain in the manufacture of the Apple iPod found that China, which is where the product is finally assembled and from where the final product is shipped, receives an estimated 2 per cent share of the Apple iPod's value capture, since final assembly of each iPod unit requires just ten minutes of labour input and the minimum monthly wage for a worker is about $100. On the other hand, the United States receives the largest share of value capture (39 per cent) based on the factory price, largely reflecting Apple's gross profit (36 per cent), which it ensures because of its control of the knowledge and the key inputs (embodying that knowledge) required for production. Key inputs account for 37 per cent of the wholesale price. If we look at the distribution of value capture among the manufacturers, Japan gets 12 per cent because it provides the hard drive.

Overall, a close examination of the evidence from China and India suggests that while knowledge is being applied in production in these countries, the United States still monopolizes the control over knowledge.

To start with, even relative to their GDP, China and India lag far behind the developed countries in terms of R&D expenditure. While the figure for 2008 is 3.4 per cent in the case of Japan and 2.8 per cent for the United States, and 2.0 and 2.6 per cent in France and Germany, it stands at 1.5 per cent in China and 0.7 in India[11] (Figure 3.10). Once we take account of GDP differences, the distribution of R&D measured using PPP exchange rates points to substantial concentration. The United States accounted for about 33 per cent of total global R&D expenditure in 2007, followed by Japan with 13 per cent. China (9 per cent) came next, followed by Germany (6 per cent) and France (4 per cent). Thus, the dominant player in the knowledge area is the United States (NSB 2010). The threat from China comes from the rapid pace at which its R&D expenditures are growing, amounting to close to 20 per cent per annum over the decade ending 2007.

Other emerging economies are increasing their expenditures, though they still remain small players. According to the NSB (2010):

> India and Brazil are among the world's larger R&D performers, although neither has yet become part of OECD's statistical system. According to the UNESCO statistics, India performed $15 billion of R&D in 2004 (current U.S. dollars, PPP) and Brazil performed $13 billion in 2005. Both figures are about double the levels of R&D performance that each country reported in the mid-1990s. These levels of R&D expenditures would put both India and Brazil in the world's top 15 R&D performers.

However, looking at the issue in terms of nations may not be that instructive, since big transnational firms are the ones that control the knowledge. For example, US TNCs spent $216.3 billion on R&D in 2006. This compares with aggregate R&D spending of $340 billion in the United States that year. Many of these TNCs individually spend more than most developing countries. According to the UNCTAD's *World Investment Report 2005*, individual firms such as Ford, Pfizer, DaimlerChrysler, Siemens, Toyota and General Motors each spent more than $5 billion on R&D in 2003 (UNCTAD 2006: ch. 4). In comparison, among the developing economies, total R&D spending exceeded $5 billion only in Brazil, China, the Republic of Korea and Taiwan Province of China.

To support its large R&D effort, there is evidence that the United States is sucking in some of the best talent from developing countries such as China and India to strengthen its hold over knowledge for production. These two countries accounted for more than 40 per cent of foreign graduate student enrolment in US universities in 2004 and 2009, with the total number of students exceeding 100,000 in both years (Table 3.6). According to the National Science Foundation, out of the approximately 270,000 foreign graduate students enrolled in US universities in 2007, 76,100 were from India and 53,800 from China. Further, a survey found that out of the 189,346 non-US citizens who received doctoral degrees in 1985–2005, 41,677 were from China and 18,712 from India. Half of these students had definite plans to stay in the United States and another 20–25 per cent were considering the possibility of staying. The United States has become a destination for some of the best talent from these two countries.

Even when talent cannot be imported into the United States to build knowledge for production in and for that country, US firms are managing to tap the best talent in the home countries themselves. Through a process of internationalization of

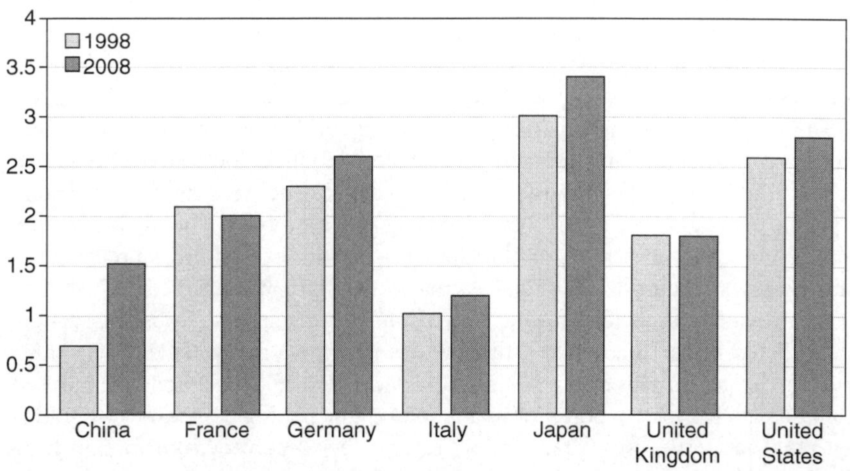

Figure 3.10 Research and development expenditure as a percentage of GDP (source: Organisation for Economic Co-operation and Development 2010).

Table 3.6 Foreign graduate student enrolment in US universities, 2004 and 2009

	2004	*2009*
All locations	279,076	270,770
India	63,013	76,100
China.	50,796	53,800
South Korea	24,757	24,150
Taiwan	15,015	15,380
Japan	8,681	5,200
Turkey	6,912	5,390
Thailand	5,708	5,094
Mexico	4,225	2,980
Germany	3,915	2,740

Source: National Science Board (2006, 2010).

R&D operations, transnational firms are exploiting that talent to retain control over knowledge. Of the $216.3 billion worth of R&D performed by US TNCs in 2006, $187.8 billion was spent in the United States by parent companies, while $28.5 billion worth was undertaken by their overseas affiliates. According to data collated by the Bureau of Economic Analysis of the US Department of Commerce, the share of R&D conducted by US multinational through their majority-owned affiliates abroad rose from 10.9 per cent in 1997 to 15.2 per cent in 2007 (Table 3.7).

Simultaneously, there has been a shift in the location of overseas R&D spending of US TNCs. The share of R&D by overseas affiliates of US TNCs undertaken in Europe, Canada and Japan fell from 90 per cent in 1994 to 80 per cent in 2006. Over the same period, the share performed in Asia (excluding Japan) rose from 5.4 per cent to 13.5 per cent, principally by affiliates' R&D spending in China, Singapore and South Korea. R&D performed by US-owned affiliates located in China and India in particular rose from less than $10 million in each country in 1994 to $804 million and $310 million, respectively, in 2006. Although these 2006 levels represented only about 3 per cent and 1 per cent, respectively, of total overseas R&D by US TNCs, their significance would have been much larger, given the lower costs of personnel, infrastructure and material in these locations (NSB 2010).

Controlling knowledge through means such as these delivers significant benefits for parent companies of US TNCs. Licensing the use of this knowledge ensures significant revenues to firms from the United States, far exceeding that received by other countries (Figure 3.11). What is noteworthy is that both receipts and payments of royalties in the case of the United States are substantially in transactions with affiliated firms. That is, the United States is reaping the benefits of its control over knowledge through transactions conducted with affiliates abroad (Table 3.8). It continues to be a net exporter of manufacturing technological know-how sold as intellectual property: on average, royalties and fees received from foreign firms were three times greater than those paid out to foreigners by US firms for access to their technology. In 2007, the data reveal, the United States earned a trade surplus of $57.6 billion, up from $15.7 billion 15 years earlier.

Table 3.7 R&D performed by majority-owned US affiliates and by all US businesses, 1997–2009

	Millions of dollars		*R&D by affiliates as percentage of R&D by all businesses*	*R&D intensity (% of value added)*		
	R&D performed by affiliates	*R&D performed by all US businesses*		*Affiliates*	*Non-bank affiliates*	*All US businesses*
1997	17,216	1,57,739	10.9	n.a.	5.5	4.6
1998	22,375	1,69,180	13.2	n.a.	6.3	4.5
1999	24,027	1,82,711	13.2	n.a.	6	4.5
2000	26,180	1,99,539	13.1	n.a.	5.9	4.4
2001	26,463	1,98,505	13.3	n.a.	6.3	4.5
2002	27,507	1,93,868	14.2	n.a.	6	4.9
2003	29,803	2,00,724	14.8	n.a.	6.3	4.8
2004	30,083	2,08,301	14.4	n.a.	5.9	5
2005	31,099	2,26,159	13.8	n.a.	5.7	4.9
2006	34,625	2,47,669	14	n.a.	5.6	4.7
2007	40,967	2,69,267	15.2	6	n.a.	4.6
2008	40,727	2,83,238	14.4	6.3	n.a.	4.4
2009	43,419	n.a.	n.a.	7.4	n.a.	n.a.

Source: US Bureau of Economic Affairs, www.bea.gov (accessed September 2011).

Table 3.8 US receipts and payments of royalties and fees associated with affiliated and unaffiliated foreign companies, 1992–2007

(Millions of current dollars)

Year	*Receipts*			*Payments*			*Balance*		
	All	*Affiliated*	*Unaffiliated*	*All*	*Affiliated*	*Unaffiliated*	*All*	*Affiliated*	*Unaffiliated*
1992	20,841	15,658	5,183	5,161	3,396	1,766	15,680	12,262	3,417
1993	21,695	15,688	5,032	5,032	3,386	1,646	16,663	12,302	3,386
1994	26,712	20,275	6,437	5,852	3,934	1,919	20,860	16,341	4,518
1995	30,289	22,859	7,430	6,919	5,256	1,663	23,370	17,603	5,767
1996	32,470	24,556	7,914	7,837	5,406	2,431	24,633	19,150	5,483
1997	33,228	24,465	8,763	9,161	6,749	2,412	24,067	17,716	6,351
1998	35,626	26,313	9,314	11,235	8,547	2,688	24,391	17,766	6,626
1999	39,670	29,275	10,395	13,107	10,374	2,733	26,563	18,901	7,662
2000	43,233	30,479	12,754	16,468	12,536	3,932	26,765	17,943	8,822
2001	40,696	29,164	11,532	16,538	13,241	3,297	24,158	15,923	8,235
2002	44,508	32,770	11,738	19,353	15,134	4,219	25,155	17,636	7,519
2003	46,988	35,539	11,449	19,033	15,179	3,854	27,955	20,360	7,595
2004	56,715	43,074	13,642	23,266	17,873	5,393	33,449	25,201	8,249
2005	64,395	48,496	15,900	24,612	20,331	4,281	39,783	28,165	11,619
2006	72,191	52,469	19,723	23,777	18,160	5,617	48,414	34,309	14,106
2007	82,614	58,881	23,733	25,048	19,653	5,396	57,566	39,228	18,337

Source: National Science Board (2010).

One consequence of internationalization is joint ownership of patents. On average, 15.6 per cent of all patents worldwide were generated in cooperation. But internationalization of R&D, as reflected in foreign ownership, varied substantially across countries. Interestingly, while the United States dominates foreign ownership of inventions in India, European countries are the main cross-border owners in China (Table 3.9).

In India, leading firms like Intel, Microsoft and Adobe have R&D operations within the country. In China too, the trend is clearly visible. According to the *Wall Street Journal*, almost all the global giants in automobiles, telecommunications technology, computers, software, machinery, electronics, biotechnology, pharmaceuticals and other major industries have made R&D investments in China. These companies include General Electric, General Motors, P&G, Unilever, Microsoft, Intel, IBM, Motorola, Siemens, Ericsson, Nortel, AT&T, Lucent Bell and Samsung.

It is indeed true that the benefits of this control of knowledge for production may not result in production and exports from the United States, since US firms could choose to locate outside their home country for cost or other reasons. But there would be a definite benefit to the firms that control such knowledge, with the country hosting production being merely the location from which these firms pursue their global strategies.

This does indeed seem to be the case in China and India, as emerges from an examination of the difference between the level of value added generated by US TNCs by country, and the pace of change of that level. While North America and Europe still dominated the level in 2004, Eurasia dominated the changes in that level between 1999 and 2004 (Table 3.10). In Asia and the Pacific, there has been a surge in production in foreign-invested firms that are involved in exports as well as sales to the burgeoning local markets. The value added in US foreign affiliates located in the region grew at an average annual rate of 9 per cent during

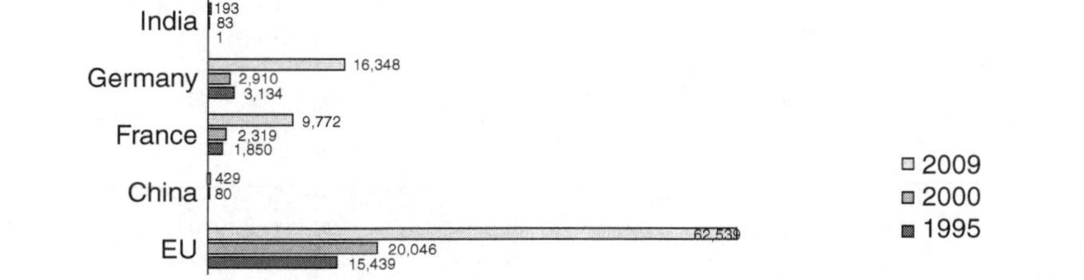

Figure 3.11 Royalty and licence fee receipts ($ million) (source: World Development Indicators Online).

Table 3.9 Foreign ownership of domestic inventions, 2008

Partner country	*Total patents*	*Total cooperation with abroad*	*Japan*	*United States*	*EU (27)*
China	7,310	1,362	34	451	621
United Kingdom	6,761	2,662	87	1,015	1,261
Brazil	598	132	–	44	77
India	1,488	592	2	285	183
Russian Federation	827	263	12	86	122
United States	45,655	5,520	398	–	3,182
European Union (27 countries)	49,679	6,163	226	3,449	6,085
OECD – total	134,784	20,006	697	5,360	10,108
Japan	26,928	1,016	–	499	316
Korea	7,257	236	52	99	53
World	145,552	22,640	793	6,495	11,195

Source: National Science Board (2010).

1999–2004, and the region's share in the value added of US foreign affiliates rose 1.2 percentage points to 19.0 per cent (Mataloni and Yorgason 2006).

The largest increases in shares were in China, India and Japan. In China, the value added of US affiliates in manufacturing accounted for more than two-thirds of the value added of all US affiliates in 2004, and during 1999–2004 the value added of affiliates in manufacturing grew at an average annual rate of 23 per cent. In 2004, more than two-thirds of the sales by Chinese affiliates in manufacturing were to customers in China, and only 7.4 per cent of these sales were to US customers, down from 16.3 per cent in 1999.

In India, the growth in value added was widespread by industry, but it was most notable in manufacturing and wholesale trade, in which affiliates sell almost exclusively to local customers, and in computer systems design and related services (part of professional, scientific and technical services), in which affiliates sell mainly to customers in the United States.

In Japan, most of the growth in value added was in manufacturing, mainly reflecting acquisition of firms or establishment of new foreign affiliates to serve the local market.

It is for this reason that we need to examine the role of foreign firms in the export performance of India and China. Foreign-funded enterprises (FFEs) accounted for 55–58 per cent of China's exports in recent years (Table 3.11). This dominance increases in the case of high-tech exports. The share of FFEs in exports of industrial machinery, which stood at $83 billion in 2003, increased from 35 per cent to 79 per cent over a decade. While exports of computer equipment rose from $716 million in 1993 to $41 billion in 2003, the FFEs' share rose from 74 per cent to 92 per cent. Similarly, the share of FFEs in China's electronics and telecom exports ($89 billion in 2003) rose from 45 per cent to 74 per cent (Gilboy 2004).

The situation appears to be similar in the case of IT services exports from India. According to NASSCOM, during 2005–06, offshore operations of global IT majors accounted for 10–15 per cent of IT services and business process outsourcing (BPO) exports, and captive BPO units accounted for 50 per cent of BPO exports.[12] Further, MNC-owned captive units have been scaling up their operations steadily.

Thus, foreign firms with control over knowledge appear to be the ones exploiting the opportunities offered by the knowledge economy, rather than countries like China and India, whose talent is being used to strengthen the control over knowledge of these firms. There is a new international division of labour emerging, in which knowledge is controlled by firms in the developed countries even while the production of knowledge-based industries and services moves to countries like India and China. What this suggests is that even while China and India are important bases for knowledge-based production of exportable goods and sources, important beneficiaries of this development are transnationals from the developed countries, even if not the mass of the workers in these countries, who fear job losses. This implies that countries like India and China are not as yet warriors in the global battle for economic supremacy, but

Table 3.10 Value added of majority-owned non-bank foreign affiliates by area, 1999 and 2004

	Millions of dollars			*Percentage*		
	1999	*2004*	*2008*	*Average annual rate of growth*	*Share of the all-areas total*	
				1999–2004	*1999*	*2004*
All areas	566,396	824,336 818,256	1,211,854	7.8 (1999–2007= 8.9)	100.0	100.0
Canada	65,780	94,205	126,352	7.4	11.6	11.4
Europe	324,634	460,010	638,280	7.2	57.3	55.8
Of which: France	37,485	47,717	56,712	4.9	6.6	5.8
Germany	61,913	74,184	94,217	3.7	10.9	9.0
Ireland	14,845	27,022		12.7	2.6	3.3
Italy	22,408	29,292		5.5	4.0	3.6
Netherlands	19,018	28,220	33,296	8.2	3.4	3.4
Norway	6,296	14,329	32,534	17.9	1.1	1.7
Poland	1,151	4,604		32.0	0.2	0.6
Russia	141	2,703		80.5	(*)	0.3
Spain	10,786	14,821		6.6	1.9	1.8
Sweden	6,198	11,028		12.2	1.1	1.3
Switzerland	8,941	17,636		14.6	1.6	2.1
United Kingdom	103,048	132,527	165,991	5.2	18.2	16.1

Latin America and other Western Hemisphere	60,641	82,181	140,149	6.3	10.7	10.0
Of which: Argentina	7,256	7,334		0.2	1.3	0.9
Bermuda	2,037	6,321		25.4	0.4	0.8
Brazil	16,593	18,261	38,915	1.9	2.9	2.2
Mexico	17,556	22,383	30,753	5.0	3.1	2.7
Africa	8,917	23,519	57,267	21.4	1.6	2.9
Middle East	5,348	7,634	21,269	7.4	0.9	0.9
Asia and Pacific	101,077	156,786	228,536	9.2	17.8	19.0
Of which: Australia	19,625	29,853	46,058	8.8	3.5	3.6
China	3,945	13,336		27.6	0.7	1.6
Hong Kong	8,011	8,345		0.8	1.4	1.0
India	1,068	3,937		29.8	0.2	0.5
Japan	30,269	46,491	44,094	9.0	5.3	5.6
Korea, Republic of	3,302	6,902		15.9	0.6	0.8
Singapore	9,848	13,353		6.3	1.7	1.6
Taiwan	6,066	5,927		-0.5	1.1	0.7

Source: Mataloni and Yorgason (2006).

Table 3.11 Role of foreign-invested firms in China's exports

	Exports: foreign-inv. enterprises: total (US$ million)	*Exports total (US$ million)*	*Proportion (%)*
1996	61,499.184	151,048.000	40.7
1997	74,935.547	182,792.000	41.0
1998	81,015.885	183,712.000	44.1
1999	88,733.353	194,931.000	45.5
2000	119,459.720	249,203.000	47.9
2001	133,333.573	266,098.000	50.1
2002	169,990.241	325,596.000	52.2
2003	240,465.065	438,228.000	54.9
2004	338,905.700	593,326.000	57.1
2005	444,391.859	761,953.000	58.3
2006	564,011.833	969,380.000	58.2
2007	695,921.661	1,217,790.000	57.1
2008	790,831.889	1,428,660.000	55.4

Source: CEIC database (accessed September 2011).

locations that serve as instruments of battle for transnational firms. The war among these firms results in strategies that may be threatening extant or future employment in the developed countries. But when faced with that prospect, it is not India and China that need to be feared by Europe and the rest of the developed world, but the United States and their own home-grown transnational companies that have taken wing.

Notes

1 Figures are based on the World Bank's *World Development Indicators Online*.
2 Figures from IMF, *International Financial Statistics Online*.
3 However, as Akyüz (2010) notes, 'The evidence suggests that in recent years the average import content of Chinese exports has been between 40 and 50 per cent; that is, domestic value-added generated by exports is less than 60 per cent of their gross value. In value-added terms the share of exports in GDP is in the order of 20 per cent.'
4 Figures computed from data reported by Reserve Bank of India at http://rbidocs.rbi.org.in/rdocs/Bulletin/PDFs/T%2042%20[Trade%20and%20Bal].pdf and Central Statistical Organisation at http://mospi.gov.in/qr_estimate_gdp_curr_prices_12march09.pdf (accessed 17 April 2009).
5 The industries identified as high-technology industries by the National Science Board consist of aerospace, pharmaceuticals, office and computing equipment, communication equipment and scientific instruments.
6 *Dataquest*, 19 (13), 15 July 2001; 20 (13), 15 July 2002; 24 (13), 15 July 2006; 26 (13), 15 July 2008. Figures on IT-enabled services are included in software exports from 2000–01 onwards.
7 Reported in balance of payments statistics available at www.rbi.org.in.
8 Figures reported on the NASSCOM website, www.nasscom.org (accessed January 2007).
9 Computed using figures from *Dataquest* and the Central Statistical Organisation.

10 Computed from figures available in *China Statistical Yearbook* (National Bureau of Statistics various years) and India's *National Accounts Statistics* (Government of India, Central Statistical Organisation) for various years.
11 The India figure relates to 2005.
12 Reported on www.nasscom.org (accessed January 2007).

References

Akyüz, Y. (2010) 'Export dependence and sustainability of growth in China and the East Asian production network', South Centre Research Papers, 27, Geneva: South Centre.

Dedrick, J., Kraemer, K. L. and Linden, G. (2008) 'Who profits from innovation in global value chains? A study of the iPod and notebook PCs', Personal Computing Industry Center, University of California–Irvine.

Engardio, P. (2005) 'A new world economy', *Business Week*, 22 August.

Gilboy, G. J. (2004) 'The myth behind China's miracle', *Foreign Affairs*, July/August. Online, available at: www.foreignaffairs.org/20040701faessay83405/george-j-gilboy/the-myth-behind-china-s-miracle.html (accessed May 2007).

Government of India, Central Statistical Organisation, *National Accounts Statistics*, New Delhi: Central Statistical Organisation.

Kaminski, B. and Ng, F. (2001) 'Trade and production fragmentation: central European Economies in European Union networks of production and marketing', vol. 1, World Bank Policy Research Working Paper 2611. Online, available at: http://go.worldbank.org/74S201OXJ0 (accessed 24 September 2009).

Karo, E. and Kattel, R. (2011) 'Should "open innovation" change innovation policy thinking in catching up economies? Considerations for policy analyses', *Innovation: The European Journal of Social Science Research*, 24 (1–2): 173–198.

Kattel, R., Reinert, E. S. and Suurna, M. (2009) 'Industrial restructuring and innovation policy in Central and Eastern Europe since 1990', Working Papers in Technology Governance and Economic Dynamics 23, The Other Canon Foundation and Tallinn University of Technology.

Mataloni, R. J. Jr and Yorgason, D. R. (2006) 'Operations of US multinational companies: preliminary results from the 2004 benchmark survey', *Survey of Current Business*, November, pp. 37–68.

National Bureau of Statistics, China (various years) *China Statistical Yearbook*.

National Science Board (2006) *Science and Engineering Indicators 2006* (2 vols), Arlington, VA: National Science Foundation.

National Science Board (2008) *Science and Engineering Indicators 2008* (2 vols), Arlington, VA: National Science Foundation

National Science Board (2010) *Science and Engineering Indicators 2010*, Arlington, VA: National Science Foundation.

OECD (2010) *Science, Technology and Industry Outlook 2010*, Paris: Organisation for Economic Co-operation and Development.

Reserve Bank of India (2009) 'Survey on computer software and information technology services exports', *Reserve Bank of India Bulletin*, September: 1517–1534.

Suurna, M. and Kattel, R. (2010) 'Europeanization of innovation policy in Central and Eastern Europe', *Science and Public Policy*, 37 (9): 646–664.

United Nations Conference on Trade and Development (UNCTAD) (2006) *World Investment Report 2005: Transnational Corporations and the Internationalization of R&D*, New York: United Nations.

4 Japanese corporations in China's developing economy

Hiroshi Itagaki

Introduction: impact of the development of China's economy

In recent years, the four countries referred to as BRICs (Brazil, China, India and Russia) have attracted significant attention for their outstanding economic development. Of the four, China and India, but particularly China, have significantly outshone their counterparts. There are a number of reasons for this. First of all, both countries have overwhelmingly large populations. In 2010, China's population reached 1.35 billion and India's 1.21 billion, placing them in a league apart from the other two BRICs, with Brazil's population of 200 million and Russia's 140 million. In fact, the combined population of China and India at 2.56 billion accounts for 37 per cent of the estimated total world population.

Another point of note about these two countries is the size of their domestic economies, and in this respect China towers over the other three BRICs. In 2009, China's nominal GDP stood at $4.98 trillion, followed by Brazil's at $1.57 trillion, India's at $1.29 trillion and Russia's at $1.23 trillion. At this time, the scale of China's economy (GDP) was surpassed only by that of the United States ($14.12 trillion) and Japan ($5.4 trillion), and in 2010 China overtook Japan to occupy the position of the world's second largest economy.

While all of the BRICs have been achieving high rates of economic growth, China's rapid rise since its decision to make the transition to a market economy has outpaced the others. In the period from 1990 to 2009, GDP in India and Brazil grew 3.9-fold and that in Russia 2.2-fold. During this same period, China's GDP expanded an astounding 12.3-fold.

China also conspicuously stands apart from the other BRICs in international trade. Exports from China in 2009 totalled $1.2 trillion, followed by Russia at $303 billion, India at $162 billion and Brazil at $153 billion. In that same year, China's imports totalled $1 trillion, India's $249 billion, Russia's $211 billion and Brazil's $134 billion. In short, China presently accounts for 9.7 per cent of the world's exports and 8.1 per cent of its imports, making it the world's leading exporter, followed by the United States (based on data or calculations based on data of the United Nations: *World Population Prospects* (www.un.org/esa/population/unpop.htm), *Monthly Bulletin of Statistics* (http://unstats.un.org) and *National Accounts Main Aggregates Database* (http://unstats.un.org)).

The impact of China and India on the rest of the world is significant not only in a quantitative but also in a qualitative sense. While both countries boast long histories stretching back several thousand years and are the birthplaces of ancient civilizations, both China and India endured long periods of hardship from the nineteenth century onwards, and it was not until the very end of the twentieth century that both countries succeeded in distinguishing themselves by joining the world's leading economies at a staggering speed. In China's case in particular, at every turning point of the twentieth century the world watched on with interest, wondering when this 'sleeping lion' would wake up, but despite the world's anticipation, the country showed little economic stirring of note. Finally, at the very end of the twentieth century this sleeping lion truly awakened. The awakening of not only the sleeping lion of China but also the 'sleeping elephant' of India – both countries that previously had a significant influence on the world as founders of ancient civilizations renowned for their culture, arts, science and religion – and their continuous steady rise as formidable economies can only be described as a major event in world history.

On the economic side, China's ability to absorb technology has been remarkable. Although it has a somewhat notorious reputation for flooding the market with copied products, the ability to achieve this feat in itself is an indication of the high level of know-how China has in absorbing technology. It must also be said that China has not been the first to produce imitation products. There was a time when Western countries ridiculed Japan as an imitator, and subsequently there was a time when Japanese firms were troubled by imitations coming onto the market from Korea and Taiwan. If we go further back in history, we will recall that even the United States, a country that prides itself as a founder of originality, was in the nineteenth century criticized by European countries for copying their products. It was only after repeatedly imitating the products of other countries that both the United States and Japan eventually achieved originality. That said, China's flooding the market with imitations as a result of its ability to absorb technology gives the impression that it is still a country worlds away from predecessors such as the United States and Japan. As a result, there have even been cases like that of Honda, which, after being plagued by imitations of its motorcycles and spare parts, decided to incorporate its imitators as joint venture partners or component suppliers. India's ability to absorb technology should not be taken lightly either. The development of India's IT industry in Bangalore is well known, but even in manufacturing, India is one or two steps ahead of China in exporting automobiles to advanced countries, particularly in Europe, where China is still fighting an uphill battle.

If we were to summarize in an impressionistic way the differences between China and India in their respective abilities to absorb technology in manufacturing, we could perhaps make the following comparisons. In a bid to quickly seize upon business opportunities, China generally focuses on imitating the form of products without paying a great deal of attention to the functions and quality of imitations. India, on the other hand, as demonstrated in its production of automobiles and motorcycles, has a tendency to build on its technology before producing imitations, working its way up from basic components. This approach is somewhat similar to the path taken by Japan in the past, by accumulating technology through reverse engineering, the method of copying made possible by retracing the process of product creation from the stages of function and material by dismantling the products of advanced countries.

Appearances, however, can be deceptive, and a country that is rapidly developing may give the appearance of being larger than it actually is, much in the same way that objects looks larger when viewed close up through binoculars. Conversely, a mature country whose growth has slowed is apt to be underestimated, much in the same way as something viewed through the reverse end of binoculars. The description of the former can be applied to China and India, and the latter to Japan. A comparison of per capita GDP of these countries in 2009 shows that in contrast to Japan's $39,500, China's was only $3,770 and India's $1,080. This is not to diminish in any way the achievements of these two countries. The point to be made here is that there is a considerable discrepancy between reality and any one-sided argument based on overestimation that gives the impression that these two countries pose a threat to other countries, or any one-sided argument based on underestimation of Japan that gives the impression that it is a country in decline.

The importance of production bases in China

China's importance to Japanese companies has been increasing significantly with the growth of China's economy, particularly the growth of the Chinese domestic market since the beginning of the twenty-first century. Despite the short-term impact on developing countries of the world financial crisis which became apparent around the autumn of 2008 and the current ongoing economic crisis in Europe, there is no doubt that economic growth in Asia as a whole – encompassing China, India, the ASEAN region, as well as Japan, Korea and Taiwan – will play an even more important role as the driver of global economic growth in the medium to long term. The global strategy of Japanese firms has consisted of a four-pronged approach centring on Japan, North America, Europe and Asia (including China). In this four-pronged strategy too, the Japanese domestic market and North America featured prominently for the majority of Japanese companies. In the future world economy, however, there is a strong possibility that a significant shift will occur in the focus of this four-pronged structure. Although China's political and social uncertainty remain factors that cannot be ignored, for Japanese companies the role of their business operations in China will continue to grow in importance in the future.

Based on an awareness of this issue, this chapter will discuss three main points. First, it will present an overview of Japanese corporate investment in China and explain how the investment objectives, the regions where companies establish bases, and the sectors of industry that Japanese firms engage in have changed over time. In discussing these aspects, the chapter will also confirm the importance of China to Japanese firms, and the importance of the presence of Japanese firms for China. Second, the chapter will take a close look at the electrical and electronics industry and the automobile industry, two core industries of direct investment in China by Japanese companies. This section of the chapter will also briefly describe the history and characteristics of the entry of Japanese firms into China's market, while correlating the competitive relationship of Japanese companies with companies of other countries and with local companies in China. Third, the chapter will discuss the characteristics of local management of Japanese companies. Here the chapter will examine the issues confronting Japanese companies and will consider possible solutions.

Trends and overview of direct investments by Japanese firms in China

After China decided to implement reforms and open its market at the end of the 1970s, Japanese companies began investing in that country. Until the 1980s, however, the majority of investments were on a small scale, and in many cases companies merely outsourced some parts of their manufacturing activities there without investing. Manufacturing at that time centred on labour-intensive industries, such as textiles, food processing and electric and electronic assembly (including the assembly of components). Japanese investment was concentrated in Guangdong Province in south China; the Pearl River Delta, notably in Shenzhen, adjacent to Hong Kong, designated as a Special Economic Zone in the 1980s; and Dalian in Liaoning Province, designated as an open coastal city in 1984.[1]

Although not direct investment per se, another point worthy of mention during this period is the exporting of factory equipment by Japan. These plant exports not only paved the way for subsequent direct investment by Japanese home electronic manufacturers but also resulted in the establishing of a technological foundation for local Chinese manufacturers, which eventually became rivals that stood up to Japanese companies (Takagi 1996; Amano and Fan 2003).

Investment in China by Japanese companies began in earnest in the first half of the 1990s after Deng Xiaoping's so-called Speech of South Cruises in 1992 and his proposal of a socialist market economy at the Fourteenth Party Congress, which removed all doubts about the possibility of a backdown on China's new open door policy. Geographically, the Pearl River Delta and Dalian continued to remain the focus of investment. The scale of investment expanded with progress in China's market economy and the development of infrastructure, and the targets of investment broadened to include electrical equipment and motorcycles in addition to textiles and sundries, and high-value-added products increasingly became the focus of investment (JETRO 2004).

The latter half of the 1990s saw a temporary decline in investment, largely due to a reaction to the sudden rush by many companies to invest in China as well as China's economic tightening policy and the worsening of Japan's domestic recession. At the beginning of the 2000s, however, when China joined the World Trade Organization, investment by Japanese companies rebounded and grew rapidly. The scale of investment also grew and investment in China began to gravitate towards eastern China, centring on Shanghai and the surrounding areas of the Changjiang

River Delta. Investment in electric and electronics and machinery remained strong but automobile assembly and parts were growing in importance. Another noticeable development at this time that is worthy of mention was the establishment of Japanese R&D bases in China. The shift in business sectors and investment locations at this time signified the transition from investment in export bases to take advantage of cheap labour to manufacturing products bound for the massive domestic market, which was rapidly growing and had enormous future potential (Itagaki 2010: ch. 2, dissertation by Dai Xiaofu).

Let us take a look at Japan's position in direct investment in China in recent years (2009–10) in comparison with the position of other countries (see Table 4.1). Hong Kong clearly leads other countries and regions with an overwhelmingly high ratio, but it must be noted that the greater part of investment from Hong Kong originates in third countries and China itself, and enters China via Hong Kong. The second leading investor is Taiwan, with Japan and Singapore following closely behind by a narrow margin. Therefore, it can be said that as a single investing country, Japan, along with Taiwan and Singapore, is among the leading investors in China.

On the other hand, let us now take a look at China's position as a recipient country of direct investment from Japan in recent years (2008–10) (see Table 4.2). Excluding investment in the Cayman Islands (a base for investment as a tax haven), the United States is the top country for Japanese direct investment, and although this may vary from year to year, China is in the second highest group along with Australia, the United Kingdom and the Netherlands. Therefore, Japan's direct investment in China accounts for a significant proportion for both Japan as an investing country and China as the recipient country.

Not only in investment but also in trade relations, Japan and China are mutually important partners (Table 4.3). China is Japan's largest export destination, now surpassing the United States. China is also Japan's top supplier of imports, while the United States trails behind as a distant second. From China's perspective, Japan is the third-largest export partner, followed by the United States and Hong Kong. However, the majority of China's exports to Hong Kong are re-exported and therefore Japan is effectively the second-largest export destination. As an import partner of China, Japan holds the top position. Therefore, rather than there being a situation where direct investment from Japan risks eliminating trade between Japan and China or vice versa, it can instead be inferred that the two countries are in a reciprocal enhancement relationship.

Next, let us take an overall look at direct investment in China by Japanese companies as summarized in Table 4.4. What is noticeable at a glance is the high ratio of investment in the manufacturing industry, which accounted for three-quarters of the direct investment in China balance at the end of 2009. This figure exceeds not only the overall world average but also the average for Asia, where the proportion of investment in the manufacturing industry is high. This tendency towards investment concentrating on manufacturing has not changed in investment trends observed from the most recent flow of investment from 2007 to 2009 (same data from the Ministry of Finance as in Table 4.4).

Table 4.1 Direct inward investment in China by country, 2009–10, (unit: %, million dollars)

Rank	*Country, region*	*2009*		*Rank*	*Country, region*	*2010*		
		Amount	*Ratio (%)*			*Amount*	*Ratio (%)*	*Growth (%)*
1	Hong Kong	53,993	60.0	1	Hong Kong	67,474	63.8	25.0
2	Taiwan	6,563	7.3	2	Taiwan	6,701	6.3	2.1
3	Singapore	4,117	4.6	3	Singapore	5,657	5.4	45.6
4	Japan	3,886	4.3	4	Japan	4,242	4.0	3.0
5	United States	3,576	4.0	5	United States	4,052	3.8	13.3
6	Korea	2,703	3.0	6	Korea	2,693	2.5	–0.4
7	Great Britain	1,469	1.6	7	Great Britain	1,642	1.6	11.8
8	France	1,227	1.4	8	France	1,239	1.2	n.a.
9	Netherlands	1,000	1.1	9	Netherlands	952	0.9	n.a.
10	Germany	959	1.1	10	Germany	933	0.9	–24.0
	Other	64,533	71.7		Other	77,624	73.4	20.3
	Total for world	90,033	100.0		Total for world	105,735	100.0	17.4

Source: 2011 JETRO Global Trade and Investment Report (previous data was China Investment Indicators, Ministry of Commerce, People's Republic of China).

Table 4.2 Trends in Japanese overseas direct investment by country/region (balance of international payments, net, flow (unit: million dollars)

Rank	*Country/ region*	*FY2008*		*FY2009*		*FY2010*		
		Amount	*Ratio*	*Amount*	*Ratio*	*Amount*	*Ratio*	*Growth*
1	Cayman Islands	22,550	17.2	12,903	17.3	−1,848	n.a	n.a
2	USA	44,674	34.2	10,660	14.3	9,193	16.1	−13.8
3	Australia	5,232	4.0	7,136	9.6	6,371	11.1	−10.7
4	China	6,496	5.0	6,899	9.2	7,252	12.7	5.1
5	Netherlands	6,514	5.0	6,698	9.0	3,288	5.7	−50.9
6	Brazil	5,371	4.1	3,753	5.0	4,316	7.5	15.0
7	India	5,551	4.2	3,664	4.9	2,864	5.0	−21.9
8	United Kingdom	6,744	5.2	2,126	2.8	4,624	8.1	117.5
9	Germany	3,905	3.0	2,089	2.8	−321	n.a.	n.a
10	Thailand	2,016	1.5	1,632	2.2	2,248	3.9	37.7
Reference	EU	22,939	17.5	17,039	22.8	8,359	14.6	−50.9
	ASEAN-10	6,309	4.8	7,002	9.4	8,930	15.6	27.5
	World total	130,801	100.0	74,650	100.0	57,223	100.0	–23.3

Source: Compiled from JETRO 2011 Global Trade and Investment Report.

Note
Some countries showed a negative net flow in 2010, therefore 2009 data were used. Growth is on a year-on-year basis.

Table 4.3 Trade relationship between Japan and China (unit: million dollars)

Japan's imports and exports in 2010

	Export			*Import*	
	Amount	*Ratio*		*Amount*	*Ratio*
World	767,025	100.0	World	691,447	100.0
China	149,086	19.4	China	152,801	22.1
USA	118,199	15.4	USA	67,171	9.7

China's imports and exports in 2010 (unit: million dollars)

	Export			*Import*	
	Amount	*Ratio*		*Amount*	*Ratio*
World	1,577,932	100.0	World	1,394,829	100.0
USA	283,304	18.0	Japan	176,707	12.7
Hong Kong	218,317	13.8	Korea	138,399	9.9
Japan	121,061	7.7	Taiwan	115,694	8.3
Korea	68,771	4.4	USA	102,038	7.3
Germany	68,047	4.3	Germany	74,342	5.3

Source: Compiled from JETRO 2011 Global Trade and Investment Report.

Table 4.4 Investment balance by region/sector (end of 2009) (unit: hundred million yen, %)

	Total		*Manufacturing*														*Non-manufacturing*					
	Amount	*Ratio*	*Amount*	*Ratio*	*Food*		*Chemical/ medicine*		*Iron/non-iron metal*		*General machinery*		*Electric machinery*		*Transport machinery*				*Wholesale/retail*		*Finance/insurance*	
					Amount	*Ratio*	*Amount*	*Ratio*	*Amount*	*Ratio*	*Amount*	*Ratio*	*Amount*	*Ratio*	*Amount*	*Ratio*	*Amount*	*Ratio*	*Amount*	*Ratio*	*Amount*	*Ratio*
Asia	16,182	100.0	104885	64.8	7,642	4.7	12,808	7.9	6,863	4.2	9,767	6.0	24,247	15.0	23,242	14.4	56,937	35.2	17963	11.1	18,609	11.5
China	50,713	100.0	37,405	73.8	2,629	5.2	3,162	6.2	2,349	4.6	4,927	9.7	8,155	16.1	8,506	16.8	13,309	26.2	5,938	11.7	4,283	8.4
North America	221,339	100.0	95,976	43.4	3,072	1.4	26,629	12.0	6,637	3.0	8,463	3.8	18,589	8.4	23,258	10.5	125,363	56.6	51265	23.2	50,798	23.0
Europe	164,961	100.0	98,090	59.5	21,762	13.2	12,325	7.5	2,213	1.3	5,484	3.3	16,701	10.1	25,093	15.2	66,870	40.5	20828	12.6	25,107	15.2
World	682,097	100.0	326,026	47.8	43,568	6.4	56,002	8.2	19,177	2.8	24,309	3.6	60,073	8.8	74,945	11.0	356,071	52.2	96984	14.2	161,925	23.7

Source: Compiled from Ministry of Finance *Statistics Monthly*, December 2010 issue.

Note
Ratio indicates percentage of sector within the region.

Electrical equipment and transport machinery (automobiles and motorcycles) account for a significant proportion of both the stock (investment balance) and the flow in the manufacturing industry. As has already been shown, it is easy to imagine that the electronics and electrical equipment industries, which led Japanese investment in China from an early stage, account for a large share. However, the transport machinery sector, led by the automobile industry, which had been slower to enter the Chinese market than its counterparts in Western countries, now occupies a more prominent position than the electrical equipment sector. In the non-manufacturing sectors, it is important to note that the wholesale and retail industries both account for a significant proportion of both investment balance and flow.

Japanese investment in regions across China in order of investment amount in 2008 was as follows: Shanghai City, Dalian City, Guangdong Province, Beijing City, Tianjin City and Shandong Province (Table 4.5). Apart from minor variations in this order, there have been no major changes to the composition of investment concentrated in eastern China, particularly around Shanghai, the south China area, including Shenzhen, Dongguan and Guangzhou, or the coastal area, including major cities such as Dalian, Beijing and Tianjin.

Consumer electronics: the entry of Japanese companies into China and the rise of Chinese companies

One of the main features of China's 'reform and open door policy' at the end of 1978 was the spelling out for the first time of the importance of consumer goods in China's economy. This was a major departure from past policies that were strongly oriented towards the heavy industry and chemical industry sectors, and this change immediately ignited demand for colour televisions and consumer electronics products. Chinese manufacturers at that time, however, were unable to cope with the surge in demand, because of low production capacity and technology standards, and this led to a rapid rise in imports. Faced with these conditions, the Chinese government adopted a policy of promoting domestic production through plant imports and the introduction of technology from foreign companies. By the middle of the 1980s, Japanese consumer electronics makers such as Matsushita, Hitachi, Sanyo Electric, Japan Victor, Toshiba and

Table 4.5 2008 Japan's investment in China by region (unit: million dollars)

Beijing	475
Tianjin	435
Shanghai	1,197
Dialian	831
Guangdong Province	530
Shandong Province	402

Source: JETRO (2009) Joint Research Report of Regional Offices in Northeast Asia: Special Feature, China and North Asia, Issues Confronting Japanese Companies.

Sony were playing a central role in plant export and technology transfer for the assembly of colour televisions and components. The introduction of equipment and technology from Japan and other countries, coupled with China's policy of high tariffs and industry protection through price control to prevent a decline in prices, many government-owned enterprises entered the colour television business in regions all across China. As a result, China's colour television production capacity mushroomed in the 1980s. To cope with this situation, Hitachi (Shenzhen) and other foreign companies began to launch joint ventures for supplying CRTs in China (Takagi 1996; Aoki 2003; Amano and Fan 2003).

For white goods such as refrigerators, washing machines and air-conditioners, plant export package arrangements that included assembly line and production equipment for main components along with production, process management and quality control technologies were implemented one after another. The Matsushita group alone organized the export of over 150 plants, several times more than other consumer electronics manufacturers (Aoki 2003).

During the 1990s, however, the Chinese government's active policy of developing the consumer electronics industry through the introduction of technology from foreign countries began to come apart at the seams. Colour televisions and VCRs exported to Hong Kong from Japan en masse began to make their way into China duty free through illegal export from Hong Kong and open utilization of clever arrangements organized through dealers in Hong Kong.[2] Because these illegally imported goods began to hit the market in large numbers, owing to robust demand for 'made-in-Japan products', which had a strong reputation for reliability, local colour television manufacturers entering the market under government protection inadvertently became exposed to severe competition. Local plants operating under planned economic regulations were unable to keep up with the rapid pace of technological innovation in the electronics and electrical industry.

Against this backdrop, China's market economy continued to accelerate following Deng Xiaoping's Speech of South Cruises, and the Chinese government eventually relaxed regulations that had impeded the inflow of foreign capital.[3] The relaxation of regulations, coupled with confidence that there would be no reversal in China's transition to a market economy, resulted in a rush by foreign companies to invest in China. Japanese and other leading foreign electronics companies established joint ventures with local companies and started local production of colour televisions (Amano and Fan 2003). Local production of white goods through foreign investment also began, largely through joint ventures with local companies. Hitachi, Mitsubishi, Toshiba and Matsushita also began local production of compressors, a core component of air conditioners (Marukawa 2007).

However, the start of local production was also the beginning of the decline of Japanese companies in the Chinese market. While many government-owned colour television manufacturers buckled under the stiff competition, other new manufacturers emerged and rose rapidly. Local television manufacturing companies rapidly expanded their market share using price competitiveness to gain an edge, and by the early 2000s the leading three local companies had captured over 40 per cent of the Chinese domestic market. Against this backdrop, the market share of Japanese colour television manufacturers declined significantly (Marukawa 2007).

Chinese manufacturers responded quickly during the start-up period of flat-panel televisions from 2005 onwards. Many companies entered the flat-panel television sector by procuring panels from manufacturers in Taiwan and South Korea. When the market for flat-panel televisions took off by the second half of 2008, the top five makers were all Chinese (including Hisense and TCL), with competitive prices. Now Chinese companies hold a 70 per cent share of the Chinese market. Japanese and Korean makers have been unable to capture a substantial share of the volume market (*Nikkei Sangyo Shimbun*, 24 May 2011).

In the white goods sector, an exactly similar pattern occurred as for colour televisions. At the beginning of the 1990s, Japanese products were very popular but by the middle of the 1990s, when Japanese white goods manufacturers made inroads into local production, local manufacturers were rapidly growing in strength and began to expand their share of the market. Local companies now lead in the local white goods market. With the exception of Panasonic, which has gained about 10 per cent of China's washing machine market, Japanese home electronic makers have been able to capture only a very modest share of China's local market in any products (market shares for 2008 by Japan Electrical Manufacturers' Association, 2009).

Three major factors can be cited to explain the rapid rise in competitiveness of Chinese companies. First, Chinese makers improved their quality. Second, they succeeded in cutting costs by achieving economies of scale through mass production without increasing the number of models unnecessarily. Third, Chinese manufacturers concentrated their efforts on strengthening their sales and service networks. Conversely, the reason why Japanese products declined in popularity was that their products were comparatively higher in price and Japanese makers were lagging in reinforcing their sales networks and after-sales services[4] (Marukawa 2007; Japan Electrical Manufacturers' Association 2009).

However, it would be a somewhat lopsided view to judge China as the winner and Japan as the loser in the market solely on the basis of trends in market shares. Japanese manufacturers still maintain a degree of competitiveness in high-function, high-end products, particularly in urban areas. Also, many Chinese consumer electronics manufacturers do not produce key components on their own, and the suppliers of these components are foreign manufacturers, including Japanese manufacturers. Finally, underlying the marked improvement in the quality of products manufactured by Chinese makers were the key components either made in Japan or made by Japanese manufacturers.

If we look at the approach of Chinese manufacturers to production, we can perhaps say that they opted for a strategy of specializing in the simple assembly of finished products without investing in the production of key components that would require the accumulation of various technologies over a long period, and costly production facilities. This is in stark contrast to the approach taken by

Japanese companies during Japan's period of high growth and afterwards, when manufacturers struggled to catch up with their European and American counterparts by homing in on cutting-edge technologies with uncertain future potential in a range of industries, including steel, electronics and electricals, and automobiles. The advantage for Chinese makers specializing in the assembly of finished products is the agility it offers, enabling makers to respond swiftly to market needs and changing technologies. On the other hand, their dependence on external suppliers for core components precludes their ability to fundamentally differentiate their products from those of their rivals. As a result, these manufacturers have no choice but to turn to cost reduction through mass production and engage in price wars. What this course of action will inevitably lead to is a negative cycle of chronic excessive production capacity, price wars and low profit margins (Marukawa 2007).

If Japanese companies are serious about closing in on the Chinese market, they will not be able to avoid becoming caught up in these price wars, and the issue for them will be the extent to which they will be able to demonstrate their competitive edge in the volume zone. In view of this market environment, the strategy of giving up on finished products in favour of specializing in the supply of core components may be considered a viable alternative. At the same time, however, producing in-house the entire finished product, which is directly exposed to changes in market needs, would also seem to enable a manufacturer to hone the main components and therefore respond appropriately to new technological changes.[5] If this is the case, selling finished products may be considered the price to pay for securing a competitive edge in key components, which are the main stronghold of Japanese companies.

The automobile industry: battleground for global and rising national corporations

In the automobile industry as well, the environment before and after the introduction of the 'reform and open door' policy changed considerably. Prior to the introduction of the policy, except for production of a very small number of automobiles such as the Hongqi (Red Flag) limousine for senior officials of the Communist Party and the Shanghai for middle-rank officials, commercial vehicles were the mainstays of the automotive industry.

During the 1980s, after reform and opening of the market, the Chinese government shifted from a policy of autonomous development of the automobile industry to promoting development through the use of foreign capital and technology. For foreign companies to be able to invest in the industry, however, the Chinese government made forming joint ventures with government-owned companies mandatory. It also limited to two the number of government companies a foreign company could invest in and set a ceiling of less than 50 per cent as the maximum amount a foreign company could invest in the joint venture. To dissolve the haphazardly established auto manufacturers, the Chinese government under the Automobile Industry Policy adopted in 1987 worked out a structure that was referred to as the 'Three Major, Three Minor' (later to become the 'Three Major, Three Minor, Two Small') by streamlining government-owned companies to reduce their overall number.[6] What this meant for foreign companies was that the potential joint venture partners were limited to these eight companies only. Essentially, it can be said that this was a policy for utilizing foreign capital in a restricted form. This situation continued until about the end of the 1990s.

Germany's Volkswagen (VW) was the first to succeed in making a foray into China ahead of the non-committal Japanese auto makers, which were giving top priority to local production in the United States. VW established Shanghai Volkswagen Automotive in a joint venture with Shanghai Automotive Industry Corporation in 1983 and commenced production of the Santana after importing used equipment and dies from overseas plants. Santana models were used as official cars for middle-rank government officials as well as for taxis, and their production almost monopolized the market (Kamiyama 2009). In addition to VW, foreign investment allowed in China's automobile industry included American Motors Corporation (later to become Chrysler) and Peugeot. This framework continued until the second half of the 1990s.

Changes in the industry first came about with the introduction of the latest models in the late 1990s by Honda with its Accord (the same as the US model) and by General Motors with the Buick. Honda succeeded Peugeot in a joint venture with Guangzhou Automotive Industry Group after the withdrawal of Peugeot, and General Motors (GM) had been granted permission to participate in a new joint venture with Shanghai Automotive Industry Group. The debut of these new models drew a favourable response from consumers, who were dissatisfied with past models that had remained unchanged for a long time. In view of this situation and conditions attendant to joining the World Trade Organization (WTO) in 2001, changes in the Chinese government's policies began to occur during the 2000s. The policy of the Three Major, Three Minor and Two Small was effectively shelved, increasing opportunities for the participation of foreign capital and the range of selection of potential joint venture partners. As a result, VW, GM and Honda were suddenly joined by other Japanese car makers such as Toyota and Nissan, Korean car makers such as Hyundai and Kia, and many other foreign car makers such as Citroën and Ford. Rapidly rising national auto makers such as Chery and Geely also joined the fray and, with its diverse variety of participants, the China auto market became one enormous automobile production base unparalleled in the world.

With the entry of a variety of global players, the market share of the Santana, which had previously enjoyed a near-monopoly position, rapidly plummeted, and from 2000 onwards the Chinese auto market was transformed into a robust competitive market where major world brands competed ruthlessly. Japanese auto makers, including Toyota, which seemed to have had a late start compared with VW and GM, have been rapidly expanding their market share in recent years and enhancing their presence in the Chinese market. Individually, even Honda and Toyota, with relatively high market shares, captured a less than 10 per cent share of the market. All Japanese makers combined, however, have captured 20–30 per cent of China's auto market in recent years. More than any other reason, high quality accounts for the popularity of Japanese cars.[7] Despite the Santana's considerable contraction of its market share, VW provides a variety of brands in China's market and it maintains the largest share of the market as a single group enterprise. GM also commands a share of the market almost equal to that of VW. Hyundai commands a market share on a par with Toyota and Honda (Kamiyama 2009; *Nippon Keizai Shimbun*, 26 April 2009; *Nikkei Sangyo Shimbun*, 16 July 2009).

On the other hand, the so-called national manufacturers that have grown significantly in the past several years are Chery, Geely and BYD Auto. These auto makers specialize in compact cars in the lower price range and boast a market share almost at the same level as Japanese auto makers combined, in terms of number of cars sold. However, these auto makers do have a number of weaknesses and issues that they must address, such as copying, very high reliance on external resources for key components and design (a weakness shared with the electrical industry), and anxiety concerning procedures for strengthening environmental regulations in the future.

The management of Japanese firms in China

This section examines the internal workings of Japanese firms that have entered China's market. The focus of this examination is the framework of local management, including the methods of entering the Chinese market, characteristics of the local management group, characteristics of personnel management compared with that in firms of other countries operating overseas, and finally, the dilemmas faced by Japanese companies and the solutions to those dilemmas.[8]

The framework of local management in China

The first point that should be mentioned in an examination of the management framework of Japanese firms in China is that many Japanese firms, unlike their counterparts in the United States, adopt a joint venture arrangement with local companies.[9] This is due to regulations established by the Chinese government with regard to the assembly of automobiles, as stated earlier. However, there are also many other cases where Japanese firms chose joint ventures even in the absence of regulations. This has been particularly the case when firms were entering the market to target China's domestic market.

The second point is the Japanese preference to establish new businesses rather than take over existing businesses. In this regard, they differ from many of their Western counterparts by adopting a gradual, steady approach to expanding the scale of their business and production bases one step at a time in line with the accumulation of technology and the experience of their local employees in what may be seen as a 'build-up approach'. This approach can be said to apply not only to Japan's manufacturing industry but also to the sales bases of supermarkets and cosmetics.

The third point about management is that although it is led by a small number of Japanese expatriates, Chinese managers with a deep understanding of Japanese-style management are also playing prominent roles in local Japanese firms. Here let us take a closer look at the characteristics of this management (see Itagaki 2010 for more details).

First of all, Japanese expatriates occupy the highest management positions in the majority of Japanese local offices. This is a common trait of Japanese firms with overseas offices, including offices in the United States. The situation is similar in Korean and Taiwanese local offices in China.

The next point is that the ratio of expatriates from Japan to the total number of employees in China is low compared with the number of Japanese expatriates found in local offices in North America. Based on the same research as is detailed in note 8, the ratio of Japanese expatriates to local employees in North America is approximately 2 per cent on average, while in many cases in China the ratio is less than 0.5 per cent.

There are several reasons for this. First, many Japanese companies in China have local staff who are quite proficient in Japanese. These staff members are able to communicate with the head office in Japan and with Japanese clients with little difficulty, thereby reducing the need for Japanese expatriates. Second, local offices have staff who not only are proficient in Japanese but also have experience studying and/or working in Japan. This experience naturally deepens their understanding of Japanese corporate management, thereby reducing the need for Japanese expatriates from Japan. Third, China is geographically in close proximity to Japan and should problems that cannot be easily solved by local staff arise in local operations, Japanese firms can respond quickly by dispatching staff from Japan.

Characteristics of local management from the perspective of personnel management

The mainstream approach to personnel management at Japanese companies in China is to implement local arrangements impartially while basing them on a traditional Japanese approach.

The first point relates to wages and salaries. During Japan's period of high economic growth in the post-war era, many companies adopted an in-house qualification system as a framework for wages and salaries. This was a system for ranking employees on the basis of the employee's age and number of years of continual service, and an evaluation of the employee's ability. This formed the basis for determining the base salary of individual employees. Under an in-house qualification-type salary system, the salary differential between the top- and the bottom-ranking employees is not significant, and the short-term achievement of employees is rarely immediately reflected in their salary. In the east China region and around Shanghai, some Japanese companies have adopted a partial performance-based pay system where incentive payments are paid to employees to reward superior performance. Even under arrangements such as this, however, unlike some Taiwanese or Chinese firms, Japanese firms rarely cut the total amount of the incentive payment when performance is poor. Furthermore, the ratio of incentive payments to total salary is generally capped at about one-third of the salary.

When it comes to promotions, the majority of companies lean towards internal promotions, and Japanese companies are generally seen as being slow to localize management (see, for example, Shiroki 2005). As previously stated, in the majority of cases companies have Japanese CEOs. However, there has been significant progress in the localization of other positions. Generally, section manager-class staff in local companies tend to be almost all Chinese, while positions in the general manager and executive director class are equally divided between Japanese and Chinese.

One visible area of divergence in local operations in China from the corporate environment in Japan is gender equality. Female managers can be found in many local offices, and the author's interviews with these employees indicate that they actively participate in the workplace as fully fledged officers. Another difference between firms in Japan and their local offices in China is that promotions occur at a faster pace in the latter.

Management's position in China regarding long-term employment coincides with that in domestic Japan. In China, a contract system for all regular employees was established under the Labour Act of 1995. Under provisions of this law, labour contracts setting out employees' tenure and applying to all employees, including irregular employees, are to be concluded between employer and employee. In reality, however, in many Japanese companies, and likewise in long-established government-owned companies of China, contracts with employees are usually renewed as a matter of course unless there is a serious problem. This reflects management's intention to offer long-term employment. However, although there are significant regional differences, employees' tendencies to change jobs are much more noticeable in China than in Japan. This is a real problem not only for Japanese firms but for all firms operating in China. Nevertheless, the situation is much more serious for Japanese firms, as I shall describe.[10]

Many American companies in China have adopted a salary system which is known as a performance-based pay system: the most recent performance is reflected in the salary and, as a result, the gap among employees' salaries widens. Therefore, a capable person who takes up a high-ranking position and achieves reasonable results will receive high remuneration. On the other hand, a person who is unable to achieve expected results may suffer the consequence of dismissal.

Many Taiwanese firms, privately owned Chinese enterprises and 'pro-reform' government-owned companies such as Haier have adopted a business system based on the principle of reward and punishment.[11] Under this system, an employee's wages consist of a basic salary (fixed salary) and an incentive (performance-based wage), and in many cases these are divided equally. An employee receives the full amount of an incentive when he or she achieves the expected results. When the employee is unable to achieve targets, however, or makes errors, the incentive is reduced or forfeited entirely (in other words, the salary is halved). Furthermore, personnel performing at the lowest performance level may be demoted or their contracts not renewed.

As this demonstrates, we can see that various personnel management systems coexist in modern China. Among these, the personnel system adopted by Japanese companies is not very popular in general. Among the reasons for this are the delay in the localization of management, salaries that are considered too low, and promotions that take a long time. Consequently, these conditions make it difficult for Japanese firms to recruit outstanding personnel (Zhao 2002; Shiroki 2005; Taura and Liu 2008). In view of this situation, should Japanese firms just adopt a personnel system similar to that of American or Taiwanese firms?

Competitiveness of Japanese firms, dilemmas Japanese firms face in China, and possible solutions

This subsection examines the strengths Japanese firms overseas have by taking a look at their assembly of finished products and components and the sales of retailers.

The main strength of major Japanese manufacturers in their assembly of products, and of large-scale retailers in sales, is their ability to produce and sell a variety of products by subdividing them into numerous small lots rather than producing or displaying one item all at once. This technique of producing limited volumes of a range of products is known as multi-item small-lot production. To realize multi-item small-lot production and sales, Japanese firms had to push their ingenuity to the limit to devise a wide range of techniques and methods. The most renowned of these is Toyota's 'just-in-time' (JIT) system (Fujimoto 1997). In the retail business, the 'tanpin-kanri' (unit control) system implemented by Seven-Eleven Japan and Ito-Yokado, whereby neither too many nor too few items are stocked by accurately determining the sales performance of each item, became globally renowned (Henmi 2008).

A drawback of multi-item small-lot production is its weakness in emergency situations, such as quality problems. Therefore, responsibility for quality control is not left to specialists and engineers alone. Employees at every level and position in the company are involved in quality control, and this is why it is referred to as total quality control (TQC) (Fujimoto 2001).

Many dissertations, explanations and manuals have been published on the subjects of JIT, 'tanpin-kanri' and TQC.[12] Strangely enough, however, these systems do not necessarily function well even when companies are familiar with their workings. There are many Japanese companies, including Toyota and Ito-Yokado, that carefully plan their work operations around these systems and use them effectively. On the other hand, General Motors, for example, once attempted to incorporate these systems into its operations in the 1990s but gave up after it was unable to achieve good results. The question, then, is why these systems failed to work for General Motors. The answer is that for these systems to function adequately, companies need back-up systems that 'are not readily visible'.

In order for JIT, 'tanpin-kanri' and TQC to function effectively, teamwork and coordinated operations are essential in work processes within the company, production site, supply division, quality control division and external main suppliers.[13] For coordinated operations to work well, workers need to know the other workers well. The best way for workers to get to know each other is for them to actually work together at the work site. Many Japanese companies have actually practised reshuffling their employees to train employees to be multi-skilled. Even if employees do not actually get to work together at a work site, they must at least know what the other employees are about to do. This is known as sharing information. The reason many firms in Japan are adept at multi-skilling and sharing information is related to the fundamental way in which they work. The key point is that the barriers between various work tasks are low. Unlike the American work style practised widely in the United States, where workers are assigned tasks that have been clearly spelled out, Japanese firms tend to allocate work to employees to suit the occasion without setting the bar of employee work tasks in a particular area of work too high. This is an important fundamental feature in creating multi-skilling and the sharing of information. Having multiple skills also implies that an employee becomes involved in tasks of varying degrees of difficulty instead of simply carrying out tasks widely across operations. In coordinated operations, it is necessary for a wide range of employees at various layers to demonstrate an attitude of actively engaging in their company's business (employee participation model business).

There is another important cornerstone. It is the need for employees to work within a framework of long-term employment and long-term, ongoing business relationships.[14] Immediately after a reshuffle of employees, work efficiency declines temporarily because of unfamiliarity of the work content. To take full advantage of the development of multi-skilled employees, firms cannot afford to lose workers shortly after a reshuffle. In this sense, long-term employment is important. Superior companies in Japan still consider long-term employment important (at least for their regular employees), and they maintain long-term business relationships with suppliers of vital components even when the suppliers are not part of their own corporate group. The basis of many Japanese firms that are successful at JIT and so on is low barriers between different work tasks and a management ethos that values long-term continuity.

Of course, the American system has its own merits.[15] The degree of self-completion of each job task increases according to the definition of the job task and the more highly specialized the work. Therefore, even when employees have to be replaced, the continuity of the organization can be maintained. Strong leadership governs the aggregate of clearly defined job tasks and authority, and decision-making does not take a long time because management is under strong leadership. This American system is also replete with cultural diversity and was developed in an environment where the movement of people is frequently observed. At the same time, it is a system that is easily understood when transplanted to countries with different cultures. Moreover, barriers between work divisions are high in many Chinese companies, and those firms that adopt top-down management systems have more in common with American firms. This makes the American management system more easily understood in China. It is a problem for any company when employee mobility is excessively high, but for reasons just stated, the setbacks Japanese firms can sustain as a result of such mobility are more serious.

Personnel management of Japanese companies, as previously noted, is closely connected with the work processes and the characteristics of the organization. Salaries that are not based on types of work are compatible with the method of assigning work and sharing information. The small disparity in salaries between the top and bottom echelons of employees is compatible with an employee participation system of management. And long-term employment and proficiency assessment as well as promotions that take a considerable time are compatible with the formation of multiple skills. To demonstrate their competitiveness, Japanese firms try to transplant systems such as JIT, 'tanpin-kanri' and TQC. For these systems to function adequately, they must introduce their proprietary work methods, such as cooperative operations with other divisions. Another reason they do so is because these systems match the personnel systems of Japanese companies.

However, it is in this area that Japanese firms encounter difficulties.[16] A visible system like JIT has a specific form and is therefore easy to introduce in China. However, the work methods, which are invisible, are difficult to understand at first. For employees familiar with a system of high barriers between work divisions and top-down decision-making, understanding Japanese work methods and systems is even more difficult. Therefore, the presence of Japanese representatives who understand the work methods is essential. To spread the practice of coordinated operations between work divisions, there is also a need to appoint to top management personnel who are well versed in such procedures (also Japanese expatriates). This is the basic reason why the ratio of Japanese representatives in local companies is higher than in local US companies, and why the top management positions of many Japanese companies are filled by Japanese personnel.

These organizational arrangements are also the source of problems, however. The presence of Japanese top management and Japanese staff on loan also means the localization of management personnel is delayed (however, changes in this area have been evident over time). Furthermore, the Japanese corporate system of evaluating competence over a period of time and the slow pace at which promotions occur are incongruent with the aspirations of young, ambitious Chinese people. Therefore, it is difficult for Japanese companies to recruit talented personnel. To maintain competitiveness, the presence of Japanese representatives and a Japanese-style personnel management system may be necessary, but such systems have the potential to reduce the motivation of capable local employees. These are the dilemmas Japanese firms face in China. To be precise, these are the dilemmas that Japanese firms have faced in many countries, but they are more noticeable in major cities of China, where young, ambitious personnel frequently transfer to other companies.

Is there a viable way of dealing with this problem? Of course there is, but there is no quick, magic solution. The only way is to make changes by taking one step at a time. First, at the time of recruitment there is a need to clarify the kind of ability the company requires of new recruits in line with the mission of the relevant local company. While talented personnel may be required, the details of what constitutes 'talented' will vary. Here I would like to relate an interesting example. A major Japanese global automobile components manufacturer in Shanghai decided to establish a new R&D centre. At first, the company hoped to recruit graduates with outstanding academic records from Tsinghua University in Beijing and Fudan University in Shanghai, and proceeded to recruit desirable graduates. However, the new recruits did not remain with the company for long. The lesson learned by the company from this experience was that the kinds of candidates it recruited were not suited to straightforward work like designing components, even though there ongoing innovations in technology were involved. As a result, the company changed its recruitment priorities to seek earnest, capable university-educated personnel hailing from universities one rank lower than the universities mentioned earlier. As the result of this shift in the company's attitude, the company was able to reduce the employee attrition rate to less than 2 per cent even though it was located in Shanghai, an area where employees are known to transfer frequently.

The next point is related to this. At the time of recruitment, Japanese firms must carefully select personnel who are suited to working in a Japanese firm and in the corporate culture of that particular firm. Likewise, they must clearly convey to candidates the type of person they are seeking to recruit (Taura and Liu 2008). The kind of person suited to working in a Japanese company is one who considers his or her career from a long-term perspective and who aspires to demonstrate his or her ability in a stable environment. It goes without saying that even among the Chinese, there are many different types of people.

In Japanese firms, where multi-skilling and teamwork are cornerstones of the organization, promotions and pay rises are apt to trail behind those in American and other firms. Therefore, Japanese firms need to create a road map that clearly shows to potential employees the kinds of positions they can hold and the work they can engage in during the course of their careers. Some Japanese firms have already initiated trials along these lines (Itagaki 2009). At the time of recruitment, firms must also explain to candidates what the firm will do to improve the career prospects of its employees. In general, Japanese companies do not adequately promote this vital public relations information (Taura and Liu 2008).

For people to understand the 'invisible work methods' of Japanese firms, Japanese firms must clearly explain why they are necessary. There are many Japanese expatriates who are not good at giving explanations. Work customs and practices that may be a routine matter for Japanese who have received a Japanese school education and worked at a workplace in Japan, and may indeed be logical, may not appear that way to people of different cultures. Therefore, expatriates must be sufficiently proficient in the Chinese language to be able to explain matters appropriately to local staff.[17]

However, words alone from an expatriate may have difficulty in striking a responsive chord in the other person's heart. On the other hand, in some successful local Japanese companies there are cases where local staff members hold top management or other important positions as key staff who have a firm understanding of Japanese corporate organizations and the characteristics of their strategies. These key staff members are capable of 'translating' this information in a local manner to colleagues and subordinates, and they have the ability to revitalize the entire organization.[18] If these local personnel are to be called 'key persons', they must be trained conscientiously. Japanese firms that have been successful in securing such staff in many cases have simply had the good fortune to come across such valuable human resources. In the future, to realize the localization of business managers, Japanese firms must seek out and nurture the development of key human resources in a deliberate and systematic manner. What will be important at that time will be to have those employees experience how talented employees in Japan would handle various situations on their own. At each turning point in their career, personnel considered to be key persons of the future must be given training and guidance and be entrusted with work at the head office or other office in Japan. Japanese employees have not learned Japanese-style working methods purely because they are Japanese; employees learn by observing the way their seniors work and by working together with senior workers within the company.

Notes

1 Special Economic Zones are places where foreign capital is given preferential treatment such as reduction in import–export duties and permission to engage in wholly owned investments as a means to attract foreign export companies. Under this scheme, in exchange for preferential treatment the export of goods is mandatory. In 1980, four cities were designated as Special Economic Zones: Shenzhen; Zhuhai, next to Macau; Xiantou, which has a close relationship with overseas Chinese (all these are in Guangdong Province); and Xiamen in Fujian Province, on the coast opposite Taiwan. In 1984, after witnessing the success of Special Economic Zones, the Chinese government further expanded the areas for preferential treatment of foreign capital and attracting foreign investments, and designated a number of port cities in the coastal areas as open coastal cities. These included Dalian, Tienjin, Shanghai, Qingdao, Ningbo and Wenzhou (Guo 1999).

2 An intermediary dealer would bring consumer electric goods imported from Japan to the Chinese border. Chinese customs would then confiscate the goods and sell them by auction. A Chinese dealer in a prearrangement with the intermediary dealer in Hong Kong would then make a successful bid. When this Chinese dealer paid the dealer in Hong Kong for the goods, the illegal import of the goods without payment of any import duties was finalized. Even as of 1992, tariffs as high as 100 per cent were imposed on colour televisions (see Marukama 2007).

3 The most significant effect it had was in 1994, when the government allowed the exchange of renminbi (RMB) from domestic sales in China to be exchanged for foreign currency. As a result, it became easier for local producers to purchase imported components for products sold on the Chinese domestic market (Marukawa 2007).

4 One of the reasons for this was that until 2001, when China joined the WTO, the Chinese government did not readily grant permits for the establishment of companies whose purpose was to engage in sales and services (Marukawa 2007).

5 Based on the opinions of engineers from several electronics manufacturers that the author interviewed.

6 The Three Major and Three Minor included three large-auto makers (First Auto Works, Dongfeng Motor Corp., Shanghai Automotive Industry Group) and three compact-car makers (Beijing Automotive Industry Group, Tianjin Automotive Industry Group, Guangzhou Automotive Industry Group). Later, makers of minicars, which were called the Two Small, were added.

7 For example, according to JD Power Asia Pacific Inc., a US research firm, in an early-stage product quality ranking targeting automobiles manufactured in China, Japanese cars held the top positions in five out of six divisions (*Nihon Keizai Shimbun*, morning edition, 25 December 2006).

8 In the depiction of circumstances in this chapter, I made use in part of some of the research results made possible through the following study grants: Musashi University Overseas Special Researcher (2006), 2003–07 Musashi University Open Research Center Project (the research theme of the business management group the author was in charge of was 'Comparative Study of Overseas Business Management of Japanese, Korean, and Taiwanese companies'), 2007–09 Science Study Fund and Overseas Academic Study (I was the representative researcher and the theme was 'The direction personnel training should aim for in Japanese companies in China from the perspective of the work management organization'), 2000–04 Academic Research Project for the Promotion of Private Universities by the Ministry of Education, Culture, Sports, Science and Technology (Academic Frontier Project) 'International joint study of international competition and cooperation in management and production systems' (Representative researcher: Professor Tetsuo Abo, Teikyo University (then)). Where there are no specific references cited in the text that follows, details are fundamentally based on information obtained through these interview studies.

9 Out of 18 Japanese companies in China targeted as subjects in the Musashi University Open Research Center Project as described in note 8, there were only six local companies where investment from the Japanese parent company was 90 per cent or higher, and out of 11 companies which have been subjects of our research to date through ongoing science research funds and overseas academic study grants also mentioned in note 8, there were only five local companies for which investment by the Japanese parent company was 90 per cent or greater (in other words, 11 out of 29 companies). On the other hand, in North America, out of 37 Japanese companies which were the subjects in a research project in which the author participated, the number of local companies where the Japanese parent company invested 90 per cent or more was as high as 31. Furthermore, there was significant overlap in companies that were research subjects in both China and North America. Therefore, these figures can be described as data indicating the characteristics of companies that entered markets in foreign countries rather than data concerning the parent companies. For data concerning the United States, see Juhn and Itagaki (2011).

10 Based on a review indicating that the existing Labour Contract Act excessively weakened the position of employees, the new Labour Contract Act was adopted in 2008. This legislation made it mandatory for companies to establish contracts that did not limit the duration of service at the time of the signing of the contract for the third time, in addition to cases of ten years of service or more, as in the past (in other words, the objective was to engage employees until retirement). For further details, see Taura and Liu (2008).

11 See Yoshiwara and Ouyang (2006) for details on Haier.

12 Fujimoto (1997) provides a representative study of Toyota's production systems, including JIT and TQC.

13 For a more detailed explanation of the following, see Itagaki (2008).

14 See Koike (1996) for the merit of long-term employment, and Asanuma (1997) for the merits of long-term business relationships.

15 For a comparison of Japanese and American corporate management, see Kagono *et al.* (1985). Although it is old, it is still a useful reference. Also, see Dore (2000).
16 See Itagaki (2009) for the following details.
17 While conducting repeated interviews at Japanese and German companies in China, I noticed an interesting difference between Japanese and German expatriates. German representatives are generally good at giving explanations to persons who unfamiliar with the internal affairs of their company (which exactly describes us as interviewers). Japanese expatriates, on the other hand, have a tendency to make the assumption that other party is aware of what is common knowledge to them (internal affairs of the company) when they speak.
18 A typical example would perhaps be Peter Wickens, who worked as the president of UK Nissan and later became the president for all of Europe (Wickens 1987).

References

Amano Tomofumi and Fan Jianting (2003) *Nicchu Kaden Sangyo Hatten no Dainamizumu – Kokusai Bungyo no Tenkai to Kyoso Yuui no Henka – (Jo) (Chu) (Ge)* (Dynamism in the development of the Japanese and Chinese consumer electronics industry: development of international division of labour and changes in competitive advantages, vols 1, 2 and 3), *Keieiron Shu Dai 58, 59, 60 go* (Theories on business management, vols 58, 59 and 60).

Aoki Shunichiro (2003) 'Matushita Denki: Chugoku deno Jigyo Tenkai' (Matsushita Electric: business development in China), in Yoshikawa Hideki, Itagaki Horoshi and Morokai Shiget (eds) *Keisu Bukku, Kokusai Keiei* (Case book of international business management), Tokyo: Yuhikaku (in Japanese).

Asanuma Banri (1997) *Nihon no Kigyou Soshiki: Kakushin-teki Tekio no Mekanizumu – Chouki Torihiki Kankei no Kouzo to Kinou* (Japanese corporate organizations: mechanism for innovative adaptation: structure and functions of long-term trading ties), Tokyo: Toyo Keizai Shinposha (in Japanese).

Dore, Ronald (2000) *Stock Market Capitalism: Welfare Capitalism: Japan and Germany versus the Anglo-Saxons*, Oxford: Oxford University Press.

Fujimoto Takahiro (1997) *Seisan Shisutemu no Shinkaron – Toyota Jidosha ni Miru Soshiki Noryoku to Sohatsu Purosesu* (The evolutionary theory of production systems: organizational ability and creative development process observed at Toyota Motor Company), Tokyo: Yuhikaku (in Japanese).

Fujimoto Takahiro (2001) *Seisan Manaijimento Nyumon 1: Seisan Shisutemu Hen* (Introduction to production management 1: edition on production systems), Tokyo: Nihon Keizai Shimbun (in Japanese).

Guo Sizhi (1999) *Nihon no Tai Chugoku Chokusetsu Toushi* (Japanese direct investments in China), Tokyo: Meitoku Shuppan (in Japanese).

Henmi Toshie (2008) *Ito Yokado: Kokyaku Manzoku no Sekkeizu, Kasetsu Kensho ni Motozuku Uriba Zukuri* (Ito-Yokado: design drawing on customer satisfaction: creating sales areas based on assumptions and inspections), Tokyo: Diamond (in Japanese).

Itagaki Hiroshi (2008) 'Nihon Seizogyo no Kyoso Yuui to Sekiyu Gasu Sangyo e no Tekiyo Kanosei' (Competitive advantage of Japanese manufacturing industries and potential for applying to oil and gas industries), in Abo Tetsuo (ed.) *Nihon Sekiyu Gasu Kigyo no Kokusai Kyoso Senryaku: Kokusai Sekiyu Meja Nihon Seiao Kigyo tono Hikaku* (International competition strategies of Japanese oil and gas industries: comparison of international oil majors and Japanese manufacturing companies), Kyoto: Minerva Shobo (in Japanese).

Itagaki, Hiroshi (2009) 'Competitiveness, localization and Japanese companies in China: realities and alternate approaches', *Asia Pacific Business Review*, 15 (3): 451–462.

Itagaki Hiroshi (2010) *Chugoku ni Okeru Nichi, Kan, Tai Kigyo no Keiei Hikaku* (Comparison of business management between Japanese, Korean, and Taiwanese companies in China), Kyoto: Minerva Shobo (in Japanese).

Japan Electrical Manufacturers' Association, Home Electrical Appliances Division (2009) *Chugoku no Shiromono Kaden no Seisan Kyoten Narabini Shijo to Shiteno Hyoka to Nikkei Meika no Kadai* (Production bases for the white goods home electrical appliances in China, assessment as the market, and tasks for Japanese-owned manufacturers), Tokyo: Japan Electrical Manufacturers' Association (in Japanese).

JETRO (2004) *Chugoku Shijo ni Idomu Nikkei kigyo: Sono Senryaku to Kadai wo Saguru* (Japanese companies taking up the challenge of the Chinese market: examining the strategies and issues), Tokyo: JETRO (in Japanese).

Juhn, Wooseok and Itagaki, Hiroshi (2011) 'Hybrid analysis of Japanese transplants in the United States', in Tetsuji Kawamura (ed.) *The Hybrid Factory in the United States: The Japanese-Style Management and Production System under the Global Economy*, Oxford: Oxford University Press.

Kagono, T., Nonaka, I., Sakakibara, K. and Okumura, A. (1985) *Strategic vs. Evolutionary Management: A U.S.–Japan Comparison of Strategy and Organization*, Amsterdam: North-Holland.

Kamiyama Kunio (ed.) (2009) *Kyodaika Suru Chugoku Jidosha Sangyo* (Enormous Chinese automotive industry), Tokyo: Nikkan Jidosha Shimbun (in Japanese).

Koike, Kazuo (1996) *The Economics of work in Japan*, Tokyo: LTCB International Library Foundation.

Marukawa Tomo (2007) *Gendai Chugoku no Sangyo: Bokko suru Chugoku Kigyo no Tsuyosa to Morosa* (Industries of modern China: strength and fragility of rising Chinese automotive industries), Tokyo: Chuokoron-Shinsha (in Japanese).

Shiroki Mitsuhide (ed.) (2005) *Chaina Shifuto no Jinteki Shigen Kanri* (Human resource management in the shift to China), Tokyo: Hakuto-Shobo.

Takagi Nobuyoshi (1996) 'Denshi Sangyo: Gijutsu Keisei to Kigyo Kaikau Gijutsu Iten' (electronics industries: technology formation and corporate reform, technology transfer), in Matsuzaki Yoshi (ed.) *Chugoku no Denshi Tekkou Sangyo* (Chinese electronics and steel industries), vol. 1, Tokyo: Hosei University Press (in Japanese).

Taura Rika and Liu Mozhen (2008) 'Chugoku Shijo no Doukou to Nihon Kigyo no Jinzai Manejimento Senryaku' (Trends in the Chinese market and human resource management strategies of Japanese companies), *Chiteki Shisan Souzou* (Intellectual assets creation), July (in Japanese).

Wickens, Peter (1987) *The Road to Nissan: Flexibility, Quality, Teamwork*, London: Macmillan.

Yoshiwara Hideki and Taohua Ouyang (2006) *Chugoku Kigyo no Shijou Shugi Kanri – Haiaru* (Market principle management of Chinese companies – Haier), Tokyo: Hakuto-Shobo.

Zhao Xiaoxia (2002) *Chugoku ni Okeru Nikkei Kigyou no Jinteki Shigen Kanri ni Tsuite no Bunseki* ('Analyses concerning Japanese companies' human resource management in China), Tokyo: Hakuto-Shobo (in Japanese).

Part II

Chinese perspective

5 China and world development

Beyond the crisis

Dic Lo

Introduction

It is widely recognized that the interaction between China and the world economy since the turn of the century has been of systematic importance in shaping the direction of globalization. The structural dynamics behind this interaction, however, has been a topical issue of scholarly debates. Recent international opinions on this issue have focused on the China–US economic nexus.

The story of 'China causing global imbalances' has been in vogue in the international arena since the outbreak of the financial crisis in the United States and other advanced capitalist countries in 2007, which has subsequently resulted in a world-scale recession. This story posits that the particular way through which China integrates itself into the world economy has been responsible for prolonging the world recession – indeed, for causing the financial crisis in the first place. The focus of the story is on the relationship of economic interdependence between China and the United States, or the so-called China–US economic nexus. And the central assertion is that this nexus is the product, unilaterally, of Chinese policy. Hence, it is concluded that China has to change course – in particular, it should adopt a range of policy measures for stimulating domestic demand. These include strongly appreciating the Chinese currency, the renminbi (the yuan), as the immediate measure. A further measure to be adopted in the near future is to speed up the liberalization of China's international finance – that is, to move towards a free-floating exchange rate regime and free cross-border capital flows. Over a longer time-span, China must fundamentally reform its economy in the direction of embracing neo-liberalism *in toto*. It is claimed that mass privatization of assets and lands, in particular, would stimulate domestic consumption and correct China's demand imbalances on both the domestic and the external fronts.[1]

Meanwhile, parallel to mainstream opinions, there exists a contrasting critical literature that is concerned with the developmental prospects for China itself and for the broader developing world. This literature was rather sceptical early on concerning the role of the China–US economic nexus, and has in recent years given rise to an alternative story of 'China facing internal and external dependence'. The story posits that the Chinese economy has been dependent on foreign trade and inward foreign direct investment on the external front, and on worsening income distribution and exploitation of labour on the internal front. The double dependency has thus been to the detriment of China's social and economic development. It has also, via international competition, squashed the developmental space for other developing economies, thus reinforcing their predicament of deindustrialization which has persisted over the era of globalization. The general conclusion from the story of double dependency is similar to that of the mainstream story, in that it sees the need for China to stimulate domestic demand. Nevertheless, the concrete policies are different. Instead of liberalization and privatization, for promoting domestic consumption what is needed for China is to strengthen the position of labour and other social underclasses. This will also have the effect of promoting industrial upgrading and lessening external dependence.[2]

The objective of this chapter is to attempt to clarify the analytical efficacy of the above two stories for the understanding of China and related economic development. As will be argued in the subsequent text, the two stories both suffer from serious flaws in terms of their analyses and policy conclusions. The neo-liberal story's emphasis on the benefits of the China–US economic nexus for Chinese economic development is found to be a gross exaggeration. The critical story's diametrically opposite judgement is also found to be excessively pessimistic. In this connection, the chapter further seeks to explore into the construction of an alternative policy line that is well founded and suits better the needs of the social and economic development of China and the developing world.

The chapter has five sections, of which this introduction is the first. The second section examines the empirical efficacy of the stories of 'China causing global imbalances' and 'China facing internal and external dependence'. The third section connects the preceding discussion to the analysis of the structural dynamics of China's prevailing development path. The fourth section seeks to construct an alternative analytical story of the Chinese experience, and derive different policy lessons. There is a final concluding section.

China in the face of global imbalances and deindustrialization

'The China–US economic nexus' refers to a structural relationship whereby China exports cheap manufactures to the United States in exchange for US government papers and other dollar-denominated financial assets. This nexus is the accumulated outcome of the particular way through which China integrates itself into the world economy. Specifically, the nexus first took shape at the turn of the century and has since expanded at tremendous speed. The general background against which this occurred is the transition of world development from the 'lost decades' of the 1980s and 1990s to the substantial growth rebound across all regions of the developing world in the period 2000–07. It is reasonable to believe that the China–US economic nexus has significantly contributed to this growth rebound. At one level, cheap imports from China have helped to hold down living costs in the United States and other advanced countries, and cheap capital from China has supported US investment and consumption. At another level, by absorbing intermediate industrial products from the rest of East Asia and raw materials from a number of developing countries, the nexus has helped to promote economic growth in the developing world. Meanwhile, the standard neo-liberal thesis of export-led growth implies that the nexus might have been conducive to China's own economic growth. There is indeed no shortage of claims that Chinese economic development over this period has been mainly export led.

The story of 'China causing global imbalances', which has emerged and gained currency since the outbreak of the financial crisis in 2007, is based on a straightforward observation: the almost symmetrical trends of China's expanding current account surplus and the United States' expanding deficits since the turn of the century (Figure 5.1). These trends reflect the deficiency of domestic investment vis-à-vis savings in China, and the opposite situation in the United States. From

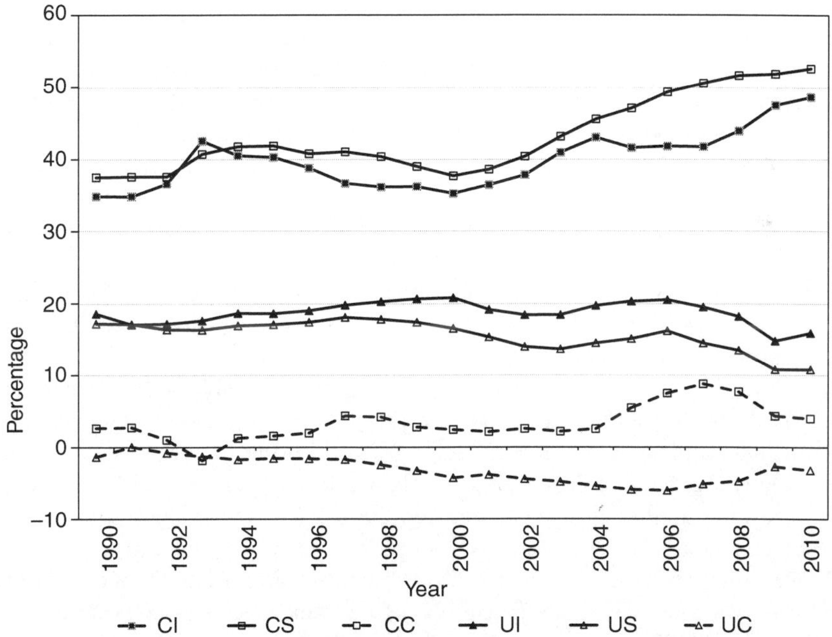

Figure 5.1 Current-Account and Savings-Investment balance (ratio to GDP, %) (sources: Chinese data from National Bureau of Statistics, *Zhongguo Tongji Zhaiyao* 2010 (China Statistical Abstract 2010); US data from IMF, *World Economic Outlook*, data bank (accessed 23 August 2010)).

Notes

CI=China's gross investment, CS=China's savings (=gross investment+current account balances), CC=China's current account balances, UI=US gross investment, US=US savings, UC=US current account balances. GDP data are of the expenditures approach.

this observation, US economic officials and mainstream media commentators assert that China's surplus has been an important cause of US deficits. And China's surplus, it is further asserted, has been caused by government exchange-rate manipulation as well as the more fundamental problem of the Chinese economic system providing insufficient protection to property rights, and therefore investment. There follow the policy demands that China ought to immediately appreciate its currency substantially and implement systemic reform measures, particularly financial liberalization, together with mass privatization over a longer time-span.

Is there really a causal relationship between China's current account surplus and US deficits? Conceptually, as McKinley (2009) has pointed out, the charge that China has caused global imbalances (and thereby the financial crisis) hinges on the theory of the so-called global savings glut. For this theory to hold, it requires either of the following conditions in the world economy: either a significant increase in the world savings to income ratio, or a stable consumption rate (and hence savings rate) in the advanced countries. Yet neither of these exists in reality. According to data from the International Monetary Fund (IMF), the world savings to income ratio has remained basically the same for a long time: 22.7 per cent in the period 1986–93, 22.1 per cent in 1994–2001 and 22.7 per cent in 2002–08. During these same periods, the savings to income ratio for the United States was 16.3 per cent, 17.0 per cent and 13.9 per cent, respectively. The same ratio for all advanced countries combined was 22.2 per cent, 21.6 per cent and 19.8 per cent, respectively. Clearly, it is excessive consumption in advanced countries, especially in the United States, that has caused global imbalances. It is also the combination of excessive consumption and deficient financial systems that has caused the financial crisis, as well as the fiscal crisis of the state in a number of European countries. In other words, China's surplus should not be held responsible for US deficits, let alone for causing the financial crisis. For the United States, the logical outcome of reducing trade deficits with China would only be a redirection towards trade deficits with other countries (Petras 2009).

This said, however, it remains true that China's massive current account surplus with the United States has been a problem in the bilateral relationship. The imbalance did, time and again, cause friction during the boom years. It is most unlikely that the imbalance can be sustained in the years of crisis and recession. According to statistical data from the US side, it was in 2000 that China first replaced Japan as the number one surplus country with the United States. By 2008, deficits with China accounted for a hefty share of almost one-third of the total of US trade deficits with the rest of the world (Kwan 2009). With the financial crisis, the US economy has suffered from serious problems of demand deficiency and unemployment. The issue of trade deficits with China has thus been injected with increased political sensitivity. No wonder that the imbalance in bilateral trade has become central to the justification for demanding that China appreciate its currency and speed up financial liberalization.

The concern of the story of 'China causing global imbalances' is over the economic impact of China on the United States and other advanced countries. In contrast, the alternative, critical story of 'China facing internal and external dependence' concerns mainly the impact of the China–US economic nexus on the development of China and the broader developing world. The writings of this latter story do not necessarily deny the contribution of the nexus to world economic growth over the 2000–07 period. Nevertheless, they are rather definitive in highlighting the negative impact of the nexus on world development over the long term.[3] The emphasis is twofold. The first element is the thesis of undercutting, meaning that the expansion of Chinese manufacturing exports has, via international competition, substantially squashed the developmental space for other developing economies. The second is the thesis of excessive (even super-) exploitation of Chinese labour during this process of expansion, which has been dominated by the operations of foreign capital investors.

The thesis of undercutting first emerged in the studies of the economic relationship between Mainland China and the rest of East Asia (Hart-Landsberg and Burkett 2004). Its empirical efficacy appears to be very limited, as it is too easy to observe that China has for a long time been persistently running trade deficits with the rest of East Asia. The application of the thesis then turns to the studies of China's large-scale importing of primary products from a number of developing countries. It is asserted that this resembles the pattern of the 'old' or 'colonial' international division of labour. Yet it is well known that China's manufacturing exports have been mostly at the lower end of the value chain of world trade and production. And along with export expansion has been a rapid deterioration in China's terms of international trade: in 1998–2008, the period with the fastest expansion of exports, the index of net barter terms of trade declined by more than 30 per cent, while the developing world as a whole showed exactly the opposite performance (Figure 5.2). It can thus be inferred that the economic relationship between China and the rest of the developing world is in no sense one of unequal exchange. It is very unlikely that the relationship has involved surplus transfer from the latter to the former. Meanwhile, however, the rapid deterioration of China's terms of trade does give support to a different, more recent argument about undercutting: that Chinese competition has tended to crowd out manufacturing exports from other developing economies in the world market, thus reinforcing the trend of deindustrialization in these economies (Jenkins 2008; Jenkins *et al.* 2008). This injects further political sensitivity to China's export expansion. In other words, the expansion is liable to affect the relationship between China and other developing countries. The fact that China has become a major target of anti-dumping charges by other semi-industrializing countries, despite the fact that its exports to their home markets have been limited, is a manifestation of this tension. The same is also indicated in the fact that countries like India and Brazil, which should have stood alongside China in the international economic orders, have time and again joined the chorus of those pressing China to appreciate its currency.

From the discussion above, it seems appropriate to say that existing evidence does not clearly back the claim that China has caused global imbalances and thereby the financial crisis. The alternative claim about China squashing the

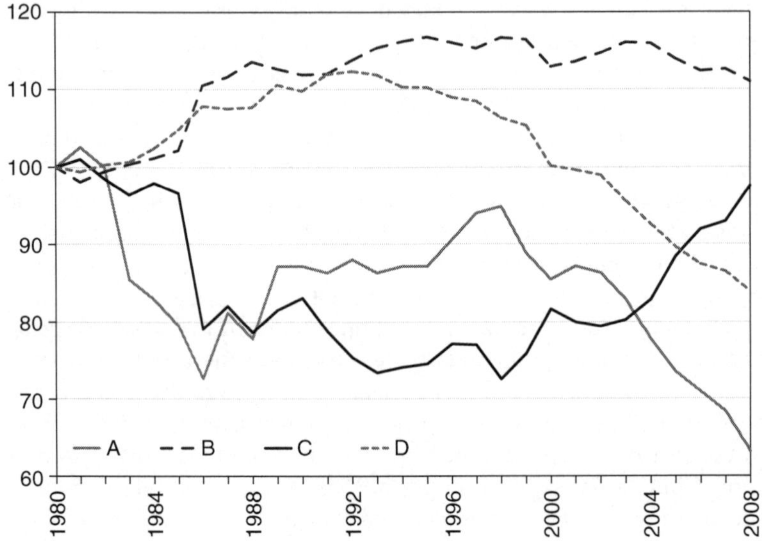

Figure 5.2 Net barter terms of international trade (1980=100) (sources: International Monetary Fund, *World Economic Outlook* data bank (accessed 23 August 2010), and *International Financial Statistics Yearbook*, various issues; World Bank, *World Development Indicators*, data bank (accessed 23 August 2010)).

Notes

A=China; B=developed countries ('industrial countries' in the IMF categorization); C=developing countries; D=East Asian newly industrializing economies (i.e. Hong Kong, Taiwan, South Korea and Singapore). East Asian newly industrializing economies data are terms of trade in goods and services; others are terms of trade in goods.

developmental space for the rest of the developing world does seem to have some elements of truth, but this has to be balanced with the positive side of the economic relationship between them. With all these considerations taken into account, however, it remains true that, for political rather than economic consideration, China still needs to strongly stimulate domestic demand and reduce its external surplus. What needs to be clarified is what the appropriate measures for achieving the target are. This requires an adequate analysis of the nature of China's prevailing path of economic development, and the role of the China–US economic nexus in the development path.

Imbalances, dependency and the structural dynamics of Chinese development

Prima facie, the China–US economic nexus as characterized in the preceding section is clearly undesirable for Chinese economic development. The nexus implies the provision of double subsidies from China, a developing economy, to the United States, a developed economy. That is to say, the former supplies first cheap products and then cheap capital to the latter. Moreover, on the Chinese side the nexus has been dominated by the operations of foreign capital investors. Yet foreign capital-invested firms (which include both foreign-owned firms and Sino-foreign joint ventures) have tended to have a slower pace of productivity growth than the rest of Chinese industry, and at the level of distribution these firms have also tended to apportion an exceedingly large share of surplus to capital (Lo *et al.* 2011). It can thus be argued that, for the benefit of China's social and economic development, this nexus needs to be weakened and restructured. The question is how. Has the Chinese economy already become structurally dependent on this nexus? And what would be the cost of breaking away from the dependence?

The critical literature does have a near-consensus that structural dependence on the nexus is a central feature of the Chinese economy. The China story that this literature has attempted to construct is typically composed of the following three propositions. First, China's expanding current account surplus is a symptom of the fact that its economic growth is dependent on the demand of the world market. This reasoning also applies to China's rapid accumulation of official foreign exchange reserves – that is, the inability of domestic demand to absorb the economic surplus that underpins the reserves, and hence the need to supporting US consumption as a means of absorbing China's economic surplus. Second, the cause of the insufficient domestic demand and structural dependence on the world market is, ultimately, underconsumption in the economy. Third, the cause of underconsumption is the small and still decreasing share of labour's compensation in the national income – that is, excessive exploitation, or even super-exploitation, of labour. Yet, the critical literature argues, it is precisely this exploitation of labour that has underpinned the competitiveness of Chinese exports – and thereby Chinese economic growth (Fischer 2010; Hung 2009; Petras 2009).

Consider, first, the proposition of export dependence. This is analytically akin to the neo-liberal theory of export-led growth, which implies that the sustainability of economic growth hinges on a comparable pace of export expansion – or even hinges on continuously increasing the ratio of trade surplus to the national output. This judgement is clearly contra to the Chinese reality. As can be seen from Figure 5.1 on p. 117, trade surplus as a share of aggregate demand has not been really large in the long term. It is only since 2004 that the share has become very large by international comparison, reaching a peak level of almost 10 per cent in 2007. In the ten years or so prior to 2004, the share did not exceed 3 per cent most of the time. And trade deficit was predominant even earlier, in most years of the first half of the reform era, i.e. 1978–92. On the whole, it is reasonable to judge that export dependence is not really a structural feature of the Chinese economy – although one need not go so far as to judge that it is import dependence that is the structural feature (Fischer 2010).

Zhu and Kotz (2011) argue that the gross measure of net exports might understate China's export dependence because some of the imports are destined for domestic consumption.[4] Akyüz (2010) further argues that it is necessary to take into account the possible crowding-in effect of exports on domestic investment and consumption. These arguments may contain elements of truth. Yet they have to be balanced by a perhaps even more significant counter-force: the fact that China's trade surplus has been mainly accounted for by processing trade. Indeed, as can be seen from Table 5.1, for most years since the early 1990s, the surplus in processing trade has even exceeded the total surplus of China's foreign trade. And the contribution of processing trade to the Chinese economy has been rather modest. A rough estimate can be computed by assuming that the domestic value added ratio of processing trade is equal to the ratio of net to gross exports. This ratio is 45 per cent at its peak in 2009, and the value added so computed is only equivalent to 5 per cent of GDP in that year – which is hardly compatible with the proposition of trade dependence. What seems more reasonable to infer from this observation is that the Chinese economy is in fact of a dualistic structure. The sector of processing trade is no more than an enclave, and is not really large enough to lead to export dependence for the Chinese economy as a whole.

Table 5.1 China's total foreign trade and processing trade (US dollars, 100 million)

	X	*PX*	*PX/X (%)*	*M*	*PM*	*PM/M (%)*	*(X − M) − (PX − PM)*	*(PX − PM)/ PX (%)*
1992	849	396	47	806	315	39	−37	20
1993	917	443	48	1,040	364	35	−201	18
1994	1,210	570	47	1,156	476	41	−40	17
1995	1,488	737	50	1,321	584	44	14	21
1996	1,511	843	56	1,388	623	45	−98	26
1997	1,828	996	54	1,424	702	49	110	30
1998	1,837	1,045	57	1,402	686	49	76	34
1999	1,949	1,109	57	1,657	736	44	−81	34
2000	2,492	1,377	55	2,251	926	41	−210	33
2001	2,661	1,474	55	2,436	940	39	−309	36
2002	3,256	1,799	55	2,952	1,222	41	−273	32
2003	4,382	2,419	55	4,128	1,629	39	−535	33
2004	5,933	3,280	55	5,612	2,217	40	−742	32
2005	7,620	4,165	55	6,600	2,740	42	−405	34
2006	9,689	5,104	53	7,915	3,215	41	−114	37
2007	12,178	6,176	51	9,560	3,685	39	127	40
2008	14,307	6,752	47	11,326	3,784	33	14	44
2009	12,016	5,870	49	10,059	3,223	32	−690	45
2010	15,778	7,403	47	13,962	4,174	30	−1,414	44

Sources: National Bureau of Statistics, *Zhongguo Tongji Nianjian* (China Statistical Yearbook) and *Zhongguo Tongji Zhaiyao* (China Statistical Abstract), various issues; Statistical Communique of Social and Economic Development 2010.

Notes
X = total exports, *PX* = processing exports, *M* = total imports, *PM* = processing imports. Note that the indicator *(X-M)-(PX-PM)* shows the balance of non-processing trade. Also note that in the year 2009, when the indicator *(PX-PM)/PX* has its highest value of 45%, the estimated value added of processing trade was, at the official exchange rate, equivalent to 5% of GDP.

Why, then, has the sector of processing trade expanded so fast in recent years, despite its limited contribution to the economy and the fact that its surplus causes serious international frictions? The consideration of job creation might be of some importance, but this importance is likely to be secondary, because as early as 2006 there were already widespread labour shortages in the labour-intensive, export-oriented industries in coastal provinces. A possibly far more important consideration is political. The sector of processing trade in Mainland China is predominantly associated with the interests of Hong Kong and Taiwan capital (mostly in the hands of junior partners of transnational corporations of advanced countries), and is indeed a significant determinant of the economic well-being of the two regions.

The proposition of underconsumption has more theoretical content than that of export dependence. In the relevant literature, particularly in the Luxemburg–Kalecki–Baran and Sweezy tradition of Marxist economics, underconsumption refers to a scenario in which the sluggish growth of consumption leads to a deficiency in aggregate demand and thereby economic stagnation. The key to this causal chain is that the expansion of investment and net export is insufficient to make up for the sluggish growth in consumption demand. But is this proposition applicable to the Chinese reality?

As was indicated earlier, up until recently, Chinese economic growth has been underpinned by domestic rather than external demand. Within domestic demand, the growth of consumption has been quite substantial throughout the reform era, but its share in aggregate demand has been decreasing. The share decreased from more than 60 per cent in the first half of the era (1978–92) to more than 50 per cent in the second half (1993–2007), and further to below 50 per cent levels after 2007. Yet all these do not necessarily imply that economic growth has thereby been bogged down in a state of underconsumption. After all, rapid economic growth has been sustained over the reform era, even in the years 2007–09, when consumption growth was far slower than the growth of aggregate demand. The crux is that investment growth has more than compensated for the sluggishness of consumption growth. Of course, whether or not this investment-led growth path – that is, a growth path that is based on 'producing investment goods for producing investment goods' (the so-called Feldman–Manalanobis–Domar model) – is sustainable in the long-term future is another matter (for an elaborate analysis and discussion of this question, see Lo and Li 2011).

Now consider the proposition of excessive exploitation, or even super-exploitation – that is, excessively low wage rates, long working hours and high work intensity. There is no doubt that the phenomenon of super-exploitation has been widespread in China, particularly in the labour-intensive, export-oriented industries in coastal provinces. The question is: has super-exploitation been the main underpinning of Chinese economic growth? The answer, quite clearly, is 'no'.

It is easily observable that throughout the reform era, and especially since the early 1990s, labour productivity growth in the Chinese economy has been extremely rapid. As can be seen from Figure 5.3, in the period 1992–2010, the index of real GDP increased from 100 to 586 while that of labour employment (in terms of the number of employees) only increased to 115. Conceptually, labour productivity growth can be based on increases in work intensity as well as technological progress. The waves of enterprise downsizing and mass privatization in the period 1993–97 probably did lead to substantial increases in work intensity. Yet it is difficult to conceive of a trend of persistently increasing work intensity over such a prolonged period, particularly in the labour-intensive, export-oriented industries, which already had high work intensity in the early 1990s. It is most unlikely that a magnitude of productivity growth such as that indicated in Figure 5.3 could be mainly attributed to increases in work intensity. Conversely, the phenomenon of super-exploitation that exists in China is mainly an issue of social fairness and justice, rather than an issue of the foundation and sustainability of economic growth. The fast productivity growth indicated in Figure 5.3 actually suggests that there is a solid material foundation for largely improving social fairness and justice: it implies that it is feasible to greatly increase labour protection and compensation.

This discussion suggests that the China–US economic nexus, and more broadly China's connection with the capitalist world economy, is of far-reaching political-economic implications. In a purely developmental sense, the judgement of structural dependence on the nexus appears to be an exaggeration. The crux of

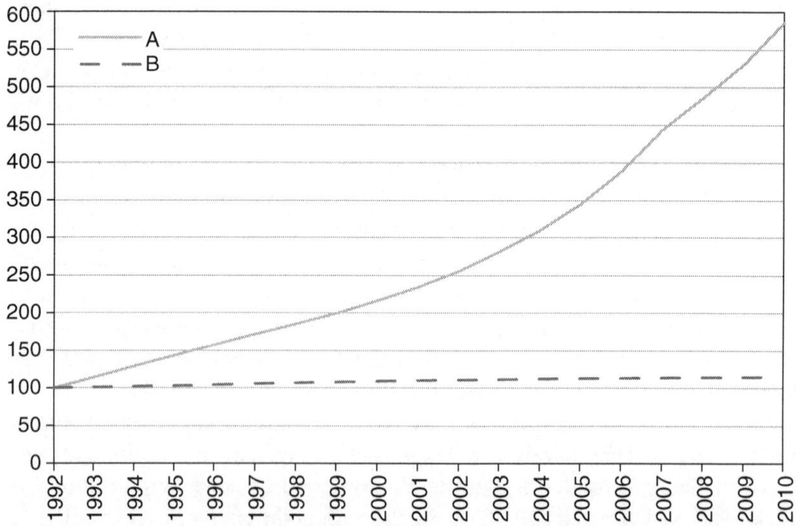

Figure 5.3 Indices of real GDP and labour employment (1992=100) (sources: National Bureau of Statistics, *Zhongguo Tongji Nianjian* (China Statistical Yearbook), various issues; *Zhongguo Tongji Zhaiyao* 2010 (China Statistical Abstract 2010)).

Notes
A=real GDP, B=labour employment (year-end number of employees).

the matter is China's fast productivity growth, which can be attributed to the improvement in various kinds of dynamic efficiency generated by the interaction between the prevailing investment-led economic growth path and the reformed economic institutions (Lo and Li 2011; Lo and Zhang 2011). The productivity growth indicates a high degree of autonomy of Chinese economic development. In other words, in so far as there is indeed some degree of structural dependence, it is likely to be bidirectional rather than unidirectional: the dependence of the capitalist world economy on China might be as strong as, or even stronger than, China's dependence on the capitalist world economy. This being the case, there exists ample scope for China to readjust its path of social and economic development. Instead of China's wholeheartedly pursuing GDP growth and integration into the world market, it is both desirable and feasible for China to embark on an alternative path of development that combines the three objectives of sustaining fast productivity growth, reducing dependence on foreign trade and foreign direct investment (and with it reduced outflows of economic surplus), and improving social fairness and justice.

China and world development dissociating from neo-liberalization

To speculate over the future prospects for Chinese economic development requires investigating into the world background. It is reasonable to say that, as the starting point of the investigation, China's rapid productivity growth over the era of globalization owes much to technology transfer and industrial relocation from the advanced capitalist countries. This judgement, in the sense that it emphasizes the importance of the external condition, is analytically akin to the neo-liberal theory of export-led growth. It is also consistent with the critical theory of undercutting, which posits that because of the fact that China has absorbed an exceedingly large share of the transferred technology and relocated industry, the rest of the developing world has had difficulty in transcending the predicament of deindustrialization.

In view of the intrinsic contradictions of the world capitalist economy as proposed in the relevant critical literature, however, the indicated technology transfer and industrial relocation are not necessarily conducive to world development – not even to the economies that receive the technology and industry. The crux is that technology transfer and industrial relocation from the advanced countries are motivated by profitability decline, and ultimately by demand deficiency in their home markets. The transfer and relocation are bound to create new productive capacity in the recipient economies. Hence, for the world economy as a whole, the transfer and relocation in effect amount to delaying rather than solving the problem of over-accumulation, and the problem is liable to become increasingly serious in subsequent periods. In this context, late-developing economies that integrate themselves into the world market by means of receiving technology transfer and industrial relocation will bear the brunt of world economic crises or severe fluctuations once the problem of over-accumulation can no longer be delayed (Harvey 2005, 2010). The so-called global imbalances can be understood as a result of the transfer and relocation. And the cost inflicted on China in the global imbalances and the resulting financial crisis and economic recession, particularly its double subsidies to the United States due to the China–US economic nexus, can be understood as the price for the way through which China integrates itself into the world market.

Central to the transition in the advanced capitalist world from the Golden Age to the era of globalization is the financialization of the economy. This process is characterized by the rising predominance of speculative financial activities, which have engulfed the economy as a whole, including the productive sector. Put another way, financialization is the result of capital increasingly avoiding being tied up with the productive sector because of the latter's decline in profitability. Financialization thus embodies an intrinsic contradiction: the speculative pursuit of profitability tends to crowd out productive activities, therefore resulting in systemic demand deficiency and undermining the sources of profitability (Lazonick 2009; Wade 2006).

Yet despite the intrinsic contradiction, the paradox is that financialization has actually been sustained for a prolonged period, at least up until the outbreak of the crisis in 2007. Key to resolving the paradox is the concept of 'accumulation by dispossession', as coined by Harvey (2005) – that is, cheapening productive inputs by means of neo-liberal policies at both the national and the international levels. Put another way, capital accumulation in the era of globalization is mainly based on the incorporation of productive resources that were previously outside the capitalist world economy. The first-generation doctrines of the Washington Consensus focusing on marketization and trade liberalization, the second-generation doctrines focusing on the privatization of public assets, and the third-generation doctrines focusing on the liberalization of international finance are means to serve this ultimate end of accumulation by dispossession. On the whole, therefore, the sustainability of capital accumulation hinges on the balance between the damage caused by speculative financial activities, on the one hand, and the supports provided by dispossessing activities, on the other hand.

But the process of financialization is prone to accelerate over time, just like any other speculative activities. As Lazonick (2009) analyses in detail, over the so-called New Economy years, US high-tech firms tended to use the profits they got from globalization in buying back their own outstanding shares instead of investing in productive activities. The rationale behind such behaviour is to boost their stock prices for the sake of satisfying the demand for shareholder value maximization. Financialization thus requires the acceleration of globalization. And the financial crisis is unlikely to reverse the process of accumulation by dispossession. On the contrary, advanced capitalist countries have incentives to press for the acceleration of this process. It is conceivable that even if the financial crisis and the associated economic recession persist, assertions such as 'we need more globalization, not less' are likely to be back in vogue in the international arena in the future.

But there is no justification whatsoever for China to continue to support such a process of globalization that has inflicted increasing damage on world development. In other words, there is no justification for Chinese workers to continue to sacrifice themselves for the sake of sustaining the hefty profits of Wall Street speculators and their agents or junior partners in various parts of the world, including China itself. No justification – that is, the prevailing trend of globalization is not only unfair and unjust but also not necessary. As has been discussed in the preceding sections, there is a solid material foundation for China to stop supporting the prevailing trend. There is unlikely to be a very heavy cost for China in rejecting or dissociating itself from neo-liberalism, such as that suggested by the critical story of 'China facing internal and external dependence'. By extension, it is feasible for China to improve its economic relationship with the rest of the developing world, while at the same time not scarifying its own development.

At the policy level, the demand for China to accelerate the reform of its external finance in the direction of liberalizing the capital account and converging towards a free-floating exchange rate regime is arguably for the purpose of serving the needs of accumulation by dispossession. International experience in the era of globalization indicates that financial liberalization in this direction has been very harmful to the economy of developing countries, or even most developed countries. Their participation in the speculative games of international finance often results in their being put in the position of being dispossessed, rather than being the dispossessor. The participation also tends to crowd out productive investment in the domestic economy, particularly through capital flight. Meanwhile, of more immediate concern, the demand for China to quickly and largely appreciate its currency also appears to be unreasonable. Such a move would be likely to invite speculative cross-border capital flows, thereby causing serious instability. More fundamentally, to the extent that appreciation does have the effect of promoting the substitution of imports for domestic production, the impact on domestic capital-intensive, high-tech industries would be devastating. This is because they are mostly infant industries that need time to gradually develop. Yet the development of these industries is necessary for the upgrading and productivity growth of the economy as a whole.

The discussion in the preceding sections indicates that there is some justification for China's reducing its external surplus. Instead of largely appreciating its currency, an alternative policy that has often been suggested in the literature is that China should substantially raise labour compensation with a view to reducing the export of labour-intensive manufactures and promoting industrial upgrading. This policy, which would raise the 'real' exchange rate without affecting the nominal exchange rate, is precisely what the Chinese government has adopted since 2009. The waves of labour unrest in foreign capital-invested enterprises in the spring of 2010 have given further impetus to the policy. According to media reports, by August 2010 a total of 27 provinces had announced that they were increasing minimum wage rates, of which 20 provinces had increased them by more than 20 per cent.[5]

Raising labour compensation is of course more than a means of reducing the external surplus. It is an important objective of social and economic development in line with the policy orientation known as 'constructing a harmonious society'. This orientation has gradually become established since the turn of the century. Related policy measures have included promoting the (re)unionization of the labour force, establishing collective bargaining mechanisms of wage settlement, enforcing the labour contract law and enhancing labour protection (Lo 2007). In connection with this orientation and the related measures, there has seen a conspicuous change in the trend of the growth of the wage rate. As is shown in Figure 5.4, before the turn of the century the growth of real wage rates was persistently below that of per capita GDP. The reverse has been the case since then. True, Figure 5.4 indicates only the wage rate growth of the formal sector of the economy, rather than the Chinese labour force as a whole. Nevertheless, it is still indicative of the direction and pace of change in China.

This change is likely of world-scale importance. It is of note that a major aspect of the process of accumulation by dispossession in the era of globalization has been precisely the very large-scale incorporation of Chinese labour into the world market. According to the IMF (*World Economic Outlook*, April 2007), if countries' labour forces are weighed by their export-to-GDP ratio, the effective global labour supply quadrupled between 1980 and 2005, with East Asia

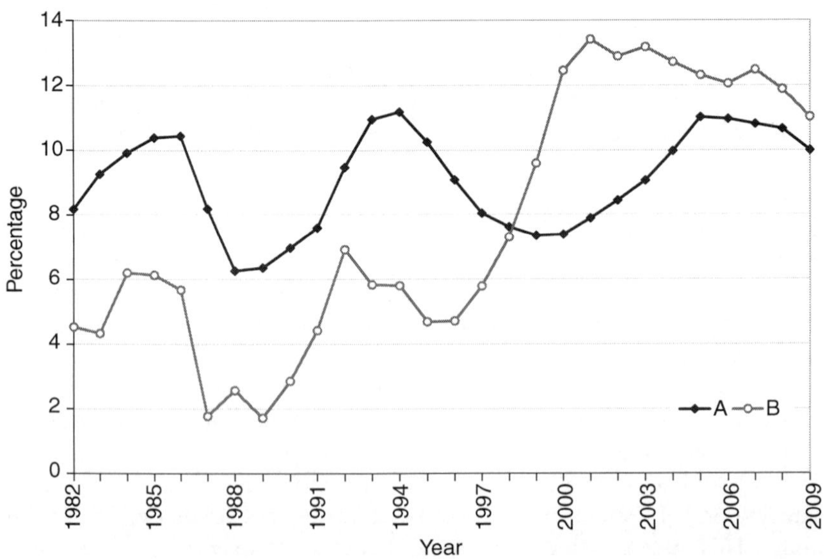

Figure 5.4 Annual growth rate of per capita real GDP and real urban wage rate (five-year moving average, %) (sources: National Bureau of Statistics, *Zhongguo Tongji Nianjian* (China Statistical Yearbook), various issues).

Note

A = per capita real GDP; B = urban real wage rate. Note that the price deflator for computing the real wage rate is the consumer price index.

contributing about half of the increase. Over this period, there was also an accelerating trend of massive relocation of industry and jobs from the rest of East Asia and beyond to Mainland China. That is to say, more than half of the increase in the labour force that produces for the world market came from China in the period 1980–2005. Using the same indicator of employment adjusted by the exports-to-GDP ratio, as of 2005 year-end China's share of the world total of workers producing for the global market reached 25 per cent. Now that Chinese labour is becoming increasingly organized, and the trend of decline in its income share is likely to reverse, the bargaining power of the world's working class as a whole is also likely to strengthen. Globalization based on accumulation by dispossession is thus likely to encounter increasingly strong resistance. This will facilitate the redirection of the world economy towards a path of social and economic development that is more stable, humane and just than the one that currently prevails.

Conclusions

Recent international opinions on China and world development have focused on the China–US economic nexus. The neo-liberal theory of 'China causing global imbalances' claims that the particular way through which China has integrated itself into the world market is to the detriment of the economies of the advanced countries. The critical theory of 'China facing internal and external dependence', in contrast, claims that the real victim has been the economic development of China itself and the majority of developing economies.

This chapter supports the policy conclusion of the critical theory: that the reasonable orientation is to serve the interests of labour, not speculative financial capital. Nevertheless, the chapter also argues that the critical story of 'internal and external dependence' is to a significant extent an exaggeration. There is good evidence that Chinese economic development does have a high degree of autonomy. This implies that the indicated policy orientation is not only desirable but also feasible.

Notes

1 Top US financial officials such as Ben Bernanke and Lawrence Summers have asserted that 'global imbalances' were crucial conditions for the eruption of the financial crisis, and have implied that China has been a cause of the imbalances. See the summaries and criticisms of these assertions by McKinley (2009) and Petras (2009). In the international media, the most outspoken commentators who blame China for causing global imbalances and thereby the financial crisis are Martin Wolf (*Financial Times*, 17 November 2009 and 8 December 2009) and Paul Krugman (*New York Times*, 31 December 2009 and 14 March 2010).

2 In the analytical sense, the story of 'China facing internal and external dependence' had actually been the dominant view in the international opinions and economic literature prior to the eruption of the financial crisis in 2007 and the subsequent world recession. Neo-liberal institutions and scholars tended to view China's performance in a favourable light, taking it as a manifestation of the notion of 'the natural path of

development' – that is, labour-intensive, export-oriented industrialization. Critical scholars, in contrast, tended to assess the experience in a negative way. Hart-Landsberg and Burkett (2004) and Harvey (2005) contend that the experience can be summarized as 'Chinese super-exploitation of labour, undercutting the world working class as a whole'. Nevertheless, Arrighi (2007) and Glyn (2006), while agreeing with the thesis of undercutting, do not accept the thesis of super-exploitation as well. They rather tend to consider that the undercutting has been due to much faster labour productivity growth in China than in other developing economies.

3 Palley (2006) provides a synthesis of, or a bridge between, the critical and neo-liberal stories of China – in the sense that his analysis is identical to the neo-liberal story whereas his policy conclusions are a mix of the two: currency appreciation, increasing wages, etc.

4 Zhu and Kotz (2011) argue that, conceptually, 'the appropriate measure of foreign demand for a country's output is the domestic content of its exports', not gross export minus import as such. This seems valid for conceptualizing the production or value added side but inadequate for conceptualizing the demand side. It begs the question as to what is the relationship between the change of export and that of import destined for domestic consumption. After all, on the demand side the relationship between exports and imports represent the exchange of demand between China and the rest of the world.

5 *Xin Jingbao* (Beijing News), 18 August 2010.

References

Akyüz, Y. (2010) 'Export dependence and sustainability of growth in China and the East Asian production network', Research Paper no. 27, South Centre, Geneva.

Arrighi, G. (2007) *Adam Smith in Beijing: Lineages of the Twenty-First Century*, London: Verso.

Fischer, A. M. (2010) 'Is China turning Latin? China's balancing act between power and dependence in the lead up to global crisis', *Journal of International Development*, 22: 739–757.

Glyn, A. (2006) *Capitalism Unleashed: Finance, Globalization, and Welfare*, Oxford: Oxford University Press.

Hart-Landsberg, M. and Burkett, P. (2004) 'China and Socialism: Market Reforms and Class Struggle', a special issue of *Monthly Review*, July–August.

Harvey, D. (2005) *A Brief History of Neoliberalism*, Oxford: Oxford University Press.

Harvey, D. (2010) *The Enigma of Capital: And the Crises of Capitalism*, London: Profile Books.

Hung, H.-F. (2009) 'American's head servant? The PRC's dilemma in the global crisis', *New Left Review*, 60: 5–25.

Jenkins, R. (2008) 'Measuring the competitive threat from China for other Southern exporters', *World Economy*, 31 (10): 1351–1366.

Jenkins, R., Peters, E. D. and Moreira, M. M. (2008) 'The impact of China on Latin America and the Caribbean', *World Development*, 36 (2): 235–253.

Kwan, C.-H. (2009) 'Redressing the global imbalance: increasing Chinese consumption and U.S. savings is the key', Research Institute of Economy, Trade and Industry. Online, available at: www.rieti.go.jp/en/china/09090301.html.

Lazonick, W. (2009) *Sustainable Prosperity in the New Economy?*, Kalamazoo, MI: W. E. Upjohn Institute for Employment Research.

Lo, D. (2007) 'China's quest for alternative to neo-liberalism: market reform, economic growth, and labor', *Kyoto Economic Review*, 76 (2): 193–210.

Lo, D. and Li, G. (2011) 'China's economic growth, 1978–2007: structural-institutional changes and efficiency attributes', *Journal of Post-Keynesian Economics*, 34 (1): 59–83.

Lo, D. and Zhang, Y. (2011) 'Making sense of China's economic transformation', *Review of Radical Political Economics*, 43 (1): 33–55.

Lo, D., Hong, F. and Li, G. (2011) 'Assessing the role of foreign direct investment in Chinese economic development: broadening the vision', unpublished paper.

McKinley, T. (2009) 'Will pinning the blame on China help correct global imbalances?', CDPR Policy Brief no. 2, Centre for Development Policy and Research, School of Oriental and African Studies, University of London.

Palley, T. I. (2006) 'External contradictions of the Chinese development model: export-led growth and the danger of global economic contraction', *Journal of Contemporary China*, 15 (46): 69–88.

Petras, J. (2009) '"Global imbalances" versus internal inequalities (understanding the world economy)', unpublished paper. Online, available at: http://www.lahaine.org/petras/b2-img/petras_global.pdf

Wade, R. (2006) 'Choking the South', *New Left Review*, 38: 115–127.

Zhu, A. and Kotz, D. M. (2011) 'The dependence of China's economic growth on exports and investment', *Review of Radical Political Economics*, 43 (1): 9–32.

6 The rise of mass capitalism in China

Tomoo Marukawa

Introduction

Many terms have been coined to describe the current economic system of China. The official description is, of course, 'socialist market economy', which has been the national goal of economic reform since 1993. Unsatisfied with the official description, however, some Western scholars have given different names to the Chinese economic system. Bremmer (2010) classifies China's system as 'state capitalism', in which the state governs the market to pursue national interest. Halper (2010) warns that China is trying to spread the model of 'state-directed capitalism', which is virtually the same as 'state capitalism', to the developing world. Huang (2008) calls China a 'commanding heights economy', because, according to him, the relative size of China's private sector is still as small as it was in the world's most statist economies in the 1970s. Prior to these arguments in the English-speaking world, some Japanese authors invented similar terms to depict China's economic system. Kojima (1997) argued that China was in the transition period to 'bureaucrat-led financial industrial capitalism', which would be dominated by large state-owned enterprise groups financed by state-owned banks. Wu (2008) asserts that China's current system is 'state-made capitalism', which is created by the will and plan of the state, and almost all of its benefits are reaped by bureaucrats and their cronies, but she predicts that along with the democratization of the political system, the economic system will evolve into a less state-directed capitalism. Although these authors use different terms, it is obvious that they share a common vision of China's system that China is (or will be) a capitalist country with strong state involvement in the economy.

It is true that China still has hundreds of thousands of state-owned enterprises and the government still designs the guiding principles of economic and social development every five years in the form of a 'five-year plan', while the banking sector is dominated by large state-owned commercial banks. With these facts, it is understandable that scholars hesitate to call China's current system simply 'capitalism'. The common problem with the above-mentioned terms, however, is that they draw too much attention to the 'state-directed' aspect of the Chinese economic system, while leading us to ignore its 'capitalistic' aspect. There may be evidence that China has stronger state involvement in the economy than a conventional capitalist country does, but at the same time there is evidence that the degree of state involvement is consistently declining. The share of state-owned and state-controlled enterprises in the gross industrial output, for example, has consistently declined from 50 per cent in 1998 to 27 per cent in 2010. The number of state-owned and state-controlled industrial enterprises decreased from 64,737 units in 1998 to 20,253 units in 2010. Although the present figures (27 per cent of industrial output and more than 20,000 state-owned industrial enterprises) may seem too high for China to be regarded as a liberal market economy, their decline does suggest that China is moving slowly but steadily towards having a more liberal economy.

This chapter tries to shed light on the growing side of the Chinese economy: the private sector. Instead of simply characterizing the sector as capitalist, I will shed light on some aspects of the sector that induce me to call it 'mass capitalism'. In applying the term to China's private sector, I use the term somewhat differently from its conventional usage. Instead of depicting a situation where a large percentage of the population own shares of public companies, I will use the term to describe a situation in which even ordinary people who have only a limited amount of money and human capital can easily become firm owners. I am not going to argue that China as a whole has a system of 'mass capitalism'; nor am I trying to argue that the Chinese economy is not a 'state capitalist' one. I believe that the term 'state capitalism' does capture a certain aspect of the Chinese economy and the aspirations of the Chinese government. The purpose of this chapter is to show that the 'mass capitalistic' side of the Chinese economy deserves as much attention as its 'state capitalistic' side.

The remainder of the chapter is structured as follows. The first section describes the present status of the private sector in the Chinese economy and briefly reviews the government's policy towards the private sector. The second section discusses the rise of mass capitalism in Wenzhou, a district famous in China for the development of the private sector, and the spread of mass capitalism from Wenzhou to other parts of the country, along with the migration of the residents of Wenzhou. The third section discusses the rise of the 'guerrilla handset' industry in Shenzhen, which is another case of mass capitalism. The fourth section describes the spread of mass capitalism to other industries, followed by the conclusion.

Present status and a brief history of the private sector in China

As was mentioned in the introduction to this chapter, the share of the state sector in China's gross industrial output[1] is consistently declining. The sector that has taken over the state sector's position is not the foreign sector: the share of industrial enterprises with Hong Kong, Macau, Taiwan and foreign investment in gross industrial output has risen only slightly, from 25 per cent in 1998 to 27 per cent in 2010, though their share once reached a peak of 33 per cent, in 2004. The share of non-state, non-foreign enterprises, on the other hand, has risen from 26 per cent in 1998 to 46 per cent in 2010.

The non-state, non-foreign sector consists of a wide variety of enterprises. Private enterprises account for 66 per cent of the total industrial output of the non-state, non-foreign sector, while limited liability corporations and joint stock companies that are neither state-controlled nor classified as 'private enterprises' account for 28 per cent. The latter are the enterprises that are partially owned but not controlled by the state or by state-owned enterprises. Collective-owned enterprises and shareholding cooperatives account for 4 per cent, and alliance firms and other types of enterprises have a 1 per cent share of the non-state, non-foreign sector's industrial output.[2] Therefore, we can fairly judge that 95 per cent of the non-state, non-foreign sector's industrial output is contributed by private or private-controlled enterprises. Considering the fact that the share of non-private enterprises within the non-state, non-foreign sector (i.e. the collective-owned enterprises, shareholding cooperatives and alliance firms) is negligible, and for the purpose of simplicity, I will hereafter call the non-state, non-foreign sector simply 'the private sector'. This practice may be regarded as an overestimate of the size of the private sector compared to the strict estimate made by Huang (2008: 13–18). He criticizes a similar estimate made by Dougherty and Herd (2005) as overestimating the size of the private sector by including legal-person shareholding firms in the category of the private sector. Excluding these firms, Huang estimates the share of the private sector in industrial value added as 22.0 per cent in 2005. In terms of Dougherty and Herd's definition, the private sector's share jumps to 50.5 per cent. My calculation stands in between the two estimates: 34.0 per cent in terms of industrial value added, or 35.0 per cent in terms of industrial output in 2005. Since value added data from 2008 onward are not available in the *Statistical Yearbook of China*, I use output data in this chapter to measure the size of the private sector. In terms of industrial output, the share of the private sector has steadily risen since 2000, reaching 46.2 per cent in 2010.

However, it is noteworthy that the shares of state, foreign and private sectors vary a great deal between different industrial sectors. Table 6.1 shows the shares of these sectors in all of the subcategories in industry. The 39 subcategories are classified into three groups, namely state-dominated industries, foreign-dominated industries and private-dominated industries, according to the sector that has the largest share in each subcategory's output. In the tobacco, petroleum and natural gas, electrical, and heat power supply industries, most of the output is produced by the state sector. The private sector is almost excluded from these industrial sectors. In 'mining of other ores', 'processing of timber, manufacture of wood, bamboo, rattan, palm and straw products', and 26 other subcategories, the private sector has a dominant share, while the state sector seems to have already withdrawn from some of these subcategories. In the manufacturing of 'communication equipment, computers and other electronic equipment' and 'articles for culture, education and sport activities', the foreign sector has a dominant share while the state sector has a very small share. To judge by the return on assets (ROA), it is not necessarily the case that the state sector is monopolizing the highly profitable industrial sectors. But we can sense the government's intention to keep the industrial sectors that relate to basic inputs such as petroleum, natural gas, electricity and water under state control, while opening up the manufacturing and mining industries to private and foreign firms.

The output shares of state, foreign and private sectors in service industries are not as easily available as in the cases of the manufacturing and mining industries. Tables 6.2 and 6.3 summarize the data for some industries that I managed to gather. In the construction industry, the rise of the private sector and the decline of the state sector during the period 2000–10 are quite obvious. The expansion of the private sector in wholesaling and retailing was not so rapid during 2004–08, but in these industries the private sector contributes around 60 per cent of the total sales value (Table 6.2). Since neither output data nor value-added data are available for transportation and postal service industries, I calculated the shares of various types of investors in the capital investments of these industries (Table 6.3). In the table, 'legal person' investors include both state-owned enterprises and private enterprises, so it is hard to judge whether or not the expansion of legal persons' investment share means the expansion of the private sector. Therefore, let us ignore the changes in legal persons' share and consider only the changes in the shares of the state and 'individual' (private) sectors. In road transportation, water transportation, air transportation, 'loading, unloading and other transport services', warehousing and postal services, the state sector's share declined and the private sector's share increased during 2004–08. In pipeline transportation and urban public transportation, on the other hand, the state sector's share increased significantly, while rail transport was still monopolized by the state sector in 2008. Generally speaking, the private sector's portion in the service industry expanded during the 2000s, though the penetration of the private sector remained low in some service industries such as rail transport, urban public transport, air transport and postal services

In total, the above data show that the private sector expanded significantly between 2000 and 2010 in the manufacturing, mining and service industries, though some industrial sectors, such as tobacco, petroleum and natural gas, the electrical industry and heat power supply, and rail transport, are still monopolized by the state sector. State monopoly of these industrial sectors may reflect the government's policy to 'promote state capital to concentrate in the important industries and crucial realms that relate to national security and the lifelines of national economy', as stipulated in the Twelfth Five-Year Plan. This statement suggests that the state sector may withdraw even further from other industrial sectors and concentrate its investments in the 'lifelines of the national economy'.

During 2000–10, there was no major policy initiative by the Chinese government to promote privatization. The fact that the private sector's share in manufacturing, mining, construction and some service industries rapidly increased even under such policy circumstances suggests the dynamism of the development of the private sector. This rise is the result of a relaxation of the suppression of the private sector, which has lasted for the greater part of China's history since 1949. After the establishment of the People's Republic, there was a short period in which the government encouraged private entrepreneurs to expand

Table 6.1 Share of industrial output of state, foreign, and private sectors in 2010

	State sector (%)	*Foreign sector (%)*	*Private sector (%)*	*ROA (%)*
Average	27	27	46	8.9
State-dominated industries				
Manufacture of tobacco	99	0	1	13.4
Extraction of petroleum and natural gas	95	5	0	18.1
Production and supply of electric power and heat power	92	7	1	2.6
Processing of petroleum, coking, processing of nuclear fuel	71	13	16	7.8
Production and supply of water	69	17	15	1.1
Mining and washing of coal	56	4	40	11.5
Manufacture of transport equipment	47	44	9	10.1
Production and supply of gas	44	36	19	8.5
Foreign-dominated industries				
Manufacture of communication equipment, computers and other electronic equipment	8	77	15	7.6
Manufacture of articles for culture, education and sport activities	1	52	47	9.1
Manufacture of measuring instruments and machinery for cultural activity and office work	10	48	42	10.4
Private-dominated industries				
Mining of other ores	2	0	98	12.2
Processing of timber, manufacture of wood, bamboo, rattan, palm and straw products	2	12	86	14.5
Mining and processing of non-metal ores	11	4	84	14.7
Mining and processing of ferrous metal ores	14	2	84	14.9
Recycling and disposal of waste	3	18	78	12.4
Manufacture of textiles	2	21	76	9.0
Manufacture of non-metallic mineral products	10	14	76	11.2

Processing of food from agricultural products	6	22	72	14.0
Manufacture of metal products	5	25	69	10.4
Mining and processing of non-ferrous metal ores	27	4	68	18.6
Manufacture of plastics	3	31	66	10.1
Manufacture of furniture	3	33	65	10.7
Printing, reproduction of recording media	12	23	64	9.6
Manufacture of general-purpose machinery	13	23	64	9.8
Manufacture of paper and paper products	8	30	62	7.5
Manufacture of textile wearing apparel, footware and caps	1	38	61	12.1
Manufacture of foods	7	32	61	14.0
Manufacture of medicines	13	27	60	12.0
Manufacture of electrical machinery and equipment	9	31	60	9.8
Manufacture of chemical fibres	9	32	60	8.5
Manufacture of artwork and other manufacturing	7	34	59	11.1
Smelting and pressing of non-ferrous metals	28	14	57	8.0
Manufacture of rubber	13	32	55	9.6
Manufacture of leather, fur, feather and related products	0	45	55	15.6
Manufacture of raw chemical materials and chemical products	19	26	54	9.4
Manufacture of special-purpose machinery	22	25	53	9.5
Manufacture of beverages	16	31	53	12.6
Smelting and pressing of ferrous metals	39	13	48	4.7

Source: Calculated from SYC (2011).

Table 6.2 Share of the state, foreign and private sectors in construction, wholesaling and retailing

Industry	*Construction (%)*			*Wholesaling (%)*		*Retailing (%)*	
Measure	*Output value*			*Sales value*		*Sales value*	
Year	*2010*	*2005*	*2000*	*2008*	*2004*	*2008*	*2004*
State sector	19	24	40	19	23	6	10
Foreign sector	1	1	1	9	7	10	6
Private sector	76	66	26	58	53	63	62
Source	1	2	2	3	4	3	4

Sources: 1 SYC (2011), 2 SYC (2006), 3 National Bureau of Statistics of China (2006), 4 National Bureau of Statistics of China (2010).

production. But in 1953, the Chinese Communist Party started the transformation of the economic system to socialism, and private enterprises were forced to turn into 'joint public–private' factories, and later transformed into state-owned or collective enterprises. Private enterprises were virtually extinguished by 1956 (Naughton 2007: 67). When China launched economic reforms at the end of 1978, one serious problem then was the massive unemployment of young people who had returned to the urban areas after staying in the countryside to work in people's communes. The official figure for urban unemployment was 5.7 million people, or 5.4 per cent of the urban workforce, in 1979, but some Chinese sources suggest that there were 15 million unemployed workers then (He 1990: 60; Cheng 2002: 120), which means that the real unemployment rate was around 13 per cent. The government encouraged unemployed youths to engage in self-employment to alleviate the pressure of excessive labour supply. By definition, self-employment businesses (*geti gongshang hu*) must not have more than seven employees, including the owner(s). Self-employment businesses which expanded their employment to more than seven employees were later allowed to register themselves as private enterprises (*siying qiye*). Until the mid-1990s, however, private enterprises faced numerous restrictions on their business. For example, they were not allowed to enter the industries which the government controlled by licensing, such as colour television manufacturing and automobile production. Owners of private enterprises were not allowed to be members of the Chinese Communist Party, while those of self-employment businesses were. Many entrepreneurs felt that to become registered as a 'private enterprise' would lead to more trouble than benefit, so they tried to disguise their businesses as other types of enterprises. One entrepreneur with whom the author had an interview in July 2001 in Wenzhou, Zhejiang Province, confessed that he kept the status of his enterprise as a self-employment business unchanged even though his business had already expanded to having more than 80 employees. Many de facto private enterprises, especially in rural areas, were registered as 'collective enterprises' because such a status was favourable for borrowing money from

Table 6.3 Shares of various types of investors in the capital investment in transportation and postal service industries, 2008 and 2004

Investor	*Rail transportation (%)*		*Road transportation (%)*		*Urban public transportation (%)*		*Water transportation (%)*		*Air transportation (%)*		*Pipeline transportation (%)*		*Loading, unloading and other transport services (%)*		*Warehousing (%)*		*Postal service (%)*	
	2008	*2004*	*2008*	*2004*	*2008*	*2004*	*2008*	*2004*	*2008*	*2004*	*2008*	*2004*	*2008*	*2004*	*2008*	*2004*	*2008*	*2004*
State	96	96	38	46	53	46	30	43	47	52	67	53	13	26	34	41	74	96
Collective	0	0	4	5	3	5	3	2	1	0	0	0	2	5	6	6	1	0
Legal-person	4	4	29	26	26	31	37	31	35	33	29	37	34	39	27	29	17	2
Individual	0	0	22	15	14	13	14	10	5	4	1	4	38	19	17	11	4	1
Foreign	0	0	7	8	4	5	16	14	12	11	4	7	13	12	17	13	4	0

Source: National Bureau of Statistics of China (2006), National Bureau of Statistics of China (2010).

banks and for entering industries that were reserved for public enterprises. Private entrepreneurs felt extremely uneasy in doing business after the June Fourth (Tiananmen Square) Incident in 1989. Some of them fled overseas, and an entrepreneur in Tianjin even donated his business to the local government.

It was not until the Fifteenth Plenum of the Chinese Communist Party in 1997 that many of the obstacles which had hampered the development of private businesses were removed. In the resolution of the plenum, it was stipulated that the 'non-public economy', meaning the private sector, formed 'an important element of the socialist economy'. Before then, the 'non-public economy' was regarded as a 'supplement' of the socialist economy in official Party documents. Private entrepreneurs have been allowed to become members of the Party since the plenum. The subtle change in status of the 'non-public sector' meant that local governments were now allowed to privatize state-owned enterprises under their jurisdiction and promote the growth of the private sector. This was a period when state-owned enterprises faced serious difficulties. Many of them found it hard to maintain their payroll. Workers of state-owned enterprises took to the streets to demand wage payment. Local governments wanted to get rid of loss-making state-owned enterprises that had turned from cash cows into burdens, so they launched a wave of privatization of small and medium-sized state-owned enterprises from 1997. Local governments started to promote the growth of the private sector, expecting that it would ease the serious unemployment problem caused by massive lay-offs in the state sector.

After the reduction of payroll and divestiture of loss-making enterprises, the profit rate of state-owned enterprises as a whole started to recover after 1999. Profitable state-owned enterprises transformed themselves into joint-stock corporations and listed their shares in stock exchanges inside and outside China, which enabled them to raise funds through initial public offerings. Most of the large state-owned enterprises have now been restructured into joint-stock corporations controlled by the state, which holds the majority of the shares but also collect investments from individual shareholders. As was indicated in Table 6.1, the state sector monopolizes several industries, and a large part of the state sector's profit comes from these industries. In 2010, for example, 47 per cent of the state sector's profit in industry came from three industrial sectors, namely petroleum and natural gas, electricity and heat power supply, and transport machinery. In the transport machinery industry, the state sector's output share is not as high as in the other two industries, but the foreign sector in this industry is partly controlled by the state because the Chinese government obliges foreign automobile manufacturers to establish joint ventures with state-owned automobile manufacturers, in which the foreign side owns less than 50 per cent of the shares, if they want to have a foothold in China.

The output share of the state sector and the foreign sector added together was 91 per cent in the transport machinery industry in 2010, which indicates a high level of state involvement in the industry. Most of the obstacles that hampered the growth of the private sector were removed after 1997, but private enterprises are still not free to enter some industries reserved for the state sector and it is widely believed that the banking system favours the state sector.

The emergence and spread of mass capitalism in Wenzhou

Wenzhou is regarded as 'the bastion of Chinese capitalism' (Huang 2008: 58). In the 1980s, Wenzhou was regarded as one of the models of rural industrialization by Chinese economists and was characterized by the prevalence of privately owned enterprises among the township and village enterprises (TVEs). Since the nationwide wave of privatizing TVEs during the 1990s, however, the prevalence of private enterprises has no longer been peculiar to Wenzhou. But Wenzhou still remains special, not because of the high proportion of privately owned enterprises in the local economy but because of the high proportion of capitalists among its population. Zhang *et al.* (2011) estimate that around half a million people were the owners of either industrial enterprises or self-employment businesses in 1988. This means that 7.6 per cent of the population of Wenzhou in 1988 were capitalists. According to the Second Economic Census, conducted in 2008, there were 46,000 private enterprises and 463,000 self-employed households in Wenzhou. Following Zhang *et al.* (2011), who assume that each private enterprise has three owners on average, there were 600,000 owners of businesses in 2008, which is equivalent to 7.8 per cent of the population. This is far higher than the national average, which was 3.0 per cent if calculated by the same method.

In Wenzhou, de facto private enterprises operated under the disguise of 'commune and brigade enterprises' even during the Cultural Revolution, when all entrepreneurial activities were suppressed. Around 1970, some commune and brigade enterprises in Oubei and Yongzhong townships in Wenzhou started producing valves for petrochemical factories. After a few years, valve production had become a very popular business in the two townships. In 1976, there were as many as 1,069 valve manufacturers in the two townships (Yu and Yu 1995: 131). Since neither private enterprise nor self-employment were allowed then, all of those manufacturers were registered as commune and brigade enterprises, but arguably those were very close to private enterprises. In Liushi, another township in Wenzhou, a commune and brigade enterprise started producing electromagnetic switches around 1972 (Huang and Luo 2002: 158–159). After a few years, several hundred manufacturers in Liushi Township were producing switches. Both cases reveal that the local people were very eager to start their own enterprise even during the period when private enterprises were strictly prohibited. Because local people lacked funds and technological expertise, these manufacturers often produced low-quality goods, leading to a crackdown by the government on unqualified manufacturers.

The surge of massive entry to a certain industry was repeated several times in various parts of Wenzhou during the 1980s. In some townships, local people rushed into shoe manufacturing; in other townships, many people started to produce clothing. Wenzhou became famous for fake and inferior goods, and the government often tried to eliminate unqualified manufacturers. A bad reputation and the crackdown, however, did not discourage Wenzhou people from establishing enterprises. While many manufacturers were forced to close down by crackdowns and competition, some turned into competitive manufacturers. Today, Oubei and Yongzhong are the largest industrial agglomeration of valves and pumps in China, and Liushi has most of the largest manufacturers of switches and breakers in China. Wenzhou also has the industrial agglomerations of leather shoes, clothing, badges, printing, artificial leather, non-woven fabrics, automobile parts and cigarette lighters, and some of the largest firms of these industries in China.

In each of these industrial agglomerations, hundreds of private enterprises are engaged in the same or similar businesses, and almost always there is a wholesale market at the centre of the agglomeration. The wholesale market is not only a place to sell the products that are produced in the agglomeration but also a place to purchase the inputs for manufacturing the products. For example, adjacent to the leather shoe industry agglomeration located in Lucheng District, Wenzhou City, there is a wholesale market of leather shoes and a market selling the materials for making leather shoes. Both the sales of products and purchasing of inputs can be done in open markets. Large shoemakers in Wenzhou, having their own sales network and supplier network, do not rely on these markets, but for small manufacturers they are a great help in their sales and procurement. With these markets, new entrants can easily start making shoes without worrying much about the procurement of materials and sales of products.

Wenzhou people are not only eager to start manufacturing businesses by themselves but also good at merchandising. Even during the Cultural Revolution, many Wenzhou people migrated to other parts of China as itinerant pedlars. Many industries were established in Wenzhou as a reaction to the information and sales opportunities brought by the pedlars. Wholesale markets at the centre of industrial agglomerations in Wenzhou work as hubs that connect the local industry with the merchants who work in other parts of China. According to the population census conducted in 2000, 1.1 million out of 7.4 million people who have household registration in Wenzhou stayed outside of the district or county in which they were registered. Many migrants from Wenzhou gather together in other cities and run their own businesses. In the suburbs of Beijing, for example, a town that was dubbed 'Zhejiang Village' was formed in the 1980s. Most of the residents of this town came from Yueqing City, Wenzhou, and engaged in the manufacturing of leather clothing (Wang 1995). The products produced in this village were sold in a huge wholesale market that was located adjacent to the village, in which many merchants from Wenzhou run their shops. It was estimated that 70,000 people lived in 'Zhejiang Village' at its peak, but after several attempts by the Beijing municipal government to shut down the village, migrants from Wenzhou disappeared from the village before 2000. During the 1990s, communities similar to 'Zhejiang Village' were created in other major cities such as Xian, Tianjin and Shenyang. Similar communities also exist in Paris, Moscow and Dubai.

Thus, the 'Wenzhou model', which started in the countryside of Wenzhou, has now spread throughout China and around the world. The common sequence of events observed in the development of the 'Wenzhou model' is as follows. First, someone in the community succeeds in a new business. Then his neighbours try to mimic his success by engaging in the same business. For example, a worker who retired from a state-owned shoe factory returned to his home in Xianjiang Township in 1979 and started to make plastic shoes by melting waste plastic and shaping it into soles, and using an iron to stick it to a leather outer. His plastic shoes sold very well because of their cheapness, so his neighbours started imitating him. In a few years, the whole village, and even neighbouring villages, were also imitating him. The number of shoe factories reached 1,500, employing more than 8,000 people in 1984. Rampant entry of new manufacturers leads to severe competition and a bad reputation, because some manufacturers produce low-grade products. Competition and shrinkage of demand due to the bad reputation lead to a decline in the profit rate of the industry. Then someone in the community tries a new line of business, which is similar to but a little different from the former business. If he succeeds, his neighbours will try to mimic his success again. For example, in Shatou Township the transfer of plastic shoe-making technology from Xianjiang Township induced some local entrepreneurs to start producing plastic shoes in 1984. Faced with a decline in the profitability of plastic shoe making, however, some manufacturers switched to rubber shoe manufacturing, and soon all the shoemakers in the township were producing rubber shoes.

The above-mentioned mechanism of innovation and mimicking explains why Wenzhou has a rich variety of industrial agglomerations. The people of Wenzhou not only create industrial agglomerations in Wenzhou but also create other kinds of agglomerations in various locations. Zhang *et al.* (2011) report that more than 5,000 people from Qiaotou Township, Wenzhou, are engaged in the agency business of international apparel and leather product brands in Guangdong Province, and 70 per cent of the population of Huadan Township run supermarkets in various locations of China.

The 'Wenzhou model' is the outcome of the extremely strong entrepreneurship of Wenzhou people, but it is a typical pattern of private enterprise development in China generally. In most cases, potential entrepreneurs only have a limited amount of financial resources and human capital. They start their own businesses by trying to mimic the success of somebody around them. Some conditions make it easy for potential entrepreneurs to start business. For example, the existence of product and input markets makes it easy for those who have just learned how to make things but do not know how to sell things to start manufacturing. The vast and growing domestic market is another condition that makes it easy for new entrants to capture a piece of the market. Such conditions lower the barriers to start a business, and lead to the emergence of 'mass capitalism'.

The rise of the 'guerrilla handset' industry in Shenzhen

The *shanzhaiji*, or 'guerrilla handset', industry which has developed recently in Shenzhen, Guangdong Province, is another typical case of 'mass capitalism'.

'Guerrilla handsets' refers to mobile handsets that are not recognized or licensed by the government. These handsets employ fake international mobile equipment identity (IMEI) numbers, which are used by wireless networks to identify valid devices, and they also carry fake network entry permit stickers. The manufacturers of these products usually evade the payment of value added taxes (Wang 2010). The guerrilla handset industry emerged in Shenzhen around 2005 and has grown rapidly since then (Figure 6.1). Wang (2010) estimates that the shipment of guerrilla handsets amounted to 145 million units in 2009, which is 13 per cent of the authorized global mobile handset business and 20 per cent of the authorized handset production in China. It has been estimated that 1 million people are engaged in the 'guerrilla handset' industry in and around Shenzhen.

The mobile handset was not initially a simple commodity that could be easily manufactured. A team consisting of dozens of engineers in a government-affiliated institute under the Ministry of Electronics Industry devoted six years to developing the first mobile handset designed and made in China in 1998 (Shiu and Imai 2010). Within ten years of the first domestically designed handset being made, however, mobile handsets had become a product that even a small private enterprise with fewer than 20 employees could design, organize the manufacturing of, and sell. The main driving force that has changed mobile handsets from a high-tech product to a commodity that is easy to design and manufacture is a Taiwanese IC vendor, Mediatek (MTK). MTK started developing baseband ICs (the core chip in mobile handsets) in 2000, but it had a hard time finding customers at first. The global market for baseband ICs was dominated by Western IC vendors, such as TI, ADI, Qualcomm, Agere, Infineon and NXP. No global handset manufacturers, not even the Taiwanese 'original design

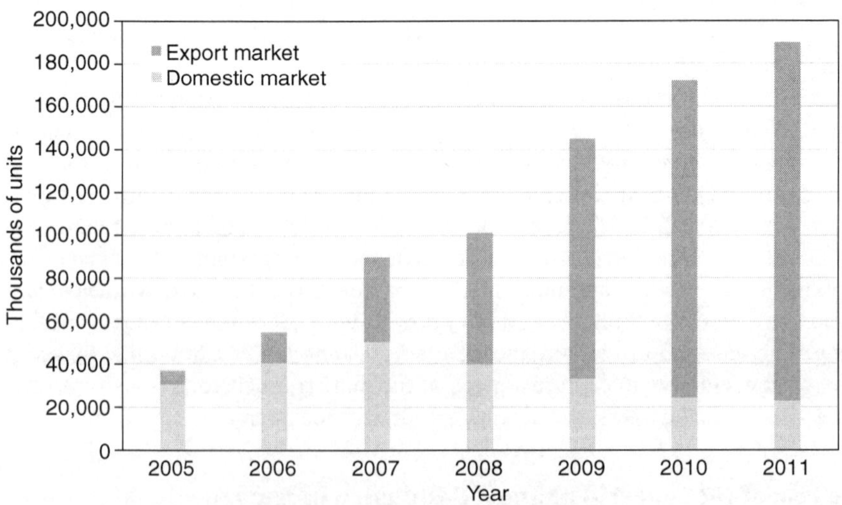

Figure 6.1 Guerrilla handset shipments in domestic and export markets (source: Wang 2010).

manufacturers' (ODMs), would take the risk of trying an immature IC made by a newcomer. Therefore, MTK began to target the Chinese market, where a lot of local handset vendors and design houses were looking for baseband ICs that were cheap and easy to handle. MTK collaborated with a design house in Shanghai named Longcheer, provided the latter with ICs and a circuit design, and let Longcheer manufacture assembled printed circuit boards (PCBAs), which are printed circuit boards mounted with ICs and other components. PCBAs sold by Longcheer were enthusiastically welcomed by local handset manufacturers because they made the manufacturing of mobile handsets very simple: all that the handset manufacturers had to do was to make the case and assemble the PCBA, liquid crystal display module and other components such as the keypad in the case. Not only the basic operation system but also application software was also bundled in the PCBA. Though MTK's baseband ICs would not allow the manufacturer to differentiate the functions of their products from other makers' handsets using the same ICs, MTK ICs were widely adopted by Chinese indigenous handset manufacturers in 2005, mainly because of their cheapness – they were US$10 cheaper than equivalent ICs made by Western vendors – and because they had popular functions such as MP3 players. It is estimated that 71 per cent of handsets shipped by indigenous manufacturers adopted MTK ICs in 2005.

The unexpected outcome of the spread of MTK's baseband ICs was the entry of many small handset manufacturers. Before their entry, there were already around 70 handset vendors, including foreign and domestic brands, in China. One reason why many small manufacturers were able to enter and survive the fierce competition from established handset makers was because the domestic market was huge and growing. The big brands of course have better advertising and marketing, but their sales network cannot cover all rural markets. It is those markets where the handsets made by small manufacturers are most welcomed. These handsets may carry some sloppy brands, or brands that resemble international brands (e.g. 'iPheno', 'Scoy Eriosscn', 'Motorcia'). Some of them utilize the cases of recycled handsets made by international manufacturers. Hundreds of small manufacturers, each having only three or four employees, buy the recycled handsets and replace the inside of the handset with a new PCBA – mounted with MTK ICs – and display. These 'renewed handsets' (*fanbanji*) are welcomed by people who want to show off that they have famous-brand handsets but do not have enough money to buy such handsets.

The small manufacturers of course cannot enjoy the same economies of scale as the big foreign and domestic manufacturers, but they employ numerous measures to offset their inferiority in scale. First, as already mentioned, they use fake IMEI numbers and fake network entry permit stickers. To acquire approval to enter wireless networks, handset manufacturers need to pay US$40,000–$50,000 to the certification institution, and it usually takes a month for the institution to finish the testing and approval process. 'Guerrilla handset' manufacturers can economize on this cost and time by bypassing the process. Second, 'guerrilla handset' manufacturers form a meticulous social division of labour among themselves, so that they can combine the agility of small enterprises and the economies of scale of mass production. Figure 6.2 shows the enterprises that constitute the supply chain of the 'guerrilla handset' industry and the division of labour among them. 'Integrators' are equivalent to mobile handset vendors such as Nokia and Samsung. They plan to develop, organize the manufacturing of, and sell handsets to merchants inside and outside China, and even to mobile service operators in developing countries. However, they outsource most of the tasks of designing and manufacturing to specialized firms. Integrators buy PCBAs from 'solution designers', which specialize in the designing of PCBAs and the development of software, and PCBAs designed by them are manufactured by 'surface mount technology (SMT) operators'. Integrators outsource the designing of handset cases to 'design companies', and then provide the blueprint to "mould-making and injection companies', which specialize in the manufacture of plastic cases. Integrators then provide PCBAs, cases, LCD displays, keypads and other components to an 'electronic manufacturing service', which assembles the components into mobile handsets. The vice-president of the handset manufacturers' association in Shenzhen, whom I interviewed in November 2010, estimated that there were 1,500–2,000 integrators in Shenzhen. There were several hundred solution designers, SMT operators and design companies. These enterprises can operate on a larger scale than integrators, because they can gather the orders from several customers. In the case of solution designers, for example, designers often sell a common PCBA to several integrators. Using a common PCBA means that handsets made from it will have the same functions and almost the same shape. SMT operators can maintain a high

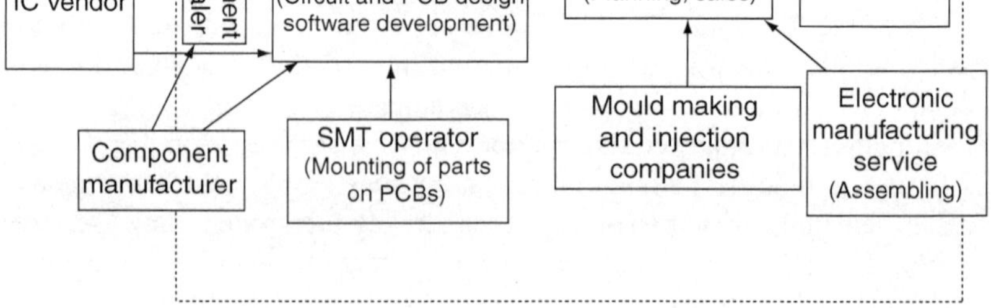

Figure 6.2 The supply chain of the 'guerrilla handset' industry.

Note

The arrows show the direction in which goods and services are provided. Enterprises within the boxed area are located in Shenzhen.

operating rate of their machinery by accepting orders not only from mobile handset integrators but also from the vendors of other electronic devices. The division of labour makes it possible for the integrators and the service suppliers that support them to operate at a different scale. The orders integrators receive are often as small as 10,000 units of handsets in total, but by gathering orders from several integrators, solution designers and SMT operators operate on a much larger scale. Since all the technological expertise that is needed to design and manufacture handsets is provided within the supply chain, one can easily become an integrator if one can invest 1 million yuan (US$160,000), which includes the cost of designing a new handset model and manufacturing 2,000 units. Consequently, many people who have work experience in the industry start their own businesses, and hence 'mass capitalism' has emerged.

The economies of scale in manufacturing and designing enable the 'guerrilla handset' industry to make handsets (with a camera and Bluetooth) as cheaply as 78 yuan (US$12) per unit. With the agility of small-scale integrators, the industry has churned out handsets catering to the demands of the world's low-income population. For example, handsets that can carry two subscriber identity module (SIM) cards were developed in the 'guerrilla handset' industry first. Such handsets enable the user to subscribe to two operators at the same time and choose the operator that offers the lowest price a particular time or place. The industry has also developed handsets that make big sounds. According to an integrator, such handsets are popular among rural Indians. Despite all efforts, however, 'guerrilla handsets' have lost ground to big international brands in the Chinese market recently (see Figure 6.1), mainly because of their unreliable quality and poor after-sales service. The industry is now turning to target overseas markets such as South-East Asia, India, the Middle East and Latin America. However, its business model does not seem to be sustainable, because, without having a fixed brand, 'guerrilla handset' manufacturers can hardly have return customers. Therefore, some of the former 'guerrillas' have now turned into normal handset vendors with fixed brands. The 'guerrilla handset' industry may be a port of entry for potential entrepreneurs, but it is not an industry in which entrepreneurs can stay for a long time.

Mass capitalism in other industries

I have described two cases of 'mass capitalism' in China, but readers may suspect that these are extreme cases and they do not represent the average situation in China. Indeed, the residents of Wenzhou seem to be more entrepreneurial than the average Chinese. The chairman of the Chamber of Wenzhou Merchants in Shenzhen estimates that half of the 'integrators' in the 'guerrilla handset' industry of Shenzhen are run by people who came from Wenzhou. Others say that people from Wenzhou and Chaozhou, Guangdong Province, constitute the two largest ethnic groups within the industry. The local economy of Chaozhou has a similar structure to that of Wenzhou, with numerous industrial agglomerations, including a stainless kitchenware industry, a ceramic industry and a confectionery industry, formed by local entrepreneurs. 'Mass capitalism' may be a phenomenon confined to some special places like Wenzhou and Chaozhou in China. It seems, however, that more and more industries in China are swarming with mass capitalists. Mass capitalism originated with some limited groups of people but its influence has now reached many industries and districts.

Rare earth mining, for example, is an industry that has recently developed thanks to the rampant entry of mass capitalists. With one-third of the world's reserve of rare earths, China accounted for 33 per cent of the global production of rare earths in 1991. In the first half of 1990s, a new method of extracting rare earths was invented in China. With this method, one can start rare earth mining with an initial investment of only 1–2 million yuan (US$160,000–US$320,000). Consequently, many entrepreneurs entered the rare earths business and produced rare earths very cheaply. Cheap rare earths exported from China have forced the rare earth mines in other countries to close down. In 2009, China accounted for 97 per cent of global rare earth production. Alarmed by the possibility of depletion of rare earth reserves, the Chinese government started to eliminate private rare earth mines in 2010 and began to try to keep rare earth resources under state control.

The Chinese bicycle industry is another industry that has grown rapidly as a result of the rampant entry of mass capitalists. Until the 1980s, the industry was dominated by a handful of big state-owned enterprises. In 1986, the top three state-owned bicycle makers, namely Yongjiu and Phoenix of Shanghai, and Pigeon of Tianjin, accounted for 35 per cent of domestic shipments. In the 1990s, however, Pigeon's sales declined sharply, forcing the company to get rid of 6,000 employees between 1990 and 1996, and eventually to stop producing bicycles altogether (Komagata 2011). And yet bicycle production in Tianjin started to grow very rapidly after that, from six million units in 1998 to 47 million units in 2007, which was 43 per cent of domestic production, or roughly 30 per cent of global bicycle production. The main driving force of Tianjin's bicycle industry was small private manufacturers, which amounted to more than 900 enterprises, including bicycle assemblers and parts makers, in 2003. According to Komagata (2011: 155), at least 80 per cent of the private bicycle manufacturers had former employees of Pigeon, who had been dismissed by the company during the 1990s, in their management. The massive level of dismissals by Pigeon has led to the diffusion of bicycle manufacturing technology from the state-owned enterprise to the private sector, and with the rampant entry of rural entrepreneurs into the bicycle industry Tianjin has become the world's largest agglomeration of bicycle industry.

Conclusion

In this chapter, I have tried to give a name to a common phenomenon that can be observed in many industries in China: the massive entry of small private businesses. This phenomenon, which I call 'mass capitalism', has a common feature.

After the massive entry, firms start to form a meticulous division of labour among them, in which various kinds of components and services are provided. By using these services, a potential entrepreneur can easily start a business with only a limited amount of capital. Hence, more entrepreneurs enter the industry and make it even larger. With the division of labour among specialized firms, 'mass capitalism' can combine the agility of small firms with the economies of scale of mass production. Thus, 'mass capitalism' can churn out competitive products that can even compete with those of global manufacturers which have established brands.

The sustainability of 'mass capitalism', however, is questionable. Since incumbent enterprises can hardly create entry barriers, they must face competition from more and more new entrants. Small enterprises in 'mass capitalism' will not be able to survive the competition from global manufacturers in the long run, because, lacking a fixed brand, they can hardly attract return customers. If some manufacturer from an industrial agglomeration sells fake and inferior products, that may ruin the reputation of all the products that come from the same district. Therefore, manufacturers in 'mass capitalism' will not survive in the long run if they remain 'mass capitalists'. 'Mass capitalism' is an entry port that invites potential entrepreneurs to start their own businesses. But entrepreneurs need to develop peculiar advantages such as brands and technological expertise if they want to survive for long in the industry.

Notes

1 The gross industrial output (*gongye zongchanzhi*) of China consists of manufacturing, mining and public utilities such as electricity and heat supply, water supply and gas supply.

2 All of the above data are calculated from the data of SYC (2011).

References

Bremmer, Ian (2010) *The End of the Free Market: Who Wins the War between States and Corporations?*, New York: Portfolio.

Cheng Liansheng (2002) *Zhongguo fanshiye zhengce yanjiu (1950–2000)* (A study of China's anti-unemployment policy), Beijing: Shehui kexue wenxian chubashe.

Dougherty, Sean and Herd, Richard (2005) *Fast-Falling Barriers and Growing Concentration: The Emergence of a Private Economy in China*, Paris: Organisation for Economic Co-operation and Development.

Halper, Stephan (2010) *The Beijing Consensus: How China's Authoritarian Model Will Dominate the Twenty-first Century*, New York: Basic Books.

He Guang (ed.) (1990) *Dangdai zhongguo de laodongli guanli* (Labour management in contemporary China). Beijing: Zhongguo shehui kexue chubanshe.

Huang Yasheng (2008) *Capitalism with Chinese Characteristics: Entrepreneurship and the State*, New York: Cambridge University Press.

Huang Yi and Luo Weidong (2002) 'Guimo jingji, lianhe jianbing yu qiyejia chuangxin' (Scale economy, alliance and merger, and entrepreneurial innovation), in Shi Jinchuan *et al.* (eds) *Zhidu bianqian yu jingji fazhan: Wenzhou moshi yanjiu* (Institutional change and economic development: a study of the Wenzhou model), Hangzhou: Zhejiang daxue chubanshe.

Kojima Reeitsu (1997) *Gendai chugoku no keizai* (Contemporary Chinese economy), Tokyo: Iwanami shoten.

Komagata Tetsuya (2011) *Chugoku no jitensha sangyo* (China's bicycle industry), Tokyo: Keio gijuku daigaku shuppankai.

National Bureau of Statistics of China (2006) *Zhongguo Jingji Pucha Nianjian* (China economic census yearbook) *2004*, Beijing: Zhongguo Tongji Chubanshe.

National Bureau of Statistics of China (2010) *Zhongguo Jingji Pucha Nianjian* (China economic census yearbook) *2008*, Beijing: Zhongguo Tongji Chubanshe.

Naughton, Barry (2007) *The Chinese Economy: Transitions and Growth*, Cambridge, MA: MIT Press.

Shiu Jing Ming and Imai, Ken (2010) 'Keitai denwa sangyo ni okeru suichoku bungyo no suishinsha' (The drivers of vertical division of labour in the mobile phone handset industry), in Marukawa Tomoo and Masanori Yasumoto (eds) *Keitai denwa sangyo no shinka purosesu* (The evolution of the mobile phone industry), Tokyo: Yuhikaku.

SYC (annual) *Zhongguo Tongji Nianjian* (Statistical yearbook of China), Beijing: Zhongguo Tongji Chubanshe.

Wang Chunguang (1995) *Shehui liudong he shehui chonggou: jingcheng 'Zhejiang cun' yanjiu* (Social mobility and reorganization of society: a study of 'Zhejiang Village' in Beijing), Hangzhou: Zhejiang renmin chubanshe.

Wang, Kevin (2010) 'China's TD-SCDMA market to take off in 2010', China Research Topical Report, Q1 2010, iSuppli. Online, available at: http://www.isuppli.com/China-Electronics-Supply-Chain/Pages/China-s-TD-SCDMA-Market-to-Take-off-in-2010.aspx

Wu Junhua (2008) *Chugoku: shizuka naru kakumei* (China: the quiet revolution), Tokyo: Nihon keizai shimbunsha.

Yu Xiong and Yu Guang (1995) *Wenzhou gongye jianshi* (A brief history of Wenzhou's industries), Shanghai: Shanghai shehui kexue chubanshe.

Zhang Yili, Ni Jing and Yu Xiangqian (2011) 'Chiiki teki na kigyoka kurasuta no keisei mekanizumu no bunseki' (An analysis of the mechanism of creating a regional entrepreneurial cluster), *Shakai Kagaku Kenkyu* (Journal of social science), 63 (2).

7 Theoretical possibilities of a socialist market economy and the Chinese road*

Makoto Itoh

The historical significance of Chinese industrialization in the context of globalization of capitalism

The capitalist market economy has intensified the global activity of multinational enterprises on the basis of microelectronic information technologies during the period of prolonged downswing and restructuring since 1973. In accordance with this trend, neo-liberalism has become dominant since the 1980s, and emphasized the rational efficiency of the market economy by reducing the economic roles of the state, privatizing public enterprises and weakening trade unions. The systemic changes after the East European revolutions in 1989 and the dissolution of the Soviet Union in 1991 proceeded under the strong influence of such neo-liberalism, and took the American model of capitalist market economy as the de facto global standard. Mainstream neo-classical economics has served as an ideological basis for such a trend across the world.

However, globalization of the capitalist market economy has not realized the economic efficiency and harmonious distribution expected by the dominant neo-liberal ideology. For instance, Japan, one of the major capitalist economies, is suffering from a severe depression following the burst of speculative bubble economy at the end of 1980s, with continuously growing unemployment during and after the lost decade of the 1990s. Not a few of the surrounding Asian countries also experienced a heavy blow from the collapse of the bubble, resulting in the monetary and financial crises of 1997–98. The 'new economy' boom in the United States had to end with the pricking of the stock market bubble, and the United States entered a phase of depression after the autumn of 2000, which was further accentuated by the attacks on the World Trade Center on 11 September 2001. The economic recovery during 2002–06 in the United States depended heavily on the housing boom promoted by the financialization of labour power by inducing workers to undertake more and more credit-driven consumption, and eventually resulted in the sub-prime world economic crisis (Itoh 2010), which was transformed further into the sovereign debt crisis of some major advanced economies. It is evident that the deregulated capitalist market economy under neo-liberalism has intensified financial instability, with disastrous effects on the economic life of working people. Neo-liberal globalization thus cannot be judged as successful in achieving stable, efficient growth and desired harmony in the advanced economies. The increasing inequalities of income and wealth, both domestically and globally, as well as poverty and starvation in not a few peripheral developing countries, suggests that it is difficult to find a hopeful way out of the current problems of the world economy.

In contrast, the Chinese economy has managed to achieve high and stable real economic growth of around 10 per cent per annum on average through the period of economic reforms since 1978, by gradually introducing market economy within the strategy of 'the Chinese road to socialism'. Even the sub-prime global crisis reduced the Chinese annual GDP growth rate merely to 9.1 per cent in 2009, as domestic demand was stimulated by the government so as to mitigate the damage of the fall in export demand. There are some serious problems to be solved in China, as we shall discuss. Nevertheless, its sustained success in economic growth by officially keeping on a socialist road is noteworthy in comparison both with the tragic confusion and collapse of economic life in Russia and several East European former socialist countries in the process of neo-liberal systemic change for a rapid and comprehensive transformation into capitalism, which was recommended as 'shock therapy', and with the unstable repetitive crises and depressions in advanced capitalist economies.

How, then, can we characterize the social order of the steadily and rapidly industrializing Chinese economy? There are three competing sets of views on this issue.

The first view asserts that China is in fact already a capitalist market economy, despite the official constitutional law of 1993, which mandates the maintenance and construction of a socialist market economy. In this view, successful Chinese industrialization indicates the victory of neo-classical economics and the effectiveness and rationality of the capitalist free market economy, which has been introduced into China through economic reforms since 1978. China will further reduce and eventually dissolve the strong political intervention of the Communist Party in the economy consistently, so as to reform the whole politico-economic system into an ordinary free and democratic society by following other advanced economies.[1] Such an argument usually assumes that the indigenous growth of market economy must form a most natural economic order best suited to human activities, and that a market economy cannot systematically work without private ownership of means of production, forming a capitalist market economy. This view lies within a narrow ideological framework that sees a capitalist market economy as the ultimate natural economic order of liberty.

The second view also argues that China is already on the path of a capitalist economy, away from the socialist road. The new elites in the Communist Party became capitalist-roaders utilizing state power. The great majority of Chinese working people are more and more exploited and oppressed under the increasing unevenness of distribution of income and wealth in the society. They have begun to fight back, as shown in a wave of strikes such as in the summer of 2010. Unlike the first view, this view underlines contradictions within Chinese capitalist economic growth, and expects them to induce a socialist revolution in accord with the historical tradition of Marxism and Maoism in China (e.g. Li 2011). This view seems to be shared by many Anglo-American Marxian political economists. A variant of this stresses the effectiveness of state intervention, including Keynesian policies for achieving stable, strong economic growth, in the Chinese model of capitalism as an example that contrasts with the failures of neo-liberal Western capitalist economies.[2]

The third view believes that there are theoretical possibilities for constructing a socialist market economy, and argues that China can still maintain such possibilities despite contradictory socio-economic problems from the standpoint of the majority of working people. As far as I know, the great majority of political economists within China, as well as a certain number of Japanese Marxian economists, including Uno theorists, basically support this view.[3]

It is not unusual for the same historical facts and data on Chinese industrialization to be differently interpreted across these various views. This chapter presents an argument for the third view, and is mostly critical of the first view. Although I am more sympathetic towards the second view, in the spirit of hoping for a more egalitarian and sounder socialist economic order for the future of China, I cannot be sure what kind of socialist economic system is more desirable: a kind of market socialism similar to the Chinese middle-term target; or an economy that would emerge after another socialist revolution, recommended by the second view. I am also concerned about the possibility that the second view would create a substantial ideological barrier to cooperation with many serious Marxian political economists in China. Furthermore, if we can recognize the theoretical possibilities for a socialist market economy in Chinese high economic growth, it must certainly be encouraging for working people in both advanced and developing countries to think of wider alternatives to the present crisis-ridden globalization of the capitalist market economy.

In order to clarify the historical significance of Chinese industrialization for the third view, what theoretical grounds can we rely on?

Marx's *Capital* (1867: 85, 94) must surely be useful. It clearly showed that the capitalist economy is not at all a natural order, but formed as a historically specific social order based upon the forms of market economy. By demonstrating the historically specific nature of capitalism, it presents us theoretical possibilities for socialism as alternatives that can overcome the historical limitations of capitalism for working people.

For about seven decades after the Russian Revolution, many people in the world used to identify Marxian socialism with the Soviet model of a comprehensive planned economy based on state ownership of means of production. As a reverse image of the comprehensive market economy in a purely capitalist society, which is analysed in Marx's *Capital*, such a model of a comprehensive planned economy without the market seems to be easily and consistently understandable. However, various models of market socialism were already present through the so-called socialist economic calculation controversy in the period when the Soviet economy was being constructed in the 1920s and 1930s. Lange (1936: 37) showed, for example, that rational prices of publicly owned means of production can be reached by a Central Planning Board (CPB) through the trial-and-error approach in market socialism. In the 1980s, in the democratization reform movements in the East European countries, such models of market socialism were recalled as desirable alternatives to the Soviet type of centrally planned statist socialism. Though they were not actually realized during and after the systemic change of the Soviet economies, the theoretical possibilities for market socialism to incorporate the flexible adjustment functions of the market economy into socialist economies with public ownership of means of production have attracted wider interest in our age, as reviewed by Itoh (1992, 1995a) and Roemer (1994).

The economic reforms in China seem to pursue more practical strategies in a large-scale social experiment that in many aspects is more complex and flexible than any theoretical models of market socialism. As the reforms in China have not been strongly based on theoretical foundations, the Chinese official position of maintaining a socialist road has globally met with doubts and criticism by the first and second views, as we have seen. Thus, how to characterize the historical significance as well as the remaining problems of Chinese industrialization from the view of the theoretical possibilities of a socialist market economy is still a challenging task.[4]

Theoretical possibilities of a socialist market economy in China

A broad historical nature for the market economy

According to Adam Smith (1776: vol. 1, ch. 2), the market economy, to promote division of labour through exchange of commodities, is a natural consequence of a propensity in human nature – that is, 'the propensity to truck, barter, and exchange one thing for another'. Commodity exchange in a market economy is thus regarded as an inevitable result of a natural human propensity to exchange that is intrinsic to human nature just as much as (or derived from) the faculties of reason and speech. Therefore, transactions in a market economy are conceived of as natural actions for human beings in general. This is a foundation for a naturalist view of the market economy, which is common to the classical and the neo-classical schools in economics, which see the natural order of liberty in a thorough market economy to form capitalism.

However, the exchange of commodities as the basic form of market economy was not actually universal to daily economic life within various communal human societies. Although commodity exchange has a long history from very ancient times, it did not spring from human relations within societies, but began 'where communities have their boundaries, at their points of contact with other communities, or with members of the latter', as Marx (1867: ch. 2) pointed out. Indeed, as happened along the Silk Road in pre-modern times, transactions of commodities formed an intersocietal economic order that externally linked different societies with various communal orders. When some products became commodities in such intersocietal transactions, a tendency to treat more and more goods as commodities penetrated societies, and occasionally it worked destructively against various traditionally communal economic orders within societies. Anyway, the central intrasocietal economic orders in pre-capitalist ages continuously maintained or reconstructed themselves as non-market communal systems even when their social forms or relation of production were altered. Human faculties of reason and speech must have existed always and everywhere in such pre-modern societies, but commodity exchange did not. The naturalist view to conceive of the propensity to exchange as an intrinsic human tendency must be a reversed overgeneralization of the individualistic and market-oriented mentality common to the way of living in modern capitalist societies.

Indeed, for the first time in human history, capitalist societies turned the market economy into a basic intrasocial economic order through the commodification of labour power. This specific historical nature of the capitalist market economy should not be identified with the much broader and older historical nature of the market economy. In view of its broader historical nature, the birth and growth of forms of the market economy were not necessarily premised on private ownership of the means of production, or, further, on a capitalist social order. Marx (1867: parts 1 and 2) presents an analysis of the forms of market economy, which are composed of commodities, money and capital, prior to the analysis of the capitalist process of production. Uno (1950, 1964) greatly respected Marx's treatment and purified these parts of *Capital* into a genuine theory of circulation without directly referring to social relations of labour as the substance of value. Such a theoretical recomposition implies an important theoretical recognition that the forms of market economy have a historical nature much broader and older than capitalist relations of production. At the same time, they must offer an important theoretical ground for the possibility of incorporating and utilizing the forms, adjustment functions, and stimulus of a market economy in a socialist economy, which is based mainly upon public ownership of the means of production being utilized by various forms of enterprise.

Contrastingly, in non-historical and naturalist theories of classical and neo-classical economics, the capitalist market economy is always identified with a market economy in general, as Takumi (2001) correctly pointed out. From such a narrow neo-classical understanding of the market economy, the historical significance and possibility of experimenting with a socialist market economy in China tend to be negated in an inelastic way, and the growth of the market economy in China is simply declared to be inconsistent with socialist public ownership of the means of production, and therefore the Chinese road to socialism is also judged simply as self-destructive.

Various types of ownership of enterprises on the road to socialism

Marx attempted to show a scientific foundation for socialism by clarifying the mechanism of development of the capitalist market economy and its internal contradictions, together with their historical characteristics. We should follow his method and examine the basic problems and possibilities for Chinese socialism in the light of critical studies of principles, history and the current situation of the capitalist market economy.

Capitalism, at the dawn of its history, dissolved the multi-layered, complicated feudal rights concerning domination over, possession of and utilization of land, and established modern private ownership of land through the historical social change that Marx (1867) called 'the process of primitive accumulation of capital'. The typical process of primitive accumulation of capital occurred in the United Kingdom, and it essentially meant 'the expropriation of the agricultural producer, the peasant, from the soil' (Marx 1867: 876), so as to create a social mass of 'free' wage workers in a dual sense. Although the mass of workers were liberated from feudal bondage, workers were also deprived of traditional access to farmland as a major means of production, and had to work as wage earners employed by the capitalists who owned the means of production. Thus, private ownership of land and other major means of production is a fundamental precondition for capitalist relations of production; it enables valorization of capital by means of purchasing and using labour power as a commodity. Therefore, the very foundation of the socialist economy as a means of transcending capitalism must lie in the public ownership of land and other major means of production. It was further believed, especially in Soviet 'orthodox Marxism', that the state ownership of means of production in combination with a centrally planned economy is the exclusively scientific road to socialism as a symmetrical negation of the anarchical private ownership of means of production under capitalism.

In retrospect, however, the ways of overcoming the capitalist private ownership of land and other major means of production and for putting them into socialist public ownership need not be limited merely to state ownership and statist control. Marx (1894: 570–573) pointed to the joint-stock corporation system and to cooperative enterprises, which 'should be viewed as transition forms from the capitalist mode of production to the associated one', either negatively or positively. Even in the Soviet economy, *kolkhoz*es remained in agriculture as social collective firms or cooperative enterprises outside of national firms, not to mention various other types of firms during the New Economic Policy (NEP) period (from 1921 to 1925).

In actual capitalist economies, moreover, there remain a wide range of different types of ownership of means of production beside the private one. For example, there are land and means of production owned by the state, local government, cooperatives, national trusts independent from government, non-profit corporations, religious organizations, political parties and non-governmental organizations. Interestingly, these non-private owners of land and other means of work have persistently sustained themselves, and even multiplied under certain circumstances through the expansion of capitalism. On the basis of such observations, it appears that the types of socialist public ownership of land and other major means of production and its management need not be narrowly limited to state ownership and its national bureaucratic administration.

Actually, in the Chinese road to a socialist market economy, diverting from the model of a centrally planned economy with comprehensive state ownership of means of production, a variety of practical possibilities are emerging for public ownership of means of production and more decentralized management. Just as we cannot deny the pivotal and basic role of capitalist private ownership of means of production among many different types of non-private ownership in an actual capitalist society, the basic pivotal nature of socialist public ownership of means of production can theoretically be maintained and conceived amid the variegated types of ownership and management of means of production in China.

We see possibilities for various types of socialist public ownership of the means of production in China more concretely in the Contract Responsibility System, which entrusts a portion of farmland to a family on the basis of the whole people's ownership of land, or entrusts to certain persons the management of state-owned enterprises by contract. Collectively owned township and village enterprises (TVEs), which are often initiated and promoted by local governments or Party bureaucrats, are another example of public ownership. Further, in the 1990s, while many state-owned enterprises were reformed into joint-stock companies, a dominant proportion of shares of those companies was still retained by the central or provincial or local governments, or partly by workers in those companies, so as to keep the nature of public ownership. A new form of joint-stock cooperative firms was created, especially among many TVEs, which gave a vote equally to each member of the firms without regard to the unequal number of shares being held among the member workers, even though this form has tended to become transformed into the ordinary joint-stock system (Ryu 1998).

The share of state-owned enterprises in Chinese industrial output declined sharply from 77.6 per cent in 1978 to 54.6 per cent in 1990 and further to 26.5 per cent in 1997, following the reform of such enterprises in 1993. In the same period, the share of collectively owned enterprises, including TVEs, increased from 22.4 per cent to 35.6 per cent and then to 40.5 per cent. As a result, the total share of both types of enterprises was still maintained at 67 per cent in 1997. Although we should note also that the share of individually owned enterprises increased from 5.4 per cent in 1990 to 15.9 per cent in 1997, this proportion was still not high enough to show a dominance of private enterprise in the Chinese economy (Ma 2000: 93).

Since the coverage of industrial output statistics had changed since 1998, the share of state-owned enterprises in industrial output jumped to 49.6 per cent in 1998. But it continuously declined thereafter, down to 26.6 per cent in 2010. The share of collectively owned enterprises declined sharply from 19.5 per cent in 1998 to 1.5 per cent in 2010, mainly as a result of the massive privatization of collectively owned TVEs. It is not easy to discover the share of indigenous private enterprises, but there are reasons to believe that most of the 46 per cent output share held by non-state, non-foreign enterprises in 2010 was contributed by indigenous private enterprises (Marukawa, this volume, Chapter 6). The role of private enterprises in China seems to be substantially increasing, though not yet becoming dominant.

Thus, after years of massive privatization the state sector's share in Chinese industrial output value has reduced to less than 30 per cent, according to Li (2011). However, it is still high in comparison with that in capitalist economies. Furthermore, in key industrial sectors forming the commanding heights, the share of the state sector in output value maintains dominant proportions: 59 per cent in coal mining and washing, 96 per cent in the extraction of petroleum and natural gas, 42 per cent in the smelting and pressing of ferrous metals, 45 per cent in the manufacturing of transport equipment and 92 per cent in the production and supply of electric power and heat (Li 2011: 44). In addition, an influential proportion of state capital continues to remain in many important joint-stock companies, including joint enterprises with foreign capital.

The share of the state sector in total wage payments was still as high as 53 per cent in 2010. Therefore, the state sector also maintained a leading role in the determination of the general level of wages (Yan 2011: 74).

Through years of reforms, big Chinese corporations either owned by the state or dominated by state capital have recently improved their competitiveness by means of advanced technologies. They have become more and more esteemed on the globalized stock market, and have increased their attraction for Chinese university graduates as desirable employers. In the world ranking of megabanks based on stock market valuation, the position of Chinese banks owned by the state has risen, especially since the sub-prime financial crisis, and Chinese banks now occupy the top three (from first to third) and the tenth positions within the top ten.

From the standpoint of proceeding on the road to a socialist market economy by keeping the dominant position of public ownership of enterprises, it must be both important and desirable for public or state enterprises quantitatively and qualitatively to maintain such leading roles. Even under the Contract Responsibility System, the socialist character of state enterprises used to be shown in the general rules determining division of profits: 55 per cent was delivered to the state, and of the remaining 45 per cent retained in the corporations, 40 per cent was devoted to the expansion of production or the business, 20 per cent was for welfare services for workers, another 20 per cent for bonuses added to wages, and 20 per cent was for research and development.

A large number of TVEs had another form of local public, cooperative and collective ownership of means of production outside of the state sector. The total number of these grew from 1.52 million, with 28 million workers, in 1978, to 18.9 million, with 95.5 million workers, by 1988, and further to 20.04 million, with 125 million workers, by 1998. Although total employment by TVEs reached 159 million in 2010, a large proportion of TVEs have been privatized since the late 1990s.

It is clear that encouragement by central and local governments to promote the creation and growth of medium-sized and small TVEs on the grounds of public ownership of the means of production, including land, was definitely an important background to such continuous development of those enterprises. Together with the state-owned big enterprises in key industries, the growth of a large number of collectively owned TVEs shows the complex variety of forms of public or semi-public ownership of means of production characteristic of the Chinese road to a socialist market economy.

This historical experience offers powerful counter-evidence against the view that socialist public ownership of means of production must inevitably cause economic stagnation, since it is unable to incorporate innovative changes, in contrast with the capitalist economy based upon private ownership of means of production. Theoretically, there can be at least two kinds of innovation to improve economic efficiency and productivity. One of them is organizational innovation in the forms of enterprises or management at workplaces to increase motivation among workers to be diligent and to cooperate with technological changes. The other is technological innovation to improve efficiency and productivity of labour. In Chinese economic reforms, organizational innovation has been clearly facilitated by public ownership of the major means of production, thereby enabling the existence and expansion of various forms of enterprises competitively modernizing the whole economy in various fields of activity. No doubt new technologies have mostly been transplanted or imported from the advanced economies, not innovatively born domestically in the rapid Chinese economic growth over more than three decades. The process, however, has been strongly guided and supported in many ways by the industrial policy of the state. It is normal in the industrial catching-up process, as experienced in the strong Japanese economic growth up to the 1970s. The comparatively powerful industrial policies that have been effectively carried out on the basis of the public ownership of land and other major means of production may also potentially be utilized for the creation of new strategies such as more eco-conscious technological development, including soft-energy paths for the future, hopefully diverting from the unhappy US experience in which large-scale military spending has been a powerful source of industrial innovation. Anyway, the source and promoter of technological innovation are theoretically and practically not narrowly limited to capitalist enterprises based upon private ownership of means of production.

At the same time, it is also noteworthy that the rapid Chinese economic growth showed much more stability even in the years of the global financial crisis, largely because of the continued strength of those publicly or collectively owned enterprises, as well as the capacity of the state to control macroeconomic activity through those enterprises, besides the usual Keynesian fiscal and monetary policies.

The possibility of a socialist labour market

Capitalist economies have grown on the basis of the commodification of the labour power of the mass of workers, who are generally excluded from private ownership of means of production. So long as labour power is available as a commodity, capital can obtain not just necessary labour time to reproduce the necessary means of consumption for workers, but also surplus labour time by utilizing the use-value of the commodity labour power, after paying its value in the form of wages to enable workers to obtain necessary labour time as the substance of value of the commodity. The entire product produced by using the commodity labour power is necessarily owned by capital, and has to be sold as commodities so as to recover the invested values of means of production together with the value of labour power, and to realize surplus value. Correspondingly, workers have to purchase the necessary means of consumption and services in a market by wages being paid to them in exchange for their labour power. Thus, a capitalist society forms a thorough market economy to treat the whole means of production and consumption as commodities.

At the same time, capital renders the mass of deskilled and homogeneous workers easily replaceable by each other or capable of being shifted from one job to another through the development of machinery and automated systems. Usually capital leaves a certain portion of workers unemployed, or in various forms of an industrial reserve army to be mobilized flexibly in the process of capital accumulation. These conditions are indispensable for capital to adjust supply to demand in an anarchical market and, further, to control workers easily in workplaces. Conversely, when a capitalist economy approaches full employment through over-accumulation of capital, wages inevitably rise and squeeze the profit rate. At the same time, the tightened labour market, with a rise in wages, creates difficulties in the adjustment of disequlibrium among industries, inducing speculative trading, and thus results in an economic crisis, as we saw at the beginning of 1970s in advanced capitalist countries (see Armstrong *et al.* 1991; Itoh 1990).

As the commodity form of labour power is thus an essential precondition for capitalism, and simultaneously a crucial source of contradiction in the capitalist economy, one of basic aims of socialism must be the abandoning of commodity labour power so as to make workers the masters of their society, on the basis of public ownership of means of production. The Soviet type of centrally planned economy, though it deprived people of the freedom to choose jobs, solved the threat of unemployment and guaranteed all the workers jobs through planned allocation of workers to necessary firms and places. At the same time, the functions of wages were reduced by increasing socially common consumption, or supplying more and more free or very cheap child care, education, medical care, public transport and housing.

Chinese socialism before the economic reforms also allocated workers to people's communes and state-owned enterprises without causing unemployment. Child care, education, medical care and housing were socially supplied within people's communes and state-owned enterprises. In such a system, however, workers were not allowed a free choice of occupation, or permitted to move for a better job. State-owned enterprises and people's communes tend to be inefficient as a result of keeping excessive workers. Therefore, in the process of economic reform of a socialist market economy, specific forms of labour market began to reappear, mainly in three aspects in the Chinese economy.

First, in agricultural villages an excessive labouring population has tended to be pushed out from agricultural family farms as labour productivity rises in limited areas for farming under the Contract Responsibility System. The growth of medium-sized and small TVEs served to absorb a large part of such excess labour power. Their share in rural industrial employment increased from 9.2 per cent in 1978 to 28.6 per cent in 1995 (Meng 2000: 37). The proportion of their workers in the total workforce in secondary and tertiary industries reached 42 per cent by 1993, close to the proportion of workers in the urban public sector, which was 49 per cent (Marukawa 2012: ch. 3). The number of their workers has continuously increased to 159 million by 2010, occupying 38.4 per cent of the total working population in rural areas (Sugawara 2011: 289; and see also Marukawa, this volume, Chapter 6). Strictly speaking, not all this flow of labour power from agricultural farms to TVEs immediately formed a market of commodity labour power, since many TVEs were initially cooperative firms and not capitalist. As a large proportion of TVEs have been privatized and turned into owner-manager-type private firms since the latter half of the 1990s, workers employed by these firms actually become wage labourers. In any case, it is remarkable to see such large flows of labour power being absorbed in rural areas outside of agricultural production.

The powerful growth of TVEs has been promoted by central and local government policies and can suggest a way to deal with the long-standing socialist problem of how to reunify agriculture and other industrial activities, given the historical tendency of capitalism to separate them geographically between remote rural villages and industrial towns.

Second, within city areas various non-state-owned enterprises grew and absorbed a large number of workers through a labour market that operated independently of the allocation of workers by the state. As a result, the share of state-owned enterprises in urban employment declined from 78.3 per cent in 1978 to 40.8 per cent in 1999, and further to 18.8 per cent in 2010 (Minami and Makino 2001: 103; Marukawa 2012). Especially through a process of modernization, state-owned enterprises have attempted to restructure, and reduce the number of excess workers, since 1993. They were allowed autonomy to determine wages, and have largely changed the nature of their employment from lifelong tenures to contract jobs lasting limited periods. The number of workers under such contract systems increased from two million in 1984 to 100.9 million in 1999. Marukawa (2012: ch. 3) estimates that 44.4 million workers were laid off from state enterprises between 1993 and 2000. Such laid-off workers cannot go back to their previous jobs in the state enterprises, though they maintain their status as workers of the state enterprises and receive severance pay (alimony) for three years, and other fringe benefits such as the right to continue living in company houses. They have to enter the labour market to seek new jobs.

Third, there has been a continuous large movement of workers with agricultural family registration from villages into towns. Their number is estimated to have increased from 78.5 million in 2000 to 137 million in 2007. Their proportion in urban employment grew from 36.9 per cent to 46.7 per cent (Sugawara

2011: 289). They still face various discriminatory restrictions in socio-economic life compared to workers with urban family registration, such as reduced access to education for their children, and to other public services, and tend to be disadvantaged in working conditions and wage rates (Sugawara 2011: ch. 12). It is clear that the abundant availability of inflow of such relatively cheap labour power to towns and urban areas through the labour market has been an essential factor in the rapid Chinese industrialization.

As a result of the emerging labour market, along with the reformation of state-owned enterprises and the increasing flow of migrant workers from rural villages, the social problem of unemployment became serious in urban areas (Marukawa 2000). In 1997, the number of registered unemployed workers in urban areas reached 5.76 million (3.1 per cent). There are also workers laid off from state-owned enterprises and collectively owned enterprises, amounting to 9.37 million in 1999. Thus, in total the number of unemployed people in urban areas is estimated to be at least 15 million (8.1 per cent). The effective rate of unemployment, including laid-off workers, continued to be at the high level of around 8 per cent in the years 1997–2000 (Marukawa 2012: ch. 3). This figure is genuinely paradoxical against the successful high economic growth rate of the Chinese socialist market economy.

It has been argued that an extensive labour market is actually emerging in China, inevitably with a certain degree of unemployment, and that a more fluid labour market with more efficient information and communication is desirable and necessary for a more efficient market economy (e.g. Meng 2000). In such an argument, the theoretical possibility of differences between the capitalist labour market and the labour market in a socialist market economy tends to be neglected.

One has to admit that a socialist labour market with some industrial reserve army must be necessary to secure the flexible adjustment of employment across various industries and firms in a socialist market economy.[5] However, unemployment in a socialist economy should be theoretically distinguished from that in a capitalist economy. In a capitalist economy, instability and difficulty in personal life in a labour market including unemployment are basically regarded as the economic problem of the individual. Social welfare policies pursued by the state may intervene and mitigate the hardship of unemployment, but they remain supplementary and not fully guaranteed. In contrast, in a socialist economy with public ownership of means of production, instability and difficulty in personal life in relation to the functioning of the labour market should not be relegated to the individual worker's risk and responsibility. Workers in a socialist economy are fundamentally masters of the society who collectively own the major means of production. They are theoretically different from proletarian workers who must survive individually, basically just by selling labour power as a commodity. In a socialist market economy, a socialist form of the labour market must be created, together with a socialist form of industrial reserve army, and must intermediate the flow of workers according to their choice of workplaces as well as changes in social demand. It must essentially be a social intermediary mechanism for movement and migration across various industries and areas for workers as masters of society. The personal life of an unemployed worker in the form of industrial reserve army should not be disastrously threatening, unlike in the case of unemployment in a capitalist economy.

We can better understand in this context the social meaning of the fact that the guarantee of basic severance pay (alimony) for three years, along with vocational retraining opportunities and housing facilities for the workers laid off from Chinese state-owned enterprises. The socialist market economy should certainly aim at a social security system for workers that is superior to the system in a capitalist economy with social democratic policies. In the Chinese socialist economy, the social guarantee or security for workers used to be generally supplied by the state-owned enterprises in urban areas and by people's communes in rural areas. As people's communes were dissolved, and as state-owned enterprises are being modernized so as to be competitive with capitalist enterprises abroad, the problem of how to secure the economic life of unemployed workers, or medical care for ordinary citizens in China, has become a serious social difficulty. The theory and practice of the social security system in China are far from what they should be in a socialist market economy. As a result, unemployment and illness can generally have disastrous consequences for individual workers. The guarantee of severance pay (alimony) for three years with company housing facilities for workers laid off from the state enterprises is not just a conventional compromise for ending the lifelong employment system, but a partial substitute for a more comprehensive social security system to be realized on the Chinese road to socialism.

Lange (1936, 1937), in his classic model of market socialism, presented an idea to compose the income of working people with a free choice of occupation in a market from two different components, one of them being remuneration for their labour and the other being derived from collectively owned capital and natural resources. In Lange's model, the latter component should not affect the choice of occupation or the social allocation of labour, and therefore can be distributed either equally to each person or according to the family structure and age of family members. This model in fact shows that the partial Basic Income system (which is designed to distribute a certain level of income unconditionally and equally to all members of a society), as is argued by Van Parijs (1995) and others in BIEN (the Basic Income Earth Network), is due to be realized in a socialist market economy in the spirit that workers are the real masters of a society with public ownership of means of production. The Chinese model of socialist market economy is still inclined to interpret the social meaning of public ownership of means of production in terms of state control of them, and does not yet fully make use of it as a basis for social security of workers' income and economic life.

Thus, the labour market in a socialist market economy is necessary, but it should be theoretically differentiated from the complete commodification of labour power in a capitalist economy. It should perform the social function of enabling the flexible and efficient movement of workers across workplaces, but should definitely be combined with a solid social security system and stability of the economic life of workers as masters of the society. We should thus be critical of the neo-liberal assertion on the basis of mainstream neo-classical economics, which one-sidedly emphasizes the efficiency of an individualistic, competitive free market including labour allocation, and the necessity to reduce the public roles of administration and social care for working people.

The Chinese task in the twenty-first century: towards a more egalitarian society

Socialism was generally grounded upon the idea of overcoming the instability, inequality and poverty of economic life among people as well as ecological destruction under capitalism, and socially achieving substantial equality in an association of free individuals. 'Collectively becoming wealthier' has been a Chinese expression of such a socialist idea.

In the process of expanding the market economy, however, unequally richer persons have emerged among managers of various types of business enterprises in coastal cities, as well as farmers in suburbs near cities. Although rural farmers' income was improved in the initial phase of Chinese economic reform until the middle of 1980s by the introduction of the Contract Responsibility System combined with political support for increasing prices of agricultural products, it thereafter faltered and was left far behind the economic growth in urban areas. This worked as an important background to continually maintain low wages and generated a large number of migrant workers from rural villages with agricultural family registration. Wage incomes became differentiated, as wages of regular workers with urban family registration tend to rise more rapidly. Although wages of migrant workers from rural areas also began to rise at an annual rate of 20 per cent after 2004 (Marukawa 2012: ch. 3), the unevenness of income and wealth distribution has conspicuously widened in China.

Li (2011) cites reports of the World Bank, among others, to state that in 2005 the wealthiest 10 per cent of households held 31 per cent of Chinese income, while the poorest 10 per cent held only 2 per cent. The ratio of average disposable income per person for urban inhabitants against that of rural village inhabitants has continuously risen, from 2.2 in 1990 to 2.8 in 2000, and further to 3.3 in 2007 in China (Yan 2011: 255).

These historical facts and trends are utterly opposite to the socialist egalitarian ideal. They are an important source of dissatisfaction among the mass of farmers and wage workers, have caused more and more rebellions and strikes, and are seen as powerful evidence of a non-socialist or capitalist economic order in China even from a Marxian standpoint (e.g. Li 2011). The increasing occurrence of economic crimes in China such as corruption (among bureaucrats and managers of enterprises), smuggling and related activities must have been induced in one way or another by the widening inequalities in distribution of income and wealth. They are therefore not easy to reduce just by emphasizing the need to re-establish socialist morals.

Thus, the Chinese government has the task of revising the increased economic unevenness and attempting to create a much more egalitarian society for the twenty-first century if it wishes to continue to pursue a socialist road for and by the working people. There are signs of political endeavour in such a direction already, in four respects.

First, the share of government budget expenditure against Chinese GDP strongly recovered from about 10 per cent in 1995 to 20 per cent in 2008, as a result of fiscal and monetary reforms since 1994. From a socialist standpoint, it was anomalous that the Chinese government had continuously allowed a wide deficit of tax revenue since the latter half of the 1980s, despite continuing high economic growth, so that the share of government revenue in Chinese GDP declined greatly from 31.2 per cent in 1978 to 11.6 per cent in 1997 (Ma 2000: 18). Although it partly reflected a result of strategic decentralization to shift various public functions to local governments, it also seemed to follow the neo-liberal trend common among the advanced capitalist countries of reducing the economic roles of the state, and taxes on corporations and wealthier individuals, so as to attract investment from abroad.

Second, on the basis of greater government revenues the implementation of a policy intentionally to develop the western inland areas has been promoted since the latter half of the 1990s by constructing new industrial cities or reconstructing old cities in those areas, and also by building networks of railways and highways so as to shift the weight of economic growth from the coastal urban areas to the inland areas.

Third, the Chinese government has increased the ratio of expenditure for education and social welfare to 27 per cent by 2007 (from 13 per cent in 1978 and 24 per cent in 1990). The proportion of expenditure on social security in the government budget grew to 11 per cent in 2006 from just 2 per cent both in 1978 and in 1990 (Marukawa 2012: ch. 4). Furthermore, the Chinese government has set up a new slogan to construct a harmonious society since 2007, and endeavours to extend a series of social security systems, including a public medical security system that also covers rural areas.

Fourth, in the face of difficulties in increasing exports, especially during and after the sub-prime world economic crisis, fiscal policies to encourage more domestic demand have been promoted, such as supporting the purchase of electric appliances by rural village families.

In order to supplement and strengthen such policies towards a more egalitarian society, it would be desirable to reconsider the following three theoretical and practical problems.

First, the Chinese tax system needs to be modernized and strengthened. It traditionally contains room for bureaucratic crony operations, and is not yet fair enough. Probably more powerful legal regulations for progressive income tax, succession tax and corporation tax are both desirable and necessary so as to realize a harmonious society in China through the socialist market economy with more satisfactory welfare policies and agrarian policies on the basis of public ownership of the means of production. It will also be desirable if a general consensus among people is established on the maximum disparity of real income after tax, although this can be altered flexibly from time to time. Economic laws, jurisdictions, and public servants and their organizations need to be modernized and strengthened in order to collect taxes fairly.

Social attempts to bring about a more egalitarian income distribution do not militate against economic growth. In the Japanese experience of the post-World War II period of high economic growth until the beginning of the 1970s, a trend for equalization of income, including the effects of redistribution policies for rural agricultural farmers, served continuously to expand domestic demand for an increasing supply of consumer durables, and substantially contributed to the high economic growth by keeping the export dependency rate (against GDP) constantly around 10 per cent. In contrast, the Chinese export dependency rate increased from 18 per cent in 1990 to 52 per cent in 2006 (Yan 2011: 24). It must be desirable for Chinese industrial firms and working people, especially in the current process of world economic crisis, as well as for surrounding Asian countries, if China can reduce such an excessively high export dependency rate by creating a more egalitarian income distribution so as to expand domestic demand. A rise in the exchange rate of the renminbi would also be desirable to bring about the same effect.

Second, in order to realize a more egalitarian economic order it must be worth reconsidering how to treat the logic of differential rent in a socialist market economy. Ground rent and a landowner class living on ground rent have traditionally been targets to abolish, as parasitic income and a parasitic social class in the ideas of socialism. Marx (1894: 799–800) also suggested that differential rent can disappear in a socialist association, by assuming that the land products would be socially estimated at the average labour cost, not at the marginal cost on the worst grade of necessary land, unlike in the capitalist market economy (Marx 1894: 799–800). So long as land is basically owned by the whole people, but utilized by individual farms and enterprises under the Contract Responsibility System, socialist forms of differential rent should explicitly be estimated and paid for by the whole society from the extra profit due to better quality or location of land.

In this regard, the terms of time periods in land use contracts do matter. The usual terms for the Contract Responsibility System on land in China now seem too long. They used to be about 15 years for farmland but have now been extended to about 30 years, and even 50–70 years for urban land for business enterprises. Although extra revenue or profit obtained because of the changed technological and locational circumstances for utilizing certain pieces of land may be counted into the new contract with the state after the terms of Contract Responsibility System have expired, for the length of the existing contract the benefit would accrue to farmers or enterprises that are fortunate enough to have rented such pieces of land near or within rapidly growing urban cities during the old terms of contract in accord with the initial conditions for expected revenue. As the Chinese coastal urban cities are rapidly expanding demand and business opportunities for suburban farmers and business enterprises in the vicinity of these cities, the logic for them to receive additional extra revenue or profit as a sort of unpaid differential rent during the long years of the terms of a contract period must work as if it were a lucky present from the whole society. It is decisively functioning to increase unevenness in income distribution, especially between rural and urban areas. Although the farmers' right to keep the farmland under the Contract Responsibility System is not very strong, and often cancelled during the terms of contract by one-sided administrative and bureaucratic decisions, the point mentioned above should surely also be taken into consideration in the reforms of the tax system.

Third, occasional rebellious social movements and strikes among rural farmers and urban workers demanding better working conditions or against uneven income distribution, as well as against corruption among administrative bureaucrats and managers in enterprises, should not be suppressed, but treated fairly in the socialist spirit to place working people in the position of real masters of society. In the same spirit, cooperative farmers' unions and trade unions should be encouraged to play more active roles to improve working and living conditions for the common people in China, as a leading model country for many other industrializing countries.

Notes

* This chapter is an extensively updated version of a paper that was first read at an international conference, 'Socialist Political Economy, Contemporary World Capitalism', held in Beijing from 22 to 24 April 2002. The original paper was translated into German by Thomas Hock and published as a Supplement der Zeitschrift, *Sozialismus*, no. 7–8, 2003, and translated also into Chinese in *Review of Political Economy*, no. 2, 2003 (Renmin University Press). Its Japanese version appeared in the *Journal of Tokyo Keizai University*, no. 233, 2003. I am grateful for T. Marukawa's generous advice and assistance in updating the paper as well as for J. Ghosh's editorial help.

1 Nakagane (1999: 207–232), for instance, argues that many people in the world interpret Deng Xiaoping's notion 'socialism with Chinese characteristics' as 'capitalism with Chinese characteristics'. In his view, public ownership of means of production cannot be consistent with a market economy, a market socialist economy cannot function, and socialism in China is in the process of self-dissolution.

2 When Harvey (2011: 270) states that '[t]he world is bifurcated between deficit paranoia in North America and Europe and a Keynesian expansionism in east Asia, led by China', he clearly seems to classify China as a central member in a group of capitalist countries in East Asia practising Keynesianism.

3 For example, Takumi (2001) and most of the 13 papers collected in Sugawara (2011) stand for this type of view among the Japanese Uno School. Yan (2011) shows a similar view in Japan, though not a member of the Uno School.

4 There is a problem as to whether and how the Chinese socialist market economy is to be distinguished from the notion of market socialism. So far as the former intends to maintain a socialist road upon the basis of public ownership of major means of production in combination with functions of a market economy, its essential character can be well understood as an actual model of the latter. In this regard, this chapter treats the former as essentially going on to construct a Chinese-characteristic market socialism, though it contains much more complex or immature aspects than any theoretical models of market socialism.

5 Reconsidering the historical experience in the Soviet, where the planned economy became so inflexible and hard to restructure with exhaustion of rural industrial reserve army in the 1970s, a socialist form of industrial reserve army must be necessary to maintain flexibility of industrial restructuring and adjustment even in a planned economy (cf. Itoh 1995b: ch. 8).

References

Armstrong, P., Glyn, A. and Harrison, J. (1991) *Capitalism since 1945*, Oxford: Basil Blackwell.

Harvey, D. (2011) *The Enigma of Capital: And the Crises of Capitalism*, London: Profile Books.

Itoh, M. (1990) *The World Economic Crisis and Japanese Capitalism*, London: Macmillan; New York: St Martin's.

Itoh, M. (1992) [*Contemporary Socialism*], Tokyo: Kodan-sha; translated into Chinese by Ro, E. [*Problems of Contemporary Socialism*]. Beijing: Social Sciences Literature Press, 1996.

Itoh, M. (1995a) *Political Economy for Socialism*, London: Macmillan; New York: St Martin's.

Itoh, M. (1995b) [*Market Economy and Socialism*], Tokyo: Heibon-sha, translated into Chinese under the same title and published Beijing: Central Party School Publishing Co., 1996.

Itoh, M. (2010) 'The historical significance and the social costs of the subprime crisis: drawing on the Japanese experience', *World Review of Political Economy*, 1 (2).

Lange, O. (1936, 1937) 'On the economic theory of socialism', *Review of Economic Studies*, October, February.

Li, M. (2011) 'The rise of the working class and the future of the Chinese Revolution', *Monthly Review*, 63 (2) (June).

Ma, J. (2000) *The Chinese Economy in the 1990s*, Basingstoke, UK: Macmillan; New York: St Martin's.

Marukawa, T. (2000) ['Present and future of the unemployment problem'], in K. Nakagane, K. (ed.) [*Structural Changes in Contemporary China*], vol. 2, Tokyo: University of Tokyo Press).

Marukawa, T. (2012) A draft of *Contemporary Chinese Economy*], Tokyo: Yuhikaku (forthcoming).

Marx, K. (1867, 1885, 1894), *Capital*, vols I, II, III, trans. B. Fowks, and D. Fernbach, Harmondsworth, UK: Penguin, 1976, 1978, 1981.

Meng, X. (2000) *Labour Market Reform in China*, Cambridge: Cambridge University Press.

Minami, R. and Makino, F. (eds) (2001) [*Introduction to Chinese Economy*], Tokyo: Nihonhyoron-sha.

Nakagane, K. (1999) [*Chinese Economic Development*], Tokyo: Yuhikaku.

Roemer, J. (1994) *A Future for Socialism*, Cambridge, MA: Harvard University Press.

Ryu, S. (1998) ['An introductory inquiry into economic reforms of public ownership and introduction of the joint-stock company system into state-owned enterprises in China'], in [*Journal of Tokyo-Keizai University*], no. 209.

Smith, A. (1776) *The Wealth of Nations*, ed. E. Cannan, 2 vols, London: Methuen, 1922.

Sugawara, Y. (ed.) (2011) [*The Present of Chinese Socialist Market Economy*], Tokyo: Ochanomizu-shobo.

Takumi, M. (2001) [What is a socialist market economy?], in Risho University, *Keizaigaku-kiho*, 50 (3/4) (March).
Uno, K. (1950, 1952) [*Principles of Political Economy*], 2 vols, Tokyo: Iwanami-shoten.
Uno, K. (1964) *Principles of Political Economy*, trans. T. Sekine, Brighton: Harvester Press, 1980.
Van Parijs, P. (1995) *Real Freedom for All: What (if Anything) Can Justify Capitalism?*, Oxford: Oxford University Press.
Yan, C. (2011) [*Economic Development and Institutional Changes in China*], Kyoto: University of Kyoto Press.

Part III

Indian perspective

8 Growth and emergent constraints in the Indian economy in the context of global uncertainty

Jayati Ghosh

Introduction

India is increasingly regarded (along with China) as one of the 'success stories' of globalization, likely to emerge as a giant economy in the twenty-first century. This perception has been bolstered by the apparent ability of the Indian economic growth process to withstand the worst effects of the global financial crisis, and to experience only a minor slowdown of output growth rather than any actual decline in national income. The subsequent post-recession resurgence has further reinforced the idea that the Indian economy is now capable of rapid expansion under its own steam, and has led some to argue that it, along with other dynamic parts of developing Asia, can become an alternative growth pole in the global economy. The country has recently experienced an economic boom that has been relatively prolonged, with a confident capitalist class increasingly taking on the world not only in exports but also through investment abroad, and growing self-confidence among the elite, professional and middle classes.

However, there are many reasons why this is at best a partial, and at worst a misleading, perception of the Indian economic reality. This is not just because economic growth has been associated with little improvement in basic social and human development indicators and material conditions for a large part of the population. It is also because the recent economic growth experience is based on a relatively fragile pattern of external dependence that may be hard to sustain over the medium term. These ideas are further developed in this chapter. In the first section, a brief historical background is provided in order to situate the recent growth process. The second section examines the nature of recent growth is examined. In the third section, the social underpinnings of the growth process are identified. The final section discusses the prospects for the future in the context of a likely global slowdown.

The historical context

India's transition in 1991 to a liberal and open economic policy regime was an event of great historical significance. The questions of why and how the transition occurred, the effects it had on the pace and pattern of growth, and the outcomes in the form of employment generation and distribution are still being debated. What is clear is that the transition did not occur because of the loss of momentum under the post-independence import substitution strategy. That loss of momentum had occurred much earlier and was heralded by the crisis of the mid-1960s, following which the Indian economy experienced a period of secular stagnation till the 1980s.

Three mutually reinforcing and interrelated contradictions in the post-independence growth strategy explain the prolonged stagnation of the mid-1960s to the early 1980s. To start with, despite talk of land reform, of providing 'land to the tiller' and curbing the concentration of economic power, little was done to attack and redress asset and income inequality in the wake of independence. One consequence of the resulting persistence of asset and income inequality was that there were definite limits to the expansion of the market for mass consumption goods in the country. The large mass of peasantry, faced with insecure conditions of tenure and often obtaining only a small share of the outputs they produced, had neither the means nor the incentive to invest. The prospect of increasing productivity and incomes in rural India, which was home to the majority of its population, in order to stimulate domestic demand was therefore limited. The absence of any radical land redistribution had meant that the domestic market, especially for industrial goods, had remained socially narrowly based.

Under these circumstances, a continuous growth in state spending was essential for the growth of the market. In the event, the stimulus to growth during the early post-independence years came from the state itself. It provided domestic capitalists with a large once-and-for-all market for manufactures by widening and intensifying protection and displacing imported goods from the domestic market. It sought to expand that market through its current and capital expenditures, and it supported the domestic capitalist class by investing in crucial infrastructural sectors and channelling household savings to finance private investment through the creation of a number of industrial development banks.

This strategy did pay dividends during the decade and a half immediately following independence, when rates of industrial growth were creditable by international standards. By the mid-1960s, however, the stimulus offered by import substitution was exhausted, because the pattern of industrialization that emerged did not generate a continuously growing domestic market. Further, the ability of the state to continue to provide the stimulus to growth was also undermined by fiscal constraints. This was related to the second of the contradictions characterizing the process of development. The state within the old economic policy regime had simultaneously to fulfil two different roles that were incompatible in the long run. On the one hand, it had to maintain growing expenditures, in particular investment expenditure, in order to keep the domestic market expanding. On the other hand, the strategy was based on transfers to capitalist groups (particularly industrial subsidies of various kinds and relatively low administered prices of important inputs such as fuel costs) that were not compensated for by increased taxes that could finance such growing subsidies. Therefore, the state exchequer was the medium through which large-scale transfers were made to the existing large capital and emerging capitalist groups. The contradiction between these two different roles of the state manifested itself in a deepening fiscal crisis that made it difficult, if not impossible, for the state to continue to fulfil both roles. The implications of this growing fiscal crisis were obvious: the government would sooner or later have to cut back its expenditure, especially investment expenditure, which would slow down the economy and eventually arouse capitalists' demands for an alternative policy regime.

The final contradiction had its roots in the cultural ambience of an ex-colonial society like India. The market for industrial goods was from its very inception, as we have seen, a socially narrowly based one. Capitalism in its metropolitan centres, however, is characterized by continuous product innovation, the phenomenon of ever newer goods being thrown onto the market, resulting in alterations of lifestyles. In an ex-colonial economy like India, the comparatively narrow social segment to whose hands additional purchasing power accrues in large measure, and whose growing consumption therefore provides the main source of the growth in demand for industrial consumer goods, is also anxious to emulate the lifestyles prevailing in the metropolitan centre. It is not satisfied with having more and more of the same goods which are domestically produced, nor is it content merely with expending its additional purchasing power upon such new goods as the domestic economy, on its own, is capable of innovating. Its demand is for the new goods which are being produced and consumed in the metropolitan centres, and which, given the constraints upon the innovative capacity of the domestic economy, are incapable of being locally produced purely on the basis of indigenous resources and indigenous technology.

An imbalance therefore inevitably arises in such economies between what the economy is capable of locally producing purely under its own steam, and what the relatively affluent sections of society who account for much of the growth of potential demand for consumer goods would like to consume. This imbalance may be kept in check by import controls, although such controls inevitably give rise to clandestine imports that are smuggled in and sold in local 'black markets'. There is therefore a basic tendency to liberalize imports. Once these contradictions are taken into account, the balance of payments crisis of the mid-1960s and the subsequent deceleration in industrial growth are explained.

Seen in this light, what was surprising was not the industrial impasse of the mid-1960s but the turnaround in industrial growth in the 1980s. The 1980s witnessed a recovery and even acceleration of industrial growth and manufacturing activity. This return to economic buoyancy cannot be attributed to the emergence of any new source of stimulus to growth. Exports during these years were by no means remarkable enough to stimulate growth in an economy as large as that of India. And the factors that had earlier constrained the expansion of the mass market were still operating. This implied that the stimulus to growth, as before, had to come from the state.

And this is essentially what happened. There were three new features that characterized the 1980s and allowed the economy to escape from the growth impasse of the earlier period. First, there was a big increase in the fiscal stimulus to the economy provided by government spending. Second, there was substantial liberalization of imports, especially of capital goods and components for manufacturing. Third, associated with both of these there was a shift to relying on external commercial borrowing by the state to finance the increases in the consequent fiscal and current account deficits.

In sum, the turnaround in the mid-1980s was a result of the ability of the Indian government to leverage external finance to drive growth in the system. The question that arises, then, is why the Indian government and capitalist class were not able to do this earlier. An answer to that question takes us to developments outside the country, developments that influenced India's medium-term growth prospects significantly. Principal among these developments was the rise to dominance of finance capital in the international economy. The major historical landmarks in the latter process are worth recalling. Till the early 1970s, the private international financial system played only a limited role in recycling financial surpluses to the developing countries. Capital flows to developing countries, barring a few unusual exceptions like South Korea, were through official bilateral and multilateral channels. The period immediately after the first oil shock saw a dramatic change in this scenario. Since oil surpluses were held in the main as deposits with the international banking system controlled in the developed world, the private financial system there became a powerful agent for recycling surpluses. This power was indeed immense. Expenditure fuelled by credit in the developed and developing world generated surpluses with the oil producers, who then deposited these surpluses with the transnational banks, who in turn could offer further doses of credit. By 1981, OPEC countries are estimated to have accumulated surpluses to the tune of $475 billion, $400 billion of which was parked in the developed industrial nations.

Two other developments contributed to the increase in international liquidity during the 1970s and 1980s. First, the United States had built up large international liabilities during the Bretton Woods years, including those resulting from expenditures on the Vietnam War and its policing efforts elsewhere in the world. The explosion of the Eurocurrency market in the 1970s reflected this. This was sustained by the confidence in the dollar stemming from the immediate post-war hegemony of the United States, which made it as good as gold. Such international confidence in its currency allowed the United States to ignore national budget constraints on its international spending and resulted in the emergence of strong banking and financial interests with an international agenda. The influence of these interests was reflected in policies that affected domestic manufacturing interests adversely, as suggested by the widening and persistent US trade deficit after the mid-1970s.

Second, there was a change in demographic structure in most of the advanced countries, with the post-war baby boomers generation reaching an age at which they would emphasize personal savings for retirement. This resulted in growing demands for more variety in savings instruments as well as higher returns, leading to the greater significance of pension funds, mutual funds and the like.

One consequence of these trends was an increase in the international assets of the big banks of the developed world. This trend has gained strength in recent years. In mid-1997, the international asset position of banks resident in 23 countries stood at $9.95 trillion. By June 2007, when 40 countries were reporting, this had risen to $33.71 trillion, with external assets totalling $29.98 trillion. The reason is obvious. Since bank profits depend on the spread between the interest they pay their depositors and the interest they charge their lenders, when deposits with banks grow, their lending must expand. Initially, this lending was within the developed world itself, but soon that was not enough. As a result, developing countries that were earlier considered too risky to lend to or invest in were rediscovered as 'emerging markets' by the international banks, and some among them were offered capital flows if they chose to open their economies. India began exploiting that opportunity in the 1980s in the form of external commercial borrowing, leading to a change in its relationship with international finance.

That change was not without its problems. Exploiting the access to foreign exchange afforded by the rise to dominance of finance internationally, the government resorted to a fiscal stimulus financed with borrowing. The demand stimulus resulting from such expenditure was serviced by domestic industry with the help of imported capital goods, intermediates and raw materials, imports of which were liberalized. This essentially meant that the import intensity of domestic production rose. But such growth was not constrained by inadequate access to foreign exchange, since it was accompanied by an increase in foreign borrowing from the IMF, the international commercial banking system and non-resident Indians. India's foreign debt to GDP ratio doubled during the 1980s. It was when international creditors chose to shut off such credit at the end of the 1980s that India ran into the balance of payments crisis of 1990–91, which provided the grounds for advocates of reform to push through an IMF-style stabilization and adjustment strategy.

It was after this crisis in the early 1990s that India entered a second phase in its relationship with international finance, when the role of other forms of capital flow, especially financial investments in equity markets, became extremely important. To facilitate such flows, regulatory controls on such flows were substantially diluted or dismantled. As a result, in the period between 1993 and 2003 there was a positive but moderate increase in the average volume of capital inflows. But since 2003, there has been a veritable surge. The perception of India as an 'emerging economic power' in the global system derives from the strength it gained from developments during the past decade, when India, like other emerging markets, has been the target of a surge in capital flows from the centres of international finance.

Recent economic growth in India

Recent high economic growth in India has been strongly related to internal and external liberalization measures that generated booms in certain types of domestic economic activity. It is commonly perceived that this reflected the impact of trade liberalization, but in fact changes in finance were probably more significant. India's success as a global player has not been because of a current account surplus resulting from its export performance. Rather, it has stemmed from inflows of capital far exceeding its current account financing requirements. Not only did India become a much-favoured destination for international investors, especially financial investors, but also these investments enabled India's foreign exchange reserves situation to become much more comfortable, thereby further increasing the perception of economic strength and resilience.

Financial deregulation allowed more capital inflows in the form especially of portfolio investment and external commercial borrowing. Domestically, it sparked a retail credit boom and this (combined with fiscal concessions that encouraged more elite consumption) spurred consumption among the richest sections of the population. This led to rapid increases in aggregate GDP growth, even though compressed public spending on basic needs, poor employment generation and persistent agrarian crisis reduced wage shares in national income and kept mass consumption demand low. There was a substantial rise in profit shares in the economy and the proliferation of financial activities. As a result, by the end of the first decade of the twenty-first century, finance and real estate accounted for more than 15 per cent of GDP. This combined with rising asset values to enable a credit-financed consumption splurge among the rich and the middle classes, especially in urban areas. And this in turn generated higher rates of investment and output over the upswing. The earlier emphasis on public spending as the principal stimulus for growth in the Indian economy was thus substituted in the 1990s with debt-financed housing investment and private consumption of the elite and burgeoning middle classes.

The recent Indian growth story in its essentials was therefore not unlike the story of speculative bubble-led expansion that marked the experience of several other developed and developing countries in the same period (Ghosh and Chandrasekhar 2009a). Both history and comparative experience tell us that such a trajectory is inevitably marked by instability, unevenness and greater vulnerability to internally and externally generated financial crises (Ghosh and Chandrasekhar 2009b; Chandrasekhar and Ghosh 2004, 2006).

Until the late 1990s, India relied on capital flows to cover a deficit in foreign exchange needed to finance its current transactions, because foreign exchange earned through exports or received as remittances fell substantially short of payments for imports, interest and dividends. More recently, however, India has been receiving excess capital. Hence, capital inflows are forcing India to export capital, not just because accumulated foreign exchange reserves need to be invested but also because it is seeking alternative ways of absorbing the excess capital that flows into the country.

Policy has had a major role in this. Underlying the surge in portfolio inflows was a continuous process of liberalization of the rules governing such investment: its sources, its ambit, the caps it was subject to and the tax laws pertaining to it. Both stock market buoyancy and volatility became phenomena typical of the post-liberalization years. The presence of foreign institutional investors generated market volatility because of the structure of India's financial markets, which are relatively thin or shallow in at least three senses. First, stocks of only a few companies are actively traded in the market. Thus, the BSE Sensex includes only 30 companies out of more than 8,000 companies listed on the stock exchange. Second, of these stocks there is only a small proportion that is routinely available for trading, with the rest being held by promoters, the financial institutions and others interested in corporate control or influence. Third, the number of players trading these stocks is also small. The net impact is that speculation and volatility are essential features of such markets, and the behaviour of a small number of foreign portfolio investors can have dramatic and magnified effects on share prices.

The growing presence of foreign portfolio investors further has a number of macroeconomic implications. Most importantly, it forces the state to adopt a fiscal stance designed to appease financial interests. Those interests are against deficit-financed spending by the state, which is seen to increase the liquidity overhang in the system, and therefore as being potentially inflationary. Inflation is anathema to finance since it erodes the real value of financial assets. Since government spending is 'autonomous' in character, the use of debt to finance such autonomous spending is seen as introducing into financial markets an arbitrary player not driven by the profit motive, whose activities can render interest rate differentials that determine financial profits more unpredictable. If deficit spending leads to a substantial build-up of the state's debt and interest burden, it may intervene in financial markets to lower interest rates with implications for financial returns. Financial interests wanting to guard against that possibility tend to oppose deficit spending. Finally, the use of deficit spending to support autonomous expenditures by the state amounts to an implicit legitimization of an interventionist state, and therefore a de-legitimization of the market. Since global finance seeks to de-legitimize the state and legitimize the market, it strongly opposes deficit-financed, autonomous state spending.

Efforts to curb the deficit inevitably involve a contraction of public expenditure, especially expenditure on capital formation, which adversely affects growth and employment; leads to a curtailment of social sector expenditures that sets back the battle against deprivation; impacts adversely on food and other subsidies that benefit the poor; and sets off a scramble to privatize profit-earning public assets, which renders the self-imposed fiscal straitjacket self-perpetuating. All the more so since the finance-induced pressure to limit deficit spending is institutionalized through legislation such as the Fiscal Responsibility and Budget Management Act passed in 2004 in India, which constitutionally binds the state to do away with revenue deficits and limit fiscal deficits to low, pre-specified levels.

All this has not received the attention it deserves, because the liquidity in the Indian economy resulting from the capital surge has helped sustain a credit-financed, private expenditure-based process of growth in the economy. Credit financed purchases of housing, automobiles, durables and ordinary goods and services has driven growth to near 9 per cent levels for the past few years, barring the period of the Great Recession. This has diverted attention from certain disconcerting features of India's external payments position, such as the excessive reliance on remittance inflows to keep the current account deficit within manageable limits; and the recent widening of that deficit on account of larger merchandise trade deficits and recent declines in revenues from services.

Ever since India opted for its first big IMF loan in 1981 in the aftermath of the second oil shock, increased dependence on foreign capital inflows has been justified on the grounds that they provide India with the wherewithal to transform its economic structure and redress what is its long-term weakness: poor export performance. It was argued that capital flows would allow the country to liberalize trade and subject domestic economic agents to efficiency-enhancing international competition; permit Indian firms to access the foreign exchange needed to import the capital and technology required to modernize their equipment and establish internationally competitive capacities that would allow them to compete in export markets; bring with them international producers intent on using India as a base and source for production for the world market; and finance any 'interim' deficit resulting from an import surge that might follow trade liberalization but precede India's transformation into a successful exporter.

What the long-term tendency in the merchandise trade deficit indicates is that close to two decades after the programme of accelerated liberalization was adopted, these expectations have remained unrealized. India has been successful as an exporter of workers who send back remittances, and as an exporter of services of various kinds, but has largely failed in its original effort to become a hub for the export of manufactures, since its manufacturing exports still are mostly concentrated in the traditional sectors like gems and jewellery, or in intermediate products. In fact, periods when the merchandise trade deficit was low were ones in which low growth or recessionary conditions were resulting in curtailed imports rather than years in which exports were booming. It was only because of the country's 'invisibles' income from remittances and services that the current account deficit for much of this period was kept low. Yet the deficit implies that India's comfortable foreign reserves are borrowed and not earned. Indeed, the period after 2004–05, when India moved onto a high-growth trajectory of between 8 per cent and 9 per cent per annum, is a period when the merchandise trade deficit widened quite sharply.

So, the recent boom has been fundamentally dependent upon greater global integration, not just in trade of goods and service, but even more significantly with respect to internationally mobile finance capital that chose to make India one of its favoured destinations among emerging markets. The dependence of GDP growth upon largely debt-fuelled consumption of a relatively small segment of the population rather than mass demand meant a more limited and ultimately more fragile domestic market. Export growth in software, IT-enabled services and some manufactures remains high but export-oriented employment is simply not large enough to counter the effects of inadequate productive employment generation in domestic sectors. High rates of investment continue to be driven by expectations of rapid growth of the domestic market as well as very substantial fiscal sops in the form of tax incentives and implicit subsidies, but these cannot increase beyond a certain point. Most of all, bubbles, whether they are driven by inflows of foreign capital or by domestic credit expansion to chosen sectors, are liable to burst, and the most adverse consequences are usually felt by those (such as workers) who did not really gain much in the period of boom.

But it is not only the fact that such growth is part of a credit-driven bubble that is a problem. It is the other major feature of the growth process, the lack of spread of its benefits, that is probably of greater concern. In fact, to paraphrase Charles Dickens, while these are the best of times for some, they are also the worst of times for others (which may well include the majority of Indians) because of the growing dichotomy in conditions of living. While this has been an unfortunate feature of the Indian development process since the start, it has reached newer and sharper levels in terms of inequality and material insecurity in the past decade.

Social underpinnings of capitalist accumulation

If we take a long view, there are some clear achievements of the Indian economy since independence – most crucially, the emergence of a reasonably diversified economy with an industrial base. The past 25 years have also witnessed rates of aggregate GDP growth that are high compared to those in the past and also compared with those in several other parts of the developing world. Significantly, this higher aggregate growth has thus far been accompanied by macroeconomic stability, with the absence of extreme volatility in the form of financial crises such as have been evident in several other emerging markets. There has also been some reduction (although not very rapid) in income poverty. However, there are also some clear failures of this growth process even from a long-run perspective. Despite more than six decades of independence, the development project is nowhere near completion in India. It is also clear that, over time, some elements of that project seem even less likely to be achieved than in the past, despite relatively rapid economic growth.

An important failure is the worrying absence of structural change, in terms of the ability to shift the labour force out of low-productivity activities, especially in agriculture, to higher-productivity and better-remunerated activities. As is evident from Table 8.1, rising investment rates have clearly contributed to GDP growth, but that growth has been concentrated in the tertiary sector, and higher investment rates have not really generated the expected expansion in industry. The share of the secondary sector in GDP has remained at around one-quarter for the past two decades. Dramatic increases in services incomes mean that these have accounted for most of the economic expansion in the recent 'high-growth' phase of the Indian economy, but the modern high-value services (especially ICT) that are seen as the growth engine account for only a relatively small proportion of employment even in services.

Table 8.1 Structural change in the Indian economy

Period	*Per cent of GDP*			
(3-year averages)	*Investment rate*	*Share of primary sector*	*Share of secondary sector*	*Share of tertiary sector*
1950–52	15.5	59	13.4	27.6
1960–62	19.4	53.1	17.3	29.6
1970–72	23.8	46.6	20.4	33
1980–82	22	41.3	21.8	36.9
1990–92	26	34.4	24	41.6
2000–02	26.2	26.1	24.7	49.2
2008–10	30.2	17.9	25.3	56.8

Source: CSO National Accounts Statistics, various issues.

Within primary activities, agriculture continues to account for around half of the total workforce and more than two-thirds of the rural workforce even though its share of GDP is now less than 15 per cent (CSO National Accounts Statistics 2010). In the past decade and a half, agrarian crisis across many parts of the country has impacted adversely on the livelihood of both cultivators and rural workers, such that cultivation is barely viable, especially in the rain-fed parts of the country. Yet the generation of more productive employment outside this sector remains woefully inadequate.

Other major failures, which are directly reflective of the still poor status of human development in most parts of the country, are in many ways related to this fundamental failure of structural transformation. These include the persistence of widespread poverty; the absence of basic food security for a significant proportion of the population, and indeed evidence of growing food insecurity in terms of nutritional outcomes; the inability to ensure that basic needs of housing, sanitation and adequate health care are provided to the population as a whole; the continuing inability to ensure universal education and the poor quality of much school education; and the sluggish widening of access to education and employment across different social groups, and for women in particular. In addition, there are problems caused by the very pattern of economic growth: aggravated regional imbalances; greater inequalities in the control over assets and in access to incomes; and dispossession and displacement without adequate compensation and rehabilitation.

Seen in this light, it becomes apparent that a basic feature of the process of economic development in India has been exclusion: exclusion from control over assets; exclusion from the benefits of economic growth; exclusion from the impact of physical and social infrastructure expansion; exclusion from education and from income-generating opportunities. This exclusion has been along class or income lines, by geographical location, by caste and community, and by gender. However, exclusion from these benefits has not meant exclusion from the system as such – rather, those who are supposedly marginalized or excluded have been affected precisely because they have been incorporated into market systems. We therefore have a process of exclusion through incorporation, a process that has actually been typical of capitalist accumulation across the world, especially in its more dynamic phases. In fact, this process of simultaneous incorporation and exclusion has been especially marked in the recent phase of rapid accumulation over the past two decades, when the Indian economy has been viewed globally as 'a success story'.

Thus, peasants facing a crisis of viability of cultivation have been integrated into a market system that has made them more reliant on purchased inputs in deregulated markets while becoming more dependent upon volatile output markets in which state protection is completely inadequate. The growing army of 'self-employed' workers, who now account for more than half of India's workforce, have been excluded from paid employment because of the sheer difficulty of finding jobs, but are nevertheless heavily involved in commercial activity and exposed to market uncertainties in the search for livelihood. Those who have been displaced by developmental projects or other processes, and subsequently have not found adequate livelihood in other activities, are victims of the process of economic integration, though excluded from the benefits.

In terms of employment patterns, the recent economic growth process in India exhibits a problem that is increasingly common throughout the developing world: the apparent inability of even high rates of output growth to generate sufficient opportunities for 'decent work' to meet the needs of the growing labour force (Figure 8.1) (Chandrasekhar and Ghosh 2007; Sharma 2006; Sundaram 2007).[1] One remarkable feature has been the deceleration and stagnation of formal employment growth despite accelerated output growth, and the lower intensity of employment in the most dynamic manufacturing and services subsectors (Kannan and Raveendran 2009; Arora 2010). Second, despite rapid

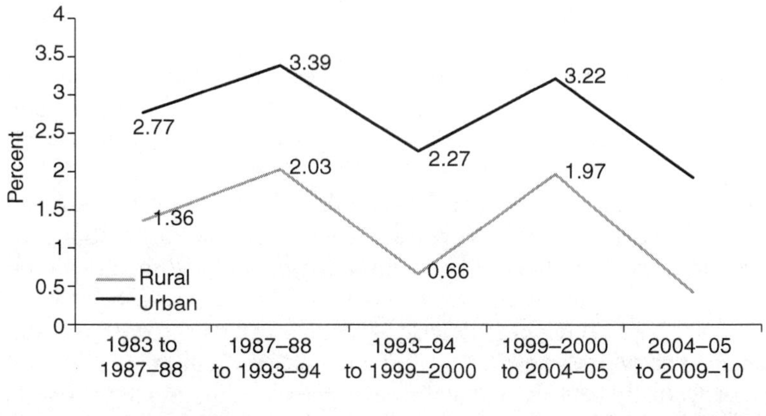

Figure 8.1 Rates of growth of unemployment in India (source: calculated from NSSO (employment rates) applied to population estimates of the Census of India).

increases in labour productivity in some sectors, as well as rapid increases in GDP growth as a whole, real wages of almost all categories of workers have barely grown and there have been increasing gender gaps, particularly in urban wages (Ghosh 2009). Third, there have been shifts in the type of employment, with declines in the proportion of all forms of wage employment and corresponding increases in self-employment, often at very low rates of remuneration. This means that around half of those making up the workforce in India currently do not work for a direct employer, and that is the case not only in agriculture but also in a wide range of non-agricultural activities.

These unfortunate features are not because of the 'failure' of the economic growth process: rather, they are fundamental to the accumulation process itself, which actually *requires* the continuing impoverishment of certain sections for its very success. This requirement also reflects the fact that the strategy is not based on the development of a domestic market based on wage demand, which would have seen wage growth as a positive feature, but on greater export competitiveness based on 'low-road' industrialization. As a result, it is the ability to rely on the surpluses generated by different categories of workers, as well as the new potential surpluses thrown up by land acquisition and various activities of the state, that has enabled Indian capitalists to invest more (both domestically and abroad) and expand production of goods and services at an increasing rate. The process of capitalist accumulation in India has utilized the agency of the state to further the project of primitive accumulation through diverse means (including land use change as well as substantial fiscal transfers) and has also exploited specific socio-cultural features, such as caste, community and gender differences, to enable greater labour exploitation and therefore higher surplus generation. This argument can be illustrated with the examples of different kinds of workers: those engaged in petty production as self-employed workers; workers operating in segmented labour markets by virtue of social discrimination and exclusion; and women workers engaged in paid and unpaid labour.

Petty production

A fundamental though apparently contradictory feature of the recent Indian accumulation process is that it has simultaneously destroyed old forms of petty production and created new ones, which are reflective of the inadequate generation of paid jobs.

The most direct evidence of this is in agriculture. The prolonged agrarian crisis is largely a policy-determined crisis reflecting the falling viability of peasant cultivation. Lack of public investment in agriculture and in agricultural research has been associated with low to poor yield increases, especially in dryland agriculture, and falling productivity of land. Greater trade openness and market orientation of farmers have led to shifts in acreage from traditional food crops that were typically better suited to the ecological conditions and the knowledge and resources of farmers, to cash crops that have increasingly relied on purchased inputs. Public provision of different inputs for cultivation and government regulation of private input provision have been progressively reduced, leaving farmers at the mercy of large seed and fertilizer companies, and input dealers. Attempts in most developing countries to reduce subsidies to farmers in the form of lower power and water prices have added to cultivation costs. Financial liberalization has moved away from policies of directed credit and provided other, more profitable (if less productive) opportunities for financial investment, so farmers are forced to opt for much more expensive informal credit networks that have added to their costs. Meanwhile, the ecological implications of pollution, degradation and over-exhaustion of nature, as well as climate change, have led to loss or declining quality of cultivable land and crop failures.

However, while this particular type of expansion of capitalism displaces and destroys the economic viability of the peasantry, it does not create an equivalent working class that finds paid employment. This is because large capital does not generate enough employment, as technological progress enables rises in labour productivity and facilitates the expansion of 'relative surplus value' in the modern sectors. So, the reserve army here is more than a disciplining device: it expands inevitably because of the nature of capitalist accumulation in the current phase. This generates the changing nature of the working class: growth of self-employment ('informal' employment) because of (underlying) growth of the reserve army, as well as due to particular relationships being developed by capital that pass on risks of production to workers, such as outsourcing.

Nevertheless, the current strength of capital therefore derives at least partly from the persistence and even expansion of petty production in some form or other. Such a category of workers, which is typically engaged in precarious and low-productivity employment, acts as an extended reserve army of labour. It was once posited that this category of work also typically had high underemployment, but it is now recognized that this is not underemployment in the traditional sense. Rather, such workers typically have to work long hours in poor conditions for very poor remuneration, as indicated by the National Sample Surveys on employment in 2004–05 and 2009–10 (NSSO 2006, 2011). Most significantly, from the point of view of the Indian corporate sector, different degrees of outsourcing have blurred the lines between formal and informal activities, and the proliferation of such low-paying self-employment has become an important means of reducing costs for the corporate sector as well passing on the risks of production to smaller units that are essentially part of the working class.

The extent to which all successful formal economic activities in India rely on the implicit subsidies provided by cheap informal labour is largely unrecognized. Yet corporate profitability in India hinges substantially on the lowering of a wide range of fixed costs through outsourcing. Thus, for example, the success of the much-lauded software industry in India has come about only partly because India's skilled IT professionals are cheaper than their international counterparts. A significant part of the lower costs comes from the entire range of support services: cleaning and maintenance of offices, transport, security, back office work, catering, and so on. These are usually outsourced to smaller companies that hire temporary workers with much lower wages, no job security, very long hours of work and hardly any form of worker protection or other benefits. Without the cost advantages indirectly conferred by these low-paid workers, the domestic software industry would find it much harder to compete internationally. The same is true of a wide range of corporate activities across both manufacturing and the newer services.

Socially segmented labour markets

These processes of direct and indirect underwriting of the costs of the corporate sector have been greatly assisted by the ability of employers in India to utilize social characteristics to ensure lower wages to certain categories of workers. Caste and other forms of social discrimination have a long tradition in India, and they have interacted with capitalist accumulation to generate peculiar forms of labour market segmentation that are probably unique to Indian society. Numerous studies (e.g. Thorat 2010) have found that social categories are strongly correlated with the incidence of poverty and that both occupation and wages differ dramatically across social categories. The National Sample Surveys reveal that the probability of being in a low-wage occupation is significantly higher for discriminated-against groups such as Scheduled Tribes, Scheduled Castes, Muslims and Other Backward Classes (in that order) compared to the general 'caste Hindu' population. This is only partly because of differences in education and skill levels, which are also important and which in turn reflect the differential provision of education across social categories.

Such caste-based discrimination has operated in both urban and rural labour markets. An earlier study (Banerjee and Knight 1985), based on a survey of workers in Delhi, showed how there was significant discrimination against Dalit workers (the Dalits being regarded as the lowest caste) operating dominantly through the mechanism of assignment to jobs, with Dalits largely entering poorly paid 'dead-end' jobs, becoming, for example, shop and sales assistants, sweepers, loaders, unskilled construction workers, and other unskilled labourers not classified elsewhere. Their jobs were thus essential ones in both production and services, but their wages were significantly lower than those of other workers, such as drivers and security guards, in even slightly more skilled activities. The study also found that methods of recruitment based on contacts, prevalent in the manual occupations, caused past discrimination to carry over to the present and thereby condemned lower-caste groups to providing poorly remunerated labour that is nonetheless essential to income generation in the economy as a whole.

Similarly, empirical studies of caste behaviour in rural India (Thorat *et al.* 2009) have found that there are many ways in which caste practices operate to reduce the access of the lower castes to local resources as well as to income-earning opportunities, thereby forcing them to provide their labour at the cheapest possible rates to employers. A study by Shah *et al.* (2006) of various caste-based practices in rural areas of 11 states (Punjab, Uttar Pradesh, Bihar, Madhya Pradesh including Chhattisgarh, Rajasthan, Maharashtra, Orissa,

Andhra Pradesh, Karnataka, Kerala and Tamil Nadu) found, in addition to the well-known lack of assets, a large number of social practices that effectively restricted the economic activity of lower-caste and Dalit groups, and forced them to supply very low-wage labour in harsh and usually precarious conditions. In 73 per cent of survey villages, Dalits could not enter non-Dalit homes. In 70 per cent of villages, Dalits could not eat with non-Dalits. In 64 per cent of villages, Dalits could not enter common temples. In 36 per cent of survey villages, Dalits could not enter village shops. In around one-third of the survey villages, Dalits were not accepted as traders dealing with commonly used items of consumption or production. These practices in turn can be used to keep wages of Dalit workers (who are extremely constrained in their choice of occupation) low, even in periods of otherwise rising wages. The persistence of such practices and their economic impact even during the period of the Indian economy's much-vaunted dynamic growth has been noted (Human Rights Watch 2007).

The point to note here is not simply that such practices continue to exist, but that they have become the base on which the economic accumulation process rests. In other words, capitalism in India, especially in its most recent globally integrated variant, has used past and current modes of social discrimination and exclusion to its own benefit to facilitate the extraction of surplus and ensure greater flexibility and bargaining to employers when dealing with workers. So, social categories are not 'independent' of the accumulation process; rather, they allow for more surplus extraction, because they reinforce low employment-generating (and therefore persistently low wage) tendencies of growth.

Women workers

With respect to women's work, there have been four apparently contradictory trends: simultaneous increases in the incidence of paid labour, underpaid labour, unpaid labour and the open unemployment of women. (These issues are elaborated upon in Ghosh 2009.) This is a paradox, since it is generally expected that when employment increases, then unemployment comes down; or when paid labour increases, then unpaid labour decreases. In any case, this marks a clear contrast with other fast-growing economies, including such economies in developing Asia. The experience of most other developing countries in phases of rapid growth has been one of rapid and often substantial increase in female overt work participation, as dynamic capitalism tends to draw in women to expand domestic labour supply for paid employment.

A significant part of the explanation for the paradoxical combination lies in the macroeconomic processes within India, described earlier. For urban women, the increase in regular work has dominantly been in services, including most importantly the relatively low-paid and less desirable activity of domestic service, along with some manufacturing. In manufacturing, there has been some recent growth of petty home-based activities of women, typically with very low remuneration, performing outsourced as part of a larger production chain. But explicitly export-oriented employment, even in special zones set up for the purpose, still accounts for only a tiny fraction of women's paid work in urban India. Meanwhile, self-employment has come to dominate women's activities even in non-agricultural occupations in both rural and urban India, largely because of the increasing difficulty of finding paid work.

A significant and disturbing trend is the evidence on wages: average real wages of women workers increased relatively little over the ten-year period 1993–94 to 2004–05 despite rapid increases in national income over this period, and for some categories of women workers (rural graduates and urban illiterate females) real wages actually declined. What is more, there were fairly sharp increases in gender gaps in wages across all categories of workers. Some of the gender gaps in wages for certain categories of workers, such as production and transport workers, are now among the highest in the world.

Unfortunately, recent public employment has not bucked the overall trend of low average real wages and casual or non-permanent contracts for women workers. While a privileged minority of women in government employment continue to access the benefits of the government's behaving as a 'model employer', new employment for the purpose of providing essential public services has been concentrated in low-remuneration activities with uncertain contracts and hardly any benefits. This is true of school education (with the employment of para-teachers without proper qualifications) as well as health and nutrition (with reliance on minimally trained local women as health workers). Indeed, the provision of basic public services in India has increasingly relied upon the underpaid labour of women workers. The recent introduction of the Mahatma Gandhi National Rural Employment Guarantee (NRGE) scheme is a different kind of public employment, which should offer a maximum of 100 days' work to rural households at minimum wages. Thus far, it has not managed to achieve this, and there are numerous other difficulties that make it difficult for women workers. Even so, it is already evident that women have been actively participating in this scheme much beyond expectation. Because of its emphasis on heavy earth work at daily wages, it typically involves self-selecting by the poor in rural India, and is likely to have the impact of significantly reducing distress migration and improving the bargaining position of workers, especially women workers. However, it is important to ensure that the scheme is made more flexible in the type of work that can be undertaken, as well as more transparent and accountable, as the NREG Act has envisaged.

Conditions of self-employment among women show many of the disturbing tendencies of wage employment. Women's self-employment in non-agricultural work is largely characterized by both low expectations regarding incomes and remuneration, and substantial non-fulfilment of even these low expectations. Despite some increase in high-remuneration self-employment among professionals and micro-entrepreneurs, in general the expansion of self-employment seems to be a distress-driven process determined by the lack of availability of sufficient paid work on acceptable terms. Case studies and evidence from large surveys carried out by the NSS both suggest that payment for home-based work, which is typically on piece rates and accounts for increasing proportions of the economic activity of women, has been declining not only in real but even in nominal terms in many urban centres, despite the economic dynamism of the areas in general.

A consideration of the extent of unpaid work by women indicates that a very substantial amount of women's time is devoted to unpaid labour, often at the cost of leisure and rest. Such unpaid labour is likely to have been increasing over time, especially in the past decade. Public policies have played a role in causing unpaid labour time of women to rise, because of either reduced social expenditure that place a larger burden of care on women, or privatized or degraded common property resources or inadequate infrastructure facilities that increase time spent on provisioning essential goods for the household, or simply because even well-meaning policies (such as for afforestation) are often gender-blind. Once again, the relevant point here is not simply that such gender differences exist, but that they – and therefore the particular forms that patriarchy takes in India – are closely intertwined with processes of capitalist accumulation.

Global uncertainties and medium-term prospects for the Indian economy

Portents for the global economy in the early years of the 2010s have been gloomy at best. It has been increasingly evident that the Indian economy will be also be affected by adverse developments in the rest of the world, whether through the impact of mobile capital flows or through exports being dragged down by the recession in Europe and the economic uncertainty in the United States. How resilient is the Indian economy at present, in the face of these negative global forces? In terms of domestic demand, it is certainly possible for the government to think of ways of rejuvenating the economy, ideally through more broad-based employment-led growth. But since the recent pattern of growth has been crucially related to India's greater global integration, it has created patterns of dependence on international markets and international capital that make the economy significantly more vulnerable.

The trade balance was negative during the first decade of this century, and progressively worsened over that period, as is evident from Figure 8.2. In the early years of the decade, this impact could be kept in check because remittance inflows and software exports ensured that the current account was either in surplus or ran small deficits. But in the second half of this period, even large remittance inflows could not prevent a substantial deterioration of the current account. Despite this, external reserves have kept growing, except for the crisis year 2008–09. This was entirely because of capital inflows, which increased over the decade except in the crisis year. The capital account peaked in 2007–08 with more than $100 billion net inflow.

This reiterates the fact that India's external reserves were effectively borrowed rather than earned, as they were largely growing because of capital inflows. In the second half of the decade, foreign investment (including private equity, which is essentially more short-term in orientation) and external

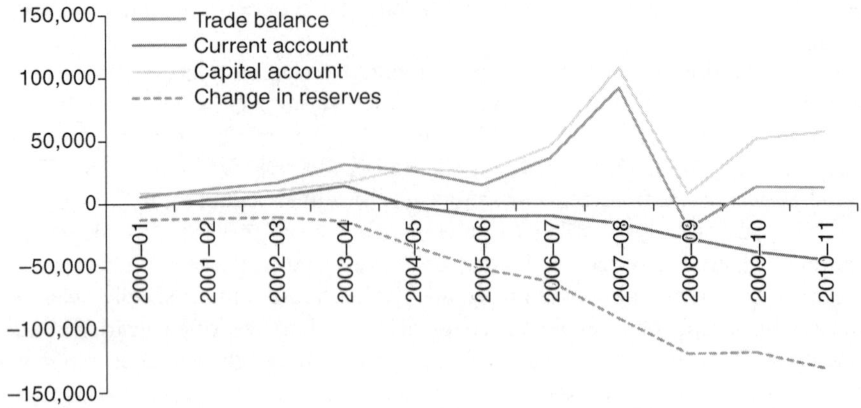

Figure 8.2 India's balance of payments ($ million) (source: Reserve Bank of India online statistical database, accessed 6 January 2012).

commercial borrowing were predominantly responsible for the inflows on the capital account. The negative trade balance indicates the extent to which import liberalization has resulted in a significantly increased propensity to import within the economy. Indeed, because import volumes have risen faster than values, the effects on import-competing activities and on employment and livelihood particularly of small producers are greater. The slow growth of non-agricultural employment despite rapid aggregate GDP growth is at least partly related to the impact of substantially increased import volumes of a wide range of manufactured commodities.

So, recent trends in the external sector were already cause for concern even before the latest impact of the ongoing global economic crisis could be felt. It is not just high energy dependence that is a strategic problem for India. The rapid expansion of non-oil imports suggests an economy that (despite two decades of liberalizing 'reforms') is becoming less externally competitive and generating trade patterns that are likely to continue to have adverse employment effects. Most of all, a trajectory of growth based on capital inflows that generate domestic finance-driven consumption, including significantly high imports and worsening trade balances, is obviously not sustainable.

The recent Indian growth story in its essentials is therefore not unlike the story of speculative bubble-led expansion that marked the experience of several other developed and developing countries, and is therefore subject to similar problems of lack of sustainability. The lack of sustainability is accentuated by the social and political problems that are increasingly emerging, driven by the unequal pattern of growth. Extremist movements are powerful and even dominate in 150 backward and relatively undeveloped districts that are nonetheless the location of extractive industries, as some segments of the local population feel not just marginalized but actively exploited by the current growth process.

Lack of productive employment generation, particularly in formal and 'decent' employment, has not only created social discontent but also directed such discontent to less progressive directions. Thus, it has given rise to powerful demands for regional autonomy and exclusion of 'non-natives' within the different states, such as demands for statehood within sub-regions such as Telengana in Andhra Pradesh and anger against migrant workers fomented by some political parties in Maharashtra and elsewhere. Other forms of criminality are increasing. There is widespread public anger not only at the evident corruption that has been characteristic of this phase but also at the explicit ways in which state policy has favoured the rich. These create potent sources of instability that may rebound on the growth process in unpredictable ways.

However, such a denouement is not inevitable, and can indeed be altered towards a more progressive direction that will allow the real potential of India's economy to be unleashed in future. The critical shift required is most of all in terms of policy orientation, to view the generation of decent work as a *means* to sustainable growth, as well as an end in itself. This approach relies on strong positive multiplier effects to create virtuous cycles of employment and productivity growth. It allows for more stable economic growth that is based on expanding the domestic market, but it does not need to conflict with increasing exports. It encourages a greater emphasis on aggregate productivity growth (rather than only through cutting-edge new technologies), thereby generating a 'high road' to industrialization from the bottom.

Even though India has a large informal sector and therefore it can be perceived that wage-led strategies are more difficult, such a strategy is possible through policies that increase the availability of consumer goods, basic services and various forms of social protection, and also improve the viability of small-scale production. Employment diversification, in terms of a long-term sustained shift of workers away from low-productivity (largely primary-sector) activities to activities with higher productivity and value added, has long been seen as a central aspect of development. The growth of good-quality wage employment in both the public and the private sectors is central to the diversification process. In addition, the conditions of self-employment have to be improved: made less insecure and fragile, and with the removal of excessive burdens of risk that are hard to bear for small producers.

There are several important elements of such a strategy. First of all, the focus of macroeconomic policies must be on the generation of decent work and on improving conditions of life, *not* on income growth per se. This is important because it makes the provision of basic needs (employment as well as access to food, sanitation, housing, health and education) and improving the quality of life of all citizens the central guiding principles. Quantitative GDP growth targets, which still tend to dominate the thinking of policymakers, are not simply distracting from these more important goals, but can even be counter-productive. For example, a chaotic, polluting and unpleasant system of privatized urban transport, involving many private vehicles and over-congested roads, actually generates more GDP than a safe, efficient, affordable and 'green' system of public transport that reduces vehicular congestion and provides a pleasant living and working environment.

Second, it is necessary to ensure the greater viability of informal and small-scale production, through better access to institutional credit to farmers and other small producers (including through directed credit, subsidies, etc.), greater integration into supply chains and marketing that improves their returns, focus on cooperative arrangements that can provide the benefits of scale economies to small producers, and technology improvements that increase labour productivity in such activities. It is particularly important to be aware of the specific needs of women producers and workers in informal activities when designing policies. Such a strategy is critical for both agriculture and other sectors, and the revival of smallholder cultivation is an essential aspect of this.

Third, the strategy must emphasize the expansion of, and better delivery systems in the provision of, public services, especially in nutrition, sanitation, health and education. Improved services allow for improved material and social conditions and have positive employment effects, directly and through the multiplier process. The required increases in public employment incidentally also set the floors for wages and improve the bargaining power of workers. This improved bargaining power is often not recognized as a crucial element in a possible wage-led strategy, but it can be extremely significant, and can be used effectively even in export-oriented economies as long as surpluses from industrialization and exports can be mobilized to provide wage goods publicly. Indeed, it has been an important and unrecognized feature of successful Asian industrialization from Japan to the East Asian NICs to (most recently) China.

Fourth, a related aspect is the need to provide much better social protection, with more funding, wider coverage and consolidation, more health spending and more robust and extensive social insurance programmes, including pensions and unemployment insurance. Such protection is important in itself, particularly for reducing human insecurity and gender gaps in living conditions, and also has great macroeconomic significance because it increases the presence of counter-cyclical buffers that reduce the negative effects of periods of economic downswing.

Obviously, such a strategy requires overall a significant increase in government spending, which seems to be almost an unrealistic demand in the current global economic context. The usual concern is that of finding the resources for it. In a context in which fiscal deficits are seen as anathema, increasing public expenditure appears to be an idealistic and impractical proposal. There are two reasons why this is not true. The first reason is that the multiplier effects of public expenditure in economies with significant unemployment and excess capacity involve increases in income and therefore also public revenues, which means that the increases in spending will not be matched by equivalent increases in deficit. The second reason – the fact that tax revenues raised from the rich can pay for this increased spending – is potentially even more significant in the current socio-political climate because it provides an opportunity to redress the dramatically increasing inequality in assets and incomes that has come to dominate the global economy. It is increasingly evident that across the world there have to be conscious attempts to reduce economic inequalities, both between countries and within countries. We have clearly crossed the limits of what is 'acceptable' inequality in most societies, and future policies will have to reverse this trend. Paradoxically, the extreme inequality that is now evident actually makes it potentially easier to raise resources through taxation, by imposing reasonable taxes on the '1 per cent' of the population that is now increasingly the target of the public protests by the '99 per cent'. Far from disrupting economic activity, as is threatened whenever such taxes are talked of, the use of such revenues in the directions mentioned here is more likely to generate more broad-based and sustainable economic expansion and improved quality of life overall.

Finally, such increased public spending must also be associated with some additional critical features. Greater state involvement must be associated with efforts to make such involvement more democratic and accountable to the people, especially those who have been marginalized or dislocated by the economic growth process. Also, it is not enough to talk about 'cleaner, greener technologies' to produce goods that are based on older and increasingly unviable patterns of consumption. Instead, we need to think creatively about such consumption itself, and work out which goods and services are more necessary and desirable for society as a whole.

Note

1 Applying the participation rates of the NSSO survey of 2009–10 to interpolated population figures from the censuses of 2001 and 2011 shows that total female employment actually declined at an annual rate of 1.72 per cent between 2004–05 and 2009–10, while male employment (mostly in casual work) showed a slight increase, albeit much lower than in the previous period, at an annual rate of 1.72 per cent.

References

Arora, A. (2010) 'Economic dualism, openness and employment in manufacturing industry in India', MPhil thesis, Jawaharlal Nehru University.

Banerjee, B. and Knight, J. B. (1985) 'Caste-based discrimination in the Indian urban labour market', *Journal of Development Economics*, 17: 277–307.

Central Statistical Organisation, Government of India (2010) Estimate of Gross Domestic Product. Online, available at: http://mospi.nic.in/.

Chandrasekhar, C. P. (2008) 'Global liquidity and financial flows to developing countries: new trends in emerging markets and their implications, G24 Working Paper, Geneva: UNCTAD.

Chandrasekhar, C. P. and Ghosh, J. (2004). *The Market That Failed: Neoliberal Economic Reforms in India*, 2nd ed., New Delhi: LeftWord Books.

Chandrasekhar, C. P. and Ghosh, J. (2006a) *Tracking the Macroeconomy*, vol. 1: *The Indian Economy*, Hyderabad: ICFAI University Press.

Chandrasekhar, C. P. and Ghosh, J. (2006b) 'Macroeconomic policy, inequality and poverty reduction in India and China', in G. A. Cornia (ed.) *Pro-poor Macroeconomics: Potential and Limitations*, Basingstoke, UK: Palgrave Macmillan.

Chandrasekhar, C. P. and Ghosh, J. (2007) 'Recent employment trends in India and China: an unfortunate convergence?', *Indian Journal of Labour Economics*, 50 (3). Online, available at: www.macroscan.org/anl/apr07/anl050407India_China.htm.

Chhibber, A., Ghosh, J. and Palanivel, T. (2009) *Asia Rebounds but Lasting Recovery Needs New Paradigm: A Synthesis Study Incorporating Evidence from Country Case Studies*, Colombo, Sri Lanka: United Nations Development Programme. Online, available at: http://web.undp.org/asia/pdf/AsiaRebounds.pdf.

Dasgupta, S. and Singh, A. (2005) 'Will services be the new engine of economic growth in India?', Working Paper 310, Centre for Business Research, University of Cambridge. Online, available at: www.cbr.cam.ac.uk/pdf/WP310.pdf.

Ghosh, J. (2009) *Never Done and Poorly Paid: Women's Work in Globalising India*, New Delhi: Women Unlimited.

Ghosh, J. and Chandraskhar, C. P. (2009a) 'The costs of coupling: the global crisis and the Indian economy', *Cambridge Journal of Economics*, 33: 725–739. doi:10.1093/cje/bep034

Ghosh, J. and Chandrasekhar, C. P. (eds) (2009b) *After Crisis: Adjustment, Recovery and Fragility in East Asia*, New Delhi: Tulika.

Human Rights Watch (2007) *India: Hidden Apartheid: Caste Discrimination against India's 'Untouchables'*, Shadow Report to the UN Committee on the Elimination of Racial Discrimination. Online, available at: www.chrgj.org/docs/IndiaCERDShadow-Report.pdf.

Kannan, K. P. and Raveendran, G. (2009) 'Growth sans employment: A quarter century of jobless growth in Indian organised manufacturing', *Economic and Political Weekly*, 7 March.

National Sample Survey Organisation (NSSO) (2006) *Report on Employment and Unemployment in India 2004–05*, New Delhi: Government of India.

National Sample Survey Organisation (2011) *Report on Employment and Unemployment in India 2009–10*, New Delhi: Government of India.

Shah, G., Mander, H., Thorat, S., Deshpande, S. and Baviskar, A. (2006) *Untouchability in Rural India*, New Delhi: Sage.

Sharma, A. N. (2006) 'Flexibility, employment and labour market reforms in India', *Economic and Political Weekly*, 41 (21) (27 May): 2078–2085.

Sundaram, K. (2007) 'Employment and poverty in India, 2000–2005', *Economic and Political Weekly*, 42 (30) (28 July): 3121–3131.

Thorat, A. (2010) 'Ethnicity, caste and religion: implications for poverty outcomes', *Economic and Political Weekly*, 18 December, pp. 47–53.

Thorat, S., Negi, P., Mahamallik, M. and Senapati, C. (2009) *Dalits in India: Search for a Common Destiny*, New Delhi: Sage.

9 The idiosyncratic nature of India's economic development

Can it be a new model of economic development?

Hideki Esho

The trajectory of economic management since independence

When India became independent in 1947, the Western countries recognized it as the most promising developing country for future economic development. Independent India was based on parliamentary democracy; it had a large economy; it had a reservoir of intellectuals such as higher-ranking officials, lawyers, researchers and journalists; and it produced entrepreneurs with funds and technology who had developed national industries to a certain level since the late nineteenth century. A representative development economist of this time, W. W. Rostow, highly appreciated India as a country on the eve of the 'take-off', along with China (1960).

Soon after independence, the first prime minister, Jawaharlal Nehru, introduced a five-year economic planning system. In the Second Five-Year Plan, which started in 1956, the two-sector growth model of Mahalanobis was introduced. This presented a theoretical pillar to support the the Second Five-Year Plan's strategy of promoting the development of heavy industry. This growth model was based on the notion that when resources were allocated with priority to heavy industries, for a certain period the nation must endure low living standards, but once heavy industries were established, then the higher rate of growth that would ensue would make possible a more affluent level of living. Also in 1956, the Industrial Policy Resolution was promulgated. According to this resolution, all basic industries, such as heavy industries, were entrusted to the public sector. On top of this, private companies were strictly regulated by licensing systems of production and imports. As a result, a mixed-economy system that combined import-substituting industrialization with a large public sector, and was characterized by planning and regulations on industry and finance, was established.

India experienced a serious politico-economic crisis in the middle of the 1960s. This crisis was the result of import-substituting industrialization in a closed economic system that suffered from a chronic shortage of foreign exchange and lagging agricultural production.[1] Soon after the start of the Second Five-Year Plan, the 'over-optimistic' (Tomlinson 1998: 181) prospects for this plan had evaporated. The Second Five-Year Plan had been drafted on the bold assumptions that agricultural production would rise smoothly and that a huge amount of aid resources was available. India faced a severe balance of payments crisis in early 1957 because of rising import costs. By 1956, the sterling balances, which had amounted to over £1,300 million at the end of World War II, had all been spent. The Plan outlay had to be cut in 1958, and in the same year the Aid-India Consortium (made up of Canada, Britain, the United States, West Germany and the World Bank) was set up (Tomlinson 1998: 182). Thereafter, India experienced a chronic foreign exchange shortage throughout the Nehru era. Nehru died in 1964. Erratic monsoon rainfall in the consecutive years of 1965 and 1966 caused a downturn of agricultural production and forced India to import food grain. On top of this, the India–China border conflict in 1962 and the India–Pakistan border conflict in 1965 affected India. As a result, India was faced with triple distress in the form of food shortage, fiscal deficit and foreign exchange shortage in 1966. The Government of India approached the World Bank to get an emergency loan. The World Bank agreed to supply the loan on condition that the government enforced a series of deregulation measures, including a drastic devaluation of the rupee, which was devalued by 37.5 per cent in June 1966. However, the US government suspended aid to India, alleging that the India–Pakistan war was still continuing, and the World Bank loan was also substantially reduced.

Prime Minister Indira Gandhi of the Congress Party, whose victory in the fourth general election in 1967 established her political power, campaigned against the United States and sought to minimize reliance on foreign capital. The Green Revolution strategy (involving a package of high-yielding seed varieties, fertilizers and pesticides to be used on irrigated lands mostly in northern India, along with credit to farmers) was introduced in a serious manner from 1967. This was based on the perception that to establish a self-sufficient food grain production system was the only way to manage India in an independent manner to avoid interventions from powerful foreign countries. In addition, she nationalized 14 major commercial banks and received support from poor farmers as well as from the left-wing political powers with the slogan 'Garibi Hatao' (eradication of poverty). Indira Gandhi concentrated power in her own hands and increased the extent of political intervention in economic management. In this period, personal connections between big business houses and government were further deepened and the black economy expanded through means such as corruption, tax evasion, bribery and smuggling.

From the mid-1960s, a medium-term trend of stagnation of the economic growth rate became conspicuous. The average annual growth rate from 1965–66 to 1979–80 stagnated at 2.94 per cent (calculated from GOI 2011: A7). The main reason for low growth rates was the nature of the economic management in a closed environment. Import-substituting industrialization was further promoted without competition with foreign products and it resulted in 'high-cost and low-quality' made-in-India products.

The 1980s was a period of economic and political turmoil characterized by high inflation (fed by the two global oil price shocks as well as domestic factors).

There were several changes of government as well as a brief attempt at authoritarian rule by Indira Gandhi during the Emergency (1975–77), which was followed by elections in which the Congress Party was soundly defeated. However, the coalition that came to power was unable to provide stability and in 1981 Indira Gandhi was returned to power. In the context of severe balance of payments problems, the government approached the IMF and got an SDR (special drawing rights) 5 billion loan commitment from the IMF. The IMF conditionalities included a series of deregulation measures, including a partial deregulation of the automobile industry. Utilizing this opportunity, the Japanese automotive company Suzuki Motors was involved in the setting up of Maruti Udyog Ltd, a public-sector joint venture company with majority government stakeholding, which started to produce a fuel-efficient 800 cc light car. Until then, the Ambassador car of the Birla group and the Fiat car of the Walchand group had monopolized the car market. The entry of Maruti Udyog introduced the first wave of competition in this market.

In October 1984, Prime Minister Indira Gandhi was assassinated by Sikh extremists involved in a separatist movement for a Sikh state. Soon after her death, her eldest son, Rajiv Gandhi, led the Congress Party to power in the next election. He promoted further deregulation and opening up of the Indian economy, especially modernization of telecommunications and electronics. However, these policy measures did not change the regulation system that had long formed the economic structure of independent India.

Transition to a full-blown economic liberalization regime

Background

In the latter half of the 1980s, the Indian government undertook huge investments based on external commercial borrowing. As a result, GDP growth rates per annum reached 5.7 per cent between 1985–86 and 1990–91. However, as the other side of the coin, fiscal deficits as well as foreign debt swelled. On top of this, the Gulf War adversely affected the Indian economy. Not only did the import bill for oil surge but remittances from migrant workers in the Middle East declined, and foreign reserves decreased to only two weeks of imports. During the general election campaign in 1991, Rajiv Gandhi was assassinated by a Tamil extremist who was fighting for independence from Sri Lanka. The Congress Party won the election by a narrow margin, largely on the basis of sympathy votes. The Congress government, led by Narasimha Rao (June 1991–May 1996) started the New Economic Policy (NEP) with the support of structural adjustment loans from the IMF. This was the beginning of the radical economic liberalization era.

As is well known, in the economic reform programmes under the structural adjustment loans the IMF and the World Bank require the recipient country to implement various conditions. Most of the economic reforms under the conditionality of the IMF and the World Bank have failed to realize the expected results in developing countries. The case of India, however, may be remembered in history as one of the most successful cases of structural adjustment. Why was India able to manage structural adjustment in such a successful manner? The first reason was that, paradoxically, India's NEP did not necessarily follow the speed, sequence and extent that the IMF and World Bank demanded, but a much more gradualist approach (Ahluwalia 2002).

Macroeconomic performance under the NEP regime

The first characteristic of economic performance of the NEP period is satisfactory and steady economic growth. The real GDP growth rates from 1992–93 to 1996–97 were 5.4 per cent, 5.7 per cent, 6.4 per cent, 7.3 per cent and 8.0 per cent. From 1997–98 to 2002–03, growth rates slowed down, but in 2003–04 there appeared a new trend. The five-year average of growth rates from 2003–04 to 2007–08 reached nearly 9 per cent, and India entered a high-growth period (Figure 9.1).

Second, the savings and investment rates have also conspicuously increased since the beginning of the NEP (Table 9.1). The growth rates of savings and investment since 2003–04 have been especially remarkable. By 2007–08, the gross savings rate had increased to 36.8 per cent of GDP and the gross fixed capital formation rate had increased to 38.1 per cent. If we look at savings rates agent-wise, although the main agent of savings remained the household sector, it is noteworthy that the savings rate of the private corporate sector increased

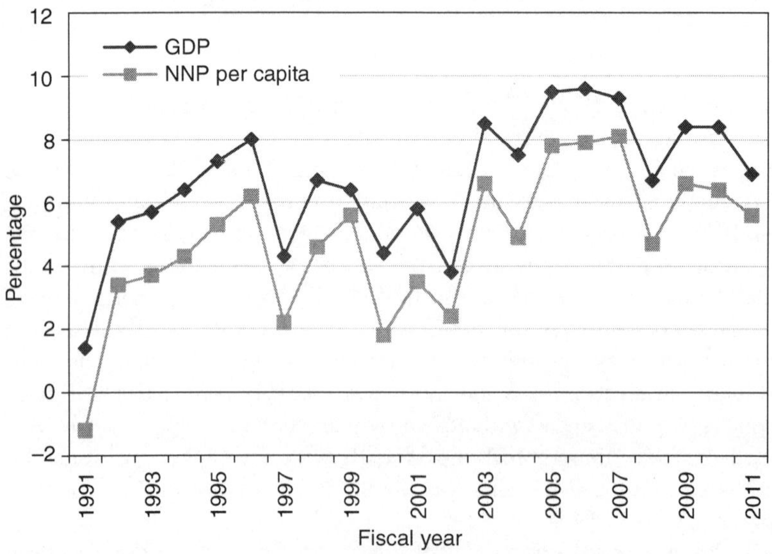

Figure 9.1 Trend of the growth rates of gross domestic product (GDP) and net national product (NNP) per capita, 1991–92 to 2009–10 (%) (source: GOI 2011: 2, A4).

substantially after 2004–05. With an increasing savings rate, the investment rate has also increased from 2002–03 and has exceeded 30 per cent since 2004–05. The importance of the public sector has decreased and the private corporate sector has taken the place of the public sector. India recorded fairly high growth rates in the 1980s, but these depended on public-sector investment, which in turn depended on huge borrowings from domestic as well as foreign markets. As a result, budget deficits were large and foreign debt accumulated, and the

Table 9.1 Gross domestic saving and gross fixed capital formation (as percentage of GDP, at current market price)

Fiscal year	*Household sector*	*Gross domestic saving*			*Gross fixed capital formation*		
		Private corporate sector	*Public sector*	*Total*	*Public sector*	*Private sector*	*Adjusted total*
1980	12.1	1.6	4.1	17.8	9.2	8.9	19.2
1981	10.8	1.5	5.2	17.5	11.0	10.8	18.9
1982	11.2	1.5	5.1	17.8	11.9	10.1	19.1
1983	11.8	1.4	3.9	17.1	10.7	9.3	18.2
1984	12.8	1.6	3.5	17.8	11.5	10.0	19.1
1985	12.7	1.9	3.9	18.4	11.9	11.5	20.6
1986	13.0	1.6	3.5	18.1	12.5	10.9	20.1
1987	15.6	1.6	2.8	20.0	10.8	11.8	21.9
1988	15.3	1.9	2.7	20.0	10.8	13.1	22.8
1989	16.5	2.4	2.4	21.3	10.8	13.1	23.7
1990	18.5	2.6	1.8	22.9	10.6	14.3	26.0
1991	15.7	3.0	2.6	21.3	10.2	12.3	21.8
1992	16.5	2.6	2.2	21.3	9.5	14.7	23.0
1993	17.0	3.4	1.3	21.7	9.1	12.2	22.2
1994	17.9	3.4	2.3	23.6	9.7	13.5	24.7
1995	16.2	4.8	2.6	23.6	8.6	17.5	25.3
1996	15.8	4.4	2.2	22.4	7.8	14.3	23.7
1997	18.1	4.2	1.9	24.2	7.4	17.1	25.6
1998	19.5	3.3	−0.2	23.2	7.3	16.3	24.2
1999	21.8	4.3	−0.5	25.7	7.7	18.5	26.8
2000	21.4	3.7	−1.3	23.8	7.2	16.4	24.4
2001	23.2	3.3	−1.6	24.9	7.2	17.8	24.3
2002	22.3	3.9	−0.3	25.9	6.5	18.0	24.8
2003	23.2	4.6	1.3	29.0	6.6	18.7	26.9
2004	23.6	6.6	2.3	32.4	7.4	23.8	32.8
2005	23.5	7.5	2.4	33.4	7.9	25.2	34.7
2006	23.2	7.9	3.6	34.6	8.3	26.4	35.7
2007	22.4	9.4	5.0	36.8	8.9	28.1	38.1
2008	23.6	7.4	1.0	32.0	9.4	24.8	34.3
2009	25.4	8.2	0.2	33.8	9.2	25.2	36.6
2010[a]	22.3	7.9	1.7	32.3	8.8	24.9	35.1

Source: GOI (2012: A10–A11).

Note
a Quick estimates.

macroeconomic imbalance was accentuated. The economic growth pattern under the NEP is quite different from the pattern observed in the 1980s. It is private corporate investment that leads the high growth under the NEP. Private corporate investment-led growth has strengthened since 1999–2000. Gross private corporate investment as a share of GDP in 2007–08 increased to 28.1 per cent, amounting to almost three-quarters of the total gross fixed capital formation.

Sector-wise, the services industry led the high economic growth during NEP era. The share of services in total GDP increased significantly from the 1990s, reaching 57.6 per cent in 2010 (Figure 9.2). Gordon and Gupta (2005) described this as the 'services revolution'.

The most important driving force that supports the services revolution in India is the conspicuous growth of the software industry and IT-enabled services. The ICT software industry is a knowledge-intensive and highly export-oriented industry. Thanks to various policies of promotion, the software industry has recorded a 30 per cent annual growth rate since 1991. Especially remarkable growth has been recorded in exports of software, which account for about three-quarters of total revenue.[2]

Exports of IT software services in 2010–11 were worth US$55.5 billion and accounted for 12.4 per cent of the total current account receipts (GOI 2012: p. 133). Employment in the IT sector increased from 284,000 in 1999–2000 to 1,287,000 in 2005–06, an annual rate of 35 per cent (GOI 2007: 147). (However, this sector still employs less than 0.5 per cent of the Indian workforce.)

With the growth of a more prosperous middle class, there is a growing demand for high-value food items such as milk and milk products, eggs and chicken, and fruits and vegetables. A 'demand-driven, consumer-dominated transformation' is under way, and the backward linkage 'from plate to plough' is increasingly important (Reardon and Gulati 2008; Gulati 2010). This marks a break with the Indian past, where the plough decided the plate, and in part has been stimulated by the development of modern retailing (Mukherjee and Patel

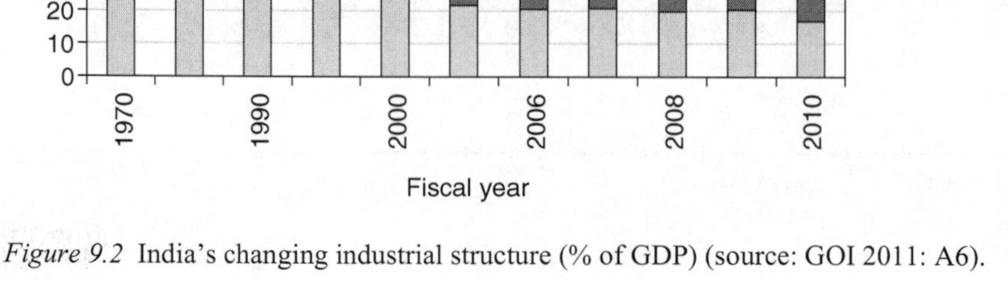

Figure 9.2 India's changing industrial structure (% of GDP) (source: GOI 2011: A6).

2005; Joseph and Soundararajan 2009). The emergence of modern retailing in cities is promoting a revolution in supply chains. New supply chains are involving the rural economy via direct procurement of vegetables and fruits or contract farming arrangement, and so on (Minten *et al.* 2009).

The Achilles heel of the Indian economy

However, the Indian high-growth experience, which is supported by the increasing savings of and investment from the private sector and the services revolution, exhibits serious vulnerabilities: growth of joblessness, underdevelopment of education, and deep-rooted poverty.

The Planning Commission was concerned about the decreasing growth rate of employment after the start of the NEP revealed by the results of the National Sample Survey Organisation 55th Round survey report *Employment and Unemployment Situation in India* (NSSO 2006). The annual employment growth decreased from 2.04 per cent in the period 1983 to 1993–94 to 0.98 per cent in the period 1993–94 to 1999–2000. The growth rate of services-sector employment decreased from 3.53 per cent to 2.42 per cent, that for the agricultural sector was −0.3 per cent and that for the manufacturing sector was stagnant at 2.05 per cent during the same period (Planning Commission 2001: 72). Elasticity of employment to GDP also conspicuously decreased, from 0.53 in the period 1977–78 to 1983 to 0.41 in the period 1983 to 1993–94, and to 0.15 in the period 1993–94 to 1999–2000 (ibid.: 71). The fact that the strong growth of the service sector could not generate enough employment created a big question mark as to the sustainability of the high Indian growth rate.

In the 1990s, there appeared a salient change of employment types. The total employment in 1999–2000 was about 397 million. Out of this, employment in the organized sector was 28.11 million, accounting for only 7 per cent of the total. The organized sector is composed of all public-sector establishments and all non-agricultural establishments in the private sector with ten or more workers. Of the 28.11 million organized-sector employees, 19.41 million were employed in the public sector. The growth rate of organized-sector employment was 1.20 per cent in the period 1983–84 to 1994–95, but it decreased to 0.53 per cent in the period 1994–95 to 1999–2000 (Planning Commission 2001: 59–60). This is called 'jobless growth' in India (Kannan and Raveendran 2009).

Since then, there have appeared two large-scale quinquennial survey reports on employment and unemployment: the National Sample Survey Organisation's 61st Round survey report (NSSO 2006) and its 66th Round survey report (NSSO 2011). So, we can trace the employment trends up to 2009–10. According to the NSSO's 61st survey, the employment growth rate increased from 1.57 per cent in the period 1993–94 to 1999–2000 to 2.48 per cent in the period 1999–2000 to 2004–05. But because the growth rate of the labour force was 2.54 per cent, which exceeds the employment growth rate, unemployment also increased, from 2.78 per cent in the period 1993–94 to 1999–2000 to 3.06 per cent in the period 1999–2000 to 2004–05 (GOI 2007: 14, 208–211) (Table 9.2).

Table 9.2 Employment and unemployment (by usual status)

	1983	*1993–94*	*1999–2000*	*2004–05*	*1983 to 1993–94*	*1993–94 to 1999–2000*	*1999–2000 to 2004–05*
		(in million)			*(Growth, per cent iper annum)*		
Labour force	277.34	343.56	377.88	428.37	2.08	1.6	2.54
Workforce	269.36	334.54	367.37	415.27	2.09	1.57	2.48
Number of unemployed	7.98	9.02	10.51	13.1	–	–	–
	(As a percentage of labour force)						
Unemployment rate	2.88	2.82	2.78	3.08	–	–	–

Source: GOI (2007: 208).

Figure 9.3 shows the change of employment per 1,000 workers from 1977–78 to 2009–10. In 2009–10, the employment ratio was 54.6 per cent for men and 22.8 per cent for women, and 39.2 per cent for the total. Compared with the same ratios for 1999–2000, men's employment had increased by 1.9 per cent but women's employment had decreased by 3.1 per cent and total employment had also decreased by 0.5 per cent. High growth rates did not generate employment at all. The overall employment ratio of 39.2 per cent in the year 2009–10 is the worst figure since 1977–78, when economic growth was much lower. The 'jobless growth' situation not only persists but is getting worse.

Indian labour markets are stratified by the education level of workers. Education level is positively related to income level, and poverty indices are negatively related to education level. Most Indian workers are still at the low education level and many are illiterate (Ghose 2004).

From the NSSO 66th Round survey *Employment and Unemployment Situation in India, 2009–2010* (NSSO 2011), we can get a rough indication of the education status of usually employed workers aged 15 years and above. Education level is classified into seven categories: (1) not literate, (2) literate and up to primary (from grade I to V), (3) middle (from grade VI to VIII, (4) secondary (from grade IX to X), (5) higher secondary (from grade XI to XII), (6) diploma certificate, and (7) graduate and above. In 2009–10, 28.3 per cent of rural males, 58.1 per cent of rural females, 11.5 per cent of urban males and 29.3 per cent of urban females were not literate. On the other hand, 4.3 per cent of rural males, 1.7 per cent of rural females, 21.1 per cent of urban males and 22.4 per cent of urban females were educated to graduate level or above in the same year (Table 9.3). From 1993–94 to 2009–10, in all categories, whether male or female, education level conspicuously went up. However, there is clearly a huge gap in education level between urban areas and rural areas, as well as between males and females. The only exception is the ratio for 'graduate and above' for urban areas, where the ratio for females is higher than that for males.

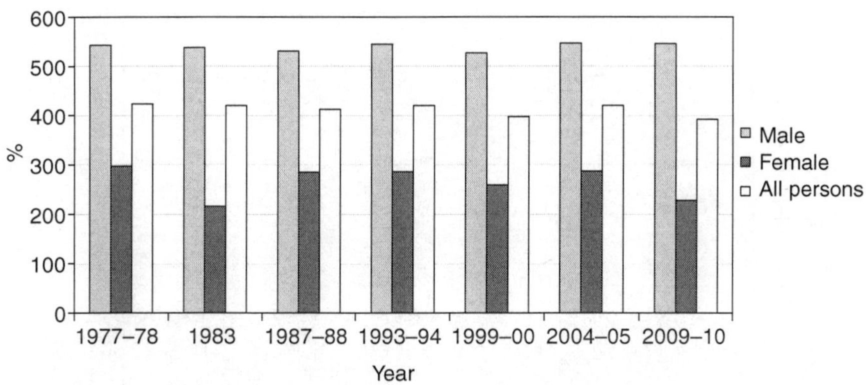

Figure 9.3 Number of persons employed per 1,000 persons according to usual status (source: NSSO 2006a: 76).

Table 9.3 Per 1,000 distribution of the usually employed of age 15 years and above by education category

	Male				*Female*			
	1993–94	*1999–00*	*2004–05*	*2009–10*	*1993–94*	*1999–00*	*2004–05*	*2009–10*
Rural								
Not literate	444	400	342	283	799	753	678	581
Literate and up to primary	294	274	296	283	138	151	181	227
Middle	134	161	180	197	37	57	80	105
Secondary	72	92	90	125	16	24	33	47
Higher secondary	31	41	44	61	6	7	13	19
Diploma/certificate	–	–	10	8	–	–	5	4
Graduate and above	25	32	38	43	5	7	10	17
All	1,000	1,000	1,000	1,000	1,000	1,000	1,000	1,000
Urban								
Not literate	185	161	132	115	483	437	376	293
Literate and up to primary	260	220	229	183	185	171	198	188
Middle	173	188	194	180	74	94	106	126
Secondary	153	169	149	176	78	87	69	82
Higher secondary	86	93	91	107	52	59	50	59
Diploma/certificate	–	–	36	28	–	–	36	30
Graduate and above	143	168	170	211	126	152	164	224
All	1,000	1,000	1,000	1,000	1,000	1,000	1,000	1,000

Source: NSSO (2011: 84).

How about poverty? The standard of minimum calorie intake settled by the Planning Commission's Expert Group on Estimation of Proportion and Number of Poor (Lakdawala Committee) in 1979 is still used as the basis of the official poverty estimate: the necessary calories per day for a man are 2,400 in the case of rural areas and 2,100 in the case of urban areas. The poverty line is decided by the estimated expenditure required to obtain these calorie intakes plus estimated expenditure on non-food items. According to these standards, the government of India (GOI) estimated the poverty ratio in 1999–2000 as 26.1 per cent (i.e. rural areas 27.1 per cent and urban areas 23.6 per cent) and the number of poor as 260.3 million (i.e. rural areas 193.2 million and urban areas 67.1 million) (Table 9.4; GOI 2003: 213). If this is so, the poverty ratio had dramatically reduced from 36.0 per cent in 1993–94 to 26.1 per cent in 1999–2000.

However, the estimated poverty ratio for 1999–2000 has been subject to several doubts and criticisms (Datt and Ravallion 2002; Deaton and Drèze 2002; Sen and Himanshu 2004a, b). The main thrust of these is related to the different methodology used for estimation. The 55th Round NSS survey on consumer expenditure used a 'mixed reference period', and this method is different from the previously used method, so that it is impossible to compare the results with previous data. The 61st Round survey on consumer expenditure collected data using a 'uniform reference period' that used to be applied before 1993–94.[3] So, if we ignore the data of 1999–2000 we can trace the change of poverty head-count ratio between 1993–94 and 2004–05 to some extent.

Using 61st Round NSS data on consumer expenditure, the Sengupta Commission Report (NCEUS 2007) made an interesting poverty estimate. It used the official poverty line and classified households into 'extremely poor' if their expenditure was less than 75 per cent of that constituting the poverty line, 'poor' if their expenditure was between 75 per cent and 100 per cent of the poverty line, 'marginal' if their expenditure was between 100 per cent and 125 per cent of poverty line, and 'vulnerable' if their expenditure was between 125 per cent and 200 per cent of the poverty line. Their results of its estimates show that the number of extremely poor was 69.7 million (6.4 per cent of the total population), poor 167.3 million (15.4 per cent of the total population), marginal 271.0 million (19.0 per

Table 9.4 Estimates of incidence of poverty in India

Year	*Poverty ratio (%)*			*Number of poor (million)*		
	Rural	*Urban*	*Combined*	*Rural*	*Urban*	*Combined*
1973–74	56.4	49.0	54.9	261.3	60.0	321.3
1977–78	53.1	45.2	51.3	264.3	64.6	328.9
1983	45.7	40.8	44.5	252.0	70.9	322.9
1987–88	39.1	38.2	38.9	231.9	75.2	307.1
1993–94	37.3	32.4	36.0	244.0	76.3	320.3
1999–2000	27.1	23.6	26.1	193.2	67.1	260.3

Source: GOI (2003: 213).

cent of the total population), vulnerable 392.0 million (36.9 per cent of the total population), middle-income 298.0 million (19.0 per cent of the total population) and high-income 43.7 million (4.0 per cent of the total population). And the commission asserted that if those ranging from the extreme poor to the vulnerable are called *aam aadmi* (common people), 76.7 per cent of the total population, 836.1 million people, fall into the category of *aam aadmi*. Their estimate seems to correspond well to common sense. (See also Sengupta *et al.* 2008.)

Transition from a supply-constrained economy to a demand-led economy

Economic crisis and the turning points of economic policy

The economic policy of India since independence has varied, with economic crises defining the turning points in 1957, 1961–62, 1965–66, 1974, 1979–80 and 1991. These crises were, among other things, balance of payments crises. The balance of payments crises of 1957 and 1961–62 during the Nehru era both resulted in the strengthening of economic regulation, especially strengthening of trade regulation. Conversely, in the case of the economic crises of 1965–66, 1974 and 1979–80 there appeared a new response that promoted economic liberalization. According to Bhagwati and Srinivasan (1975) the politico-economic crisis of 1965–66 led to a strengthening of regulation under the political pressures of the anti-US movement. Although the policy responses were different, the main reason for the balance of payment crises from 1957 to 1979–80 was shortage of food grain. On top of this, various exogenous factors such as war and oil crises aggravated the crisis. In case of the 1985 liberalization under Rajiv Gandhi and the politico-economic crisis of 1991, we cannot see the oft-repeated 'traditional pattern' whereby drought brings a shortage of food grain and a steep rise in prices, triggering a balance of payments crisis.

For the most part, the government responded to these crises either by strengthening economic regulation (up to 1966) or by promoting economic liberalization (since 1974). But there was no balance of payments crisis at the time when Rajiv Gandhi promoted economic liberalization in 1985, and the main reason for the balance of payments crisis in 1991 was not a food grain shortage. These facts suggest that something changed during the period from the late 1970s to early 1980s.

Turning points of economic growth in the long run

Deepak Nayyar (2006) suggests that in seeking turning points in Indian economic performance, it is not appropriate to evaluate them by focusing merely on the period since 1950; rather, they should be situated in a longer-run historical perspective starting during the colonial era.

The Indian economy stagnated in the colonial period. The most reliable estimate of economic growth rates from the colonial period up to today is that of Sivasubramonian (2000). According to his estimate, the growth rate of GDP from 1900–01 to 1946–47 was 0.93–1.05 per cent, and that of per capita GDP was 0.14–0.25 per cent. However, the growth rate of GDP from 1950–51 to 1964–65 substantially increased to 4.0 per cent and that of per capita GDP to 1.9 per cent. If we compare sectoral growth rates, in the colonial period the growth rate of the primary sector was 0.41–0.42 per cent, that of the secondary sector was 1.54–1.72 per cent and that of the tertiary sector was 1.72–1.73 per cent; but in the Nehru era, the growth rate of the primary sector increased to 2.6 per cent, that of the secondary sector to 6.8 per cent and that of the tertiary sector to 4.5 per cent. It is notable that not only did the growth rate of the primary sector increase sixfold compared to the colonial period, but also the growth rate of the secondary sector exceeded that of the tertiary sector (Table 9.5). Nayyar (2006) concluded that the most important structural break for the growth rate occurred in 1951–52. We can call this the first turning point of economic growth in modern Indian history. Nayyar continued by saying that the turning point in the growth trend since independence was *c.*1980, more than a decade before the 1991 economic liberalization. This is the second turning point of economic growth in modern Indian history. He divided the period from 1950–51 to 2004–05 into two sub-periods, 1950–51 to 1979–80 and 1980–81 to 2004–05, and estimated the growth rate of GDP as 3.5 per cent for the first period and 5.6 per cent for the second.

Using the more rigorous Bai and Perron method to identify structural breaks, which can estimate simultaneously multiple structural breaks in a series, Balakrishnan and Parameswaran (2007) concluded that a structural break in the growth rate of GDP occurred only once, in 1978–79. The factors that have accelerated the growth rate since 1978–79, they propose, have been acceleration of growth in the primary and services sectors; the growth rate of the manufacturing sector accelerated after the other sectors. This suggests that services-led growth started at least 12 years before 1991.

Nayyar, and Balakrishnan and Parameshwaran, made clear that it is undeniable that the most important turning point of economic growth in India occurred *c.*1950 and that the biggest turning point for economic growth was *c.*1980. These findings are valuable; however, we cannot read nuances of history merely by analysing the growth trend.

Table 9.5 Estimate of growth rates by Sivasubramonian

Sector	*1900–01 to 1946–47*		*1950–51 to 1964–65*
	1938–39 prices	*1948–49 prices*	*1948–49 prices*
Primary	0.42	0.41	2.6
Secondary	1.72	1.54	6.8
Tertiary	1.73	1.72	4.5
Total GDP	1.05	0.93	4.0
Per capita GDP	0.25	0.14	1.9

Source: Sivasubramonian (2000: 443, 565–566).

Transition from a supply-constrained economy to a demand-led economy

Development economics during 1950s and 1960s, using a broadly structuralist approach, reflected Indian development experience and, conversely, Indian development planners and economists were under the influence of structuralist development economics.[4] Among others, the 'economic development with unlimited supply of labour' idea of W. Arthur Lewis, the 'take-off' theory of W. W. Rostow, the 'big push' theory of P. N. Rosenstein-Rodan and the export pessimism of Hans Singer exerted a huge influence on planning during the Nehru era. For these development economists of the early period, 'turning point' meant a critical process or jumping-off point from the low-level income equilibrium. Rostow (1956) described this process as 'the take-off' from the traditional society, and he assumed that after the take-off, 'self-sustaining growth' could be attained. On the other hand, Lewis understood the turning point of the economy as the period when unlimited supply of labour vanished; after the turning point, real wages would rise in response to demand. Although Rostow's and Lewis's approaches are different, they shared a common understanding: both thought that capital scarcity is the most crucial factor leading to low-level equilibrium. Lewis (1954) regarded 'the central problem in the theory of development' as

> the process by which a community which was previously saving and investing 4 to 5 per cent of its national income or less, converts itself into an economy where voluntary saving is running at about 12 to 15 per cent of national income or more.

On the other hand, Rostow (1956) also regarded the most important definition of the take-off of the economy as 'a rise in the rate of productive investment from (say) 5 per cent or less to over 10 per cent of national income (or net national product)'. Both attached importance to capital accumulation (saving and investment) as the most crucial factor that made economic growth possible.

On the other hand, there was a big difference in their understanding of the role of agriculture in the development process. Rostow (1960) thought that a steep rise in agricultural production (an agricultural revolution) was a necessary precondition for take-off. He believed that for industrialization to be successful, industrialization alone was insufficient and that during the period of take-off, agriculture had to increase food supply to the industrial sector, expand the market for industrial goods and increase loanable funds to the modern sector. In contrast, Lewis thought that an increase of agricultural productivity in the traditional subsistence sector would increase the real wage rate in the modern capitalist sector and as a result would decrease profit (economic surplus) in the capitalist sector, and would ultimately hamper the possibility of economic development based on low-level wage labourers – that is, the unlimited supply of labour at subsistence-level wages.

Evaluating the Nehru–Mahalanobis development framework, Chakravarty (1987: 14) commented that it was better viewed as 'a variant of the Lewis model'. The variation relates, first, to the introduction of the two-sector model by Mahalanobis and, second, to the role in development that was assigned not only to capitalists but also to bureaucracy. Also, he pointed out that in the Nehru–Mahalanobis development framework, the possibility that domestic demand would constrain economic development was never considered. The Nehru–Mahalanobis development framework attached importance only to the supply-side constraints, a reflection of the supply-constrained economy during the Nehru era.

When, in that case, did the supply-constrained economy vanish? And what does 'the self-sustaining economy' after 'the take-off' or 'the turning point' look like? To investigate these issues, it is useful to examine some indicators such as savings to investment ratio, agricultural production and foreign exchange reserves.

Figure 9.4 shows the trend of gross domestic saving and gross fixed capital formation as per cent of GDP from 1950–51 to 2009–10. If the long-term incremental capital–output ratio is around 4 (Mohan 2008), then a 5 per cent growth rate can be attainable when the gross fixed capital formation reaches 20 per cent of GDP. And if we suppose that secular 5 per cent annual growth rate is the minimum necessary for take-off, then it was 1985 when the fixed capital formation exceeded 20 per cent. On the other hand, it was 1978 when the gross domestic saving rate exceeded 20 per cent. However, it fell to less than 20 per cent after that, and did not exceed 20 per cent again until 1987. So, we can say that it was between 1980 and 1985 that the Indian economy took off.

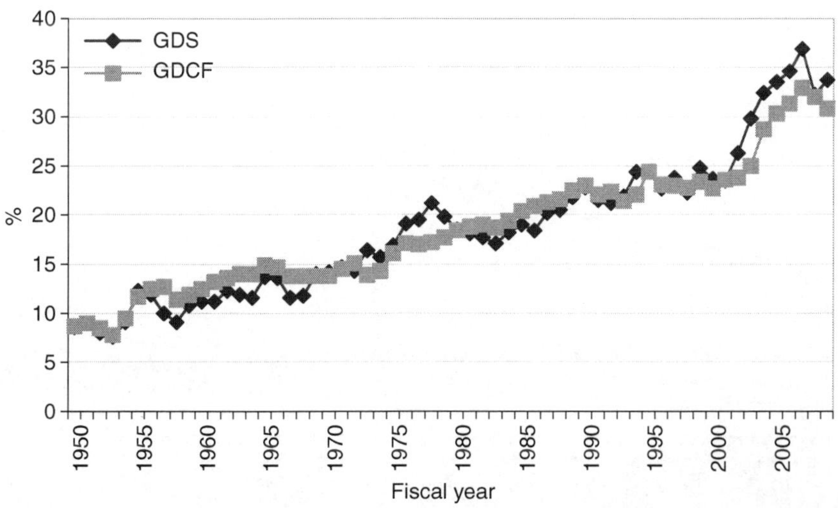

Figure 9.4 Gross domestic savings (GDS) and gross fixed capital formation (GDCF) as percentages of GDP (source: GOI 2011: A10).

Figure 9.5 shows the trend of net production and net imports of food grains from 1951 to 2009. India faced food grain shortages many times after independence, which in turn triggered economic crisis. Figure 9.5 shows that the net production of food grains exceeded 100 million tonnes in 1978, and that India became a net exporter of food grains in the same year. Since then, although net production and net imports have been fluctuating, we can say from the end of the 1970s onwards, the agricultural bottleneck for economic development had vanished.

Figure 9.6 shows the trend of foreign exchange reserves from 1950–51 to 2009–10. Foreign exchange reserves declined during the 1960s, increased from 1975–76 to 1979–80, decreased from 1980–81 to 1990–91, again conspicuously increased after 1991–92 and accelerated from 2001–02 to 2007–08. The foreign exchange bottleneck for economic development seems to have almost disappeared in the past decade. However, it is necessary to see foreign exchange reserves in relation to imports. Figure 9.7 shows the trend of the foreign exchange reserves/imports ratio. Without exception, when this ratio decreased to less than 0.4, a balance of payments crisis occurred: ten consecutive years from 1959–60 to 1969–70, three consecutive years from 1973–74 to 1975–76, three consecutive years from 1981–82 to 1983–84, and four consecutive years from 1987–88 to 1990–91. Especially in 1964–65 and 1989–90, this ratio decreased to below 0.2. This suggests that the years 1964–65 and 1989–90 were when the most severe balance of payments crises occurred. On the other hand, in seven consecutive years from 1950–51 to 1956–57, soon after independence, two years

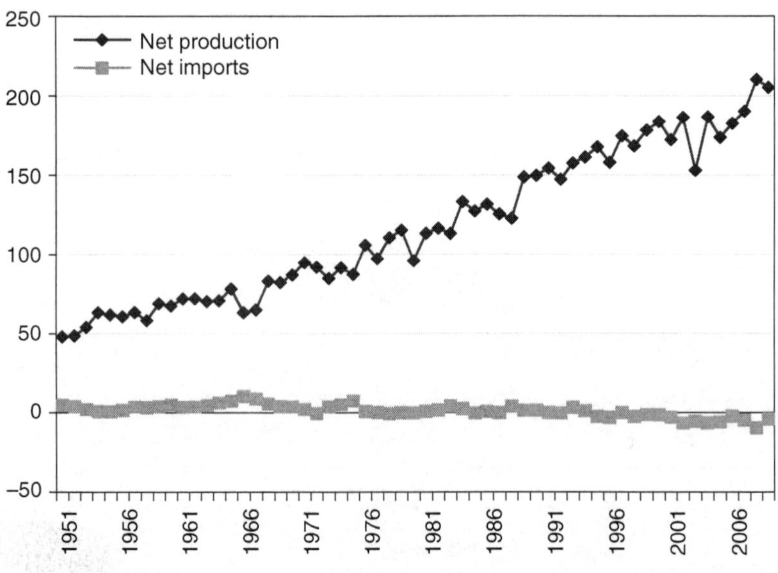

Figure 9.5 Net production and net imports of food grains (million tonnes) (source: GOI 2011: A22).

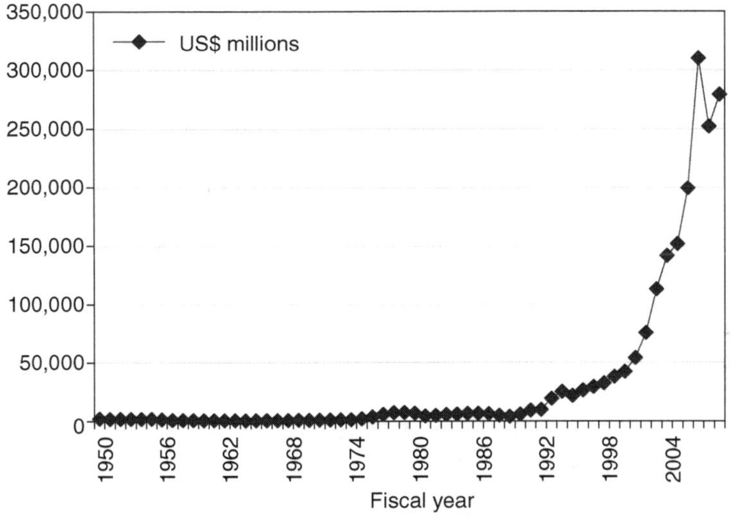

Figure 9.6 Trend of foreign exchange reserves (US$ million) (source: GOI 2011: A70).

from 1977–78 to 1978–79, two years from 1993–94 to 1994–95, and ten consecutive years following 2000–01, this ratio exceeded 0.8, so that India was free from foreign exchange crises. The fluctuations are fairly large, so the secular trend is not so clear, but this ratio has exceeded 0.7 since 1993. Thus, we can say that around 1993 the Indian economy was freed from the foreign exchange bottleneck.

Turning points in terms of economic policy, economic growth and economic structure do not necessarily occur simultaneously, although turning points in these three dimensions have some close connections. It is quite natural that turning points in terms of economic policy do not coincide with those of economic growth. It takes time to implement a new economic policy. There are time lags needed to set up new institutions or organizations and to adjust markets to realize a new economic policy. On top of this, economic policy is one of the important factors that influence economic growth, but surely not the only one. Also, it is clear that turning points of economic policy do not coincide with those of economic structure. Because change of economic structure is a long-run historical process, we cannot specify the date when it occurs. However, it is clear that from the late 1970s onwards, India gradually overcame the supply-side shortages of the 1950s and 1960s, and as economic liberalization progressed during the 1980s and 1990s, India become a more and more demand-led economy. It was the green revolution that brought the beginning of this transformation and, after that, the service revolution, followed by increasing income, savings and capital formation.

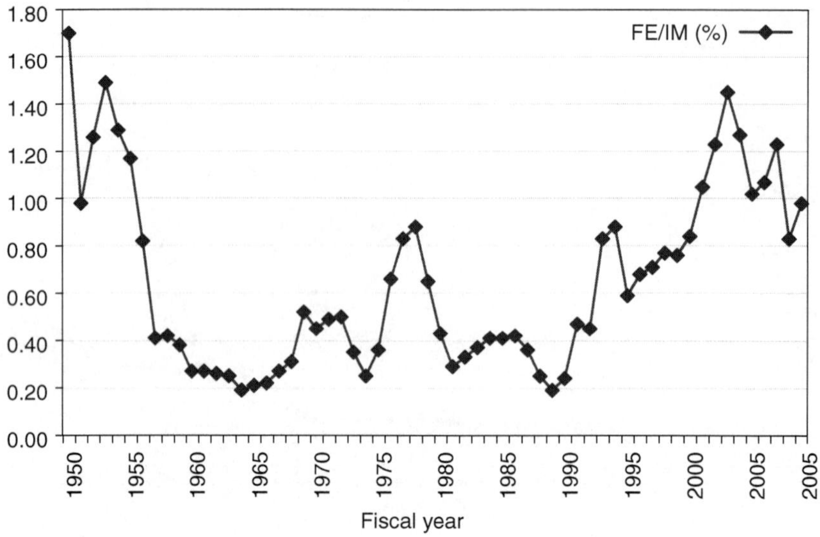

Figure 9.7 Foreign exchange reserves/imports ratio (%) (source: GOI 2011: A70, A81).

Impacts of Indian economic growth

So far, I have outlined some salient features of Indian economic performance since the beginning of the liberalization in 1991. What kind of implications can we draw from these features? Can the Indian experience of strong economic growth be a new model of development?

The idiosyncratic nature of India's economic development process

The first issue to be discussed is whether India's economic growth is sustainable or not. The first and foremost characteristic of India's economic growth is that it is a service sector-led growth, which can be contrasted with the situation in the East Asian countries, including China. In other words, the share of manufacturing in GDP has not been growing smoothly. The share of the secondary industries in GDP was 21.6 per cent in 1980–81, 24.5 per cent in 1990–91 and 24.9 per cent in 2000–01, only a minimal increase. It was mainly the declining share of the primary sector that resulted in the substantial increase in the share of service activities. This type of changing industrial structure is quite different from the experience of Japan, South Korea, Taiwan or China. In those cases, the industrial structure developed from primary to secondary and then tertiary activities, the same pattern as is found in industrial countries of today, as Colin Clark (1957) indicated. However, India has not followed this development sequence. In terms of output, India's development has followed a leapfrogging pattern that jumped from primary activities to knowledge-intensive IT service industries without there being a sufficient development of manufacturing industries.

This development sequence of India is just the reverse of 'the natural course of events' that Adam Smith described. If we look back at the economic history of India since independence, the economic planning of the Nehru era, which gave priority to public investment in the heavy industries, as suggested by the Mahalanobis growth model, was also the reverse of 'the natural course of events'. The time is different, but both cases of development experience – that of the Nehru era and the service-led growth since the 1990s – share a common character: the elite-oriented character of Indian society. There are the same vulnerabilities such as weak employment generation, unresolved poverty and widening income disparity.

However, we should not jump to the conclusion that India's ongoing economic growth is unsustainable. In the substantially globalizing world economy, as the experiences of the 'East Asian miracle', including that of China, tell us, economic growth heavily depends on foreign capital, and foreign markets do not simply result in a dependent development but rather make possible a sustainable high rate of growth.

It is true that Indian manufacturing industries lost international competitiveness under the long-lasting import-substituting industrialization strategy, which was continued after the Nehru era. The quality of products was bad and there was almost no technological innovation in many manufacturing activities. In spite of this, some Indian companies in some industrial areas are increasing their exports and international competitiveness under the new economic environments that were created from the 1990s onwards.[5] We can say that Indian companies were able to attain 'know-why' – that is, basic technological development capabilities – when they were under the long-lasting import-substituting industrialization period in a closed economy (Lall 1985: chs 8–10). Because of this, Indian companies could easily cope with a sudden change of management environment under economic liberalization.

The emergence of Indian multinationals (MNCs) is also remarkable. Foreign direct investment from India has increased sharply since 2000. Most of the Indian FDI takes the form of mergers and acquisitions (M&A) of manufacturing companies in developed countries. Among the big-deal M&A are the acquisition of Corus by Tata Steel in 2007 ($12.1 billion), the acquisition of Noveris by Hindalco in 2007 ($6 billion) and the acquisition of Jaguar Land Rover by Tata Motors in 2008 ($2.5 billion). These are the results of the international strategy of Indian companies: to try to enter the world economy at a stroke by acquiring brands and technology of the developed companies. It is noteworthy that in the case of India, the main agents of M&A are big private companies. In China, by contrast, the main agents of M&A are state corporations.

IT software and information technology-based business process outsourcing (ITES/BPO) services are knowledge-intensive industries carried out by the elite, and the numbers who can reap benefits from these industries are limited. In terms of employment generation and the nurturing of manufacturing industries with international competitiveness, it is important for India to link these industries with domestic manufacturing industries. Using panel data relating to 148 manufacturing industries, Banga and Goldar (2007) show that the contribution of services to the growth of manufacturing industries dramatically increased from 0.8 per cent in the 1980s to 25.5 per cent in the 1990s. As this study shows, the collaboration between manufacturing industries and services industries seems to have already been progressing. However, such manufacturing industries as have international competitiveness are still limited to a part of certain capital-intensive or knowledge-intensive industries. If, and only if, these collaborations further extend to labour-intensive industries, then 'the Indian growth' could be a new development model. However, for this to be realized, the development of infrastructure and educational as well as health revolutions, especially in backward states, are necessary preconditions.[6]

Political systems and economic growth

Deepak Lal once asserted that democratic government is the source of irrational economic policy because it is compelled to conciliate competing interest groups, and concluded that 'a courageous, ruthless and perhaps undemocratic government is required to ride roughshod over these newly-created special interest groups' (1983: 33). This is quite out of order for the world's biggest democratic country, India. However, Lal's observation seems to fit well with the high growth experiences of some of the East Asian countries, such as South Korea, Singapore and China.

Since then, Przeworski and Limongi (1993), who conducted research on the relation between political system and economic growth, summarized by saying that 'the critics argue that dictatorships are better at mobilizing savings; the defenders argue that democracies are better at allocating investment. Both arguments can be true but, the statistical evidence is inconclusive and studies producing it are all seriously flawed', and concluded that 'the simple answer to the question is that we do not know whether democracy fosters or hinders economic growth'. Robert Barro (1996) came to more nuanced conclusions. Analysing a group of about 100 countries from 1960 to 1990, he asserted that an increase in the standard of living tends to generate a gradual rise in democracy in such countries as Chile, Korea, Taiwan, Spain and Portugal. In contrast, democracies that arise without prior economic development tend not to last, as seen in many African countries, such as Malawi, Mali, Mozambique, Benin, Zambia, Niger, the Central African Republic, Guinea-Bissau and Congo. He suggested there is a non-linear relationship between democracy and standard of living, and asserted that 'if economic freedom can be established in a poor country, then growth would be encouraged, and the country would tend eventually to become more democratic on its own'. Then the United Nations Development Programme noted that

> while the economic performance of dictatorships varies from terrible to excellent, democracies tend to cluster in the middle. The fastest-growing

countries have typically been dictatorships, but no democracy has ever performed as badly as the worst dictatorships.... Thus democracy appears to prevent the worst outcomes, even if it does not guarantee the best ones.

(UNDP 2002: box 2.4)

India's combination of high economic growth and a democratic political system since 1990s onwards does not fit well with any of the analytical frameworks that previous studies have presented. It challenges the claim that authoritarianism along East Asian lines is a precondition for rapid economic development. It also challenges the Barro-type notion that 'industrialization should precede democracy'. Although it is true that there is some relationship between politics and economic performance, India's experience shows that their relationship is much more nuanced and complicated than we tend to think.

Notes

1 As Chakravarty pointed out, the agricultural sector was recognized as 'a bargain sector' (1987: 94n). This expression was coined by S. R. Sen, then an agricultural adviser to the Planning Commission, and it meant 'a sector with large unexploited potential which can provide the requisite surplus with relatively low investment and in a comparatively short time' (Sen 1962: p. 3).

2 However, we must take care to note that, unlike all other economic activities, GDP in this sector is not measured by value added but by gross value of output as given by figures provided by the industry association NASSCOM.

3 Data from the uniform reference period are based on a 30-day recall period for all food and non-food items. On the other hand, data from the mixed reference period use both the past 7 days and 30 days recall period for food and alcohol and the 365-day recall period for five non-food items such as clothing, footwear, durable goods, education, and medical expenditure (institutional).

4 The standard text of development economics in those days was Agarwala and Singh's *Economics of Underdevelopment*, which is packed with papers by the structuralist economists.

5 Representative cases are Tata Motors and Mahindra & Mahindra in the automobile sector, Bajaj Auto in the two-wheeler sector, Bharat Forge, Brakes India, Sundaram Fasteners in the automobile components sector, and SAIL (a public-sector company) and Tata Steel in the steel sector.

6 The Cabinet approved the National Manufacturing Policy (NMC) on 28 October 2011. The NMC seeks to enhance the share of manufacturing in the GDP to 25 per cent within a decade and create 100 million jobs. The policy envisages large integrated industrial townships, national investment and manufacturing zones (NIMZs) with state-of-the-art infrastructure, a lesser regulatory and compliance burden, faster clearances and fiscal incentives. This is a welcome move, but to make this idea meaningful it is necessary to enhance the education and health status of the common people.

References

Agarwala, A. N. and Singh, S. P. (eds) (1958) *The Economics of Underdevelopment*, London: Oxford University Press.

Ahluwalia, M. S. (2002) 'Economic reforms in India since 1991: has gradualism worked?', *Journal of Economic Perspectives*, 16 (3): 67–88.

Balakrishnan, P. and Parameswaran, M. (2007) 'Understanding economic growth in India: a prerequisite', *Economic and Political Weekly*, 14 July: 2915–2922.

Banga, R. and Goldar, B. (2007) 'Contribution of services to output growth and productivity in Indian manufacturing: pre- and post-reforms', *Economic and Political Weekly*, 30 June: 2769–2777.

Barro, R. (1996) 'Democracy and growth', *Journal of Economic Growth*, 1: 1–27.

Bhagwati, J. N. and Srinivasan, T. N. (1975) *Foreign Trade Regimes and Economic Development: India*, New York: Columbia University Press.

Chakravarty, S. (1987) *Development Planning: The Indian Experience*, Oxford: Clarendon Press.

Clark, C. (1957) *The Conditions of Economic Progress*, London: Macmillan

Datt, G. and Ravallion, M. (2002) 'Has India's post-reform economic growth left the poor behind?', *Journal of Economic Perspectives*, 16 (3): 89–108.

Deaton, A. and Drèze, J. (2002) 'Poverty and inequality in India: a re-examination', *Economic and Political Weekly*, 7 September: 3729–3748

Ghose, A. K. (2004) 'The employment challenge in India', *Economic and Political Weekly*, 27 November: 5106–5116.

GOI (Government of India) (2003) *Economic Survey 2002–03*, New Delhi: GOI.

GOI (Government of India) (2007) *Economic Survey 2006–07*, New Delhi: GOI.

GOI (Government of India) (2011) *Economic Survey 2010–11*, New Delhi: GOI.

GOI (Government of India) (2012) *Economic Survey 2011–12*, New Delhi: GOI.

Gordon, J. and Gupta, P. (2005) 'Understanding India's services revolution', in W. Tseng and D. Cowen (eds) *India's and China's Recent Experience with Reform and Growth*, Basingstoke, UK: Palgrave Macmillan and IMF.

Gulati, A. (2010) 'Accelerating agricultural growth: moving from farming to value chain', in S. Acharya and R. Mohan (eds) *India's Economy: Performance and Challenges*, New Delhi: Oxford University Press.

Joseph, M. C. and Soundararajan, N. (2009) *Retail in India: A Critical Assessment*, ICRIER, New Delhi: Academic Foundation.

Kannan, K. P. and Raveendran, G. (2009) 'Growth sans employment: a quarter century of jobless growth in India's organised manufacturing', *Economic and Political Weekly*, 7 March: 80–91.

Lal, D. (1983) *The Poverty of 'Development Economics'*, London: Institute of Economic Affairs.

Lall, S. (1985) *Multinationals, Technology and Exports*, Basingstoke, UK: Macmillan.

Lewis, A. (1954) 'Economic development with unlimited supplies of labour', *The Manchester School*, May: 400–449. Reprinted in A. N. Agarwala and S. P. Singh (eds) (1958) *The Economics of Underdevelopment*, London: Oxford University Press.

Minten, B., Reardon, T. and Vandeplas, A. 2009. *Linking Urban Consumers and Rural Farmers in India: A Comparison of Traditional and Modern Food Supply Chains*, IFPRI Discussion Paper 00883, New Delhi Office.

Mohan, R. (2008) 'Growth record of the Indian economy, 1950–2008: a story of sustained savings and investment', *Economic and Political Weekly*, 10 May: 373–397.

Mukherjee, M. and Patel, N. (2005) *FDI in Retail Sector: India*, ICRIER, New Delhi: Academic Foundation.

Nayyar, D. (2006) 'Economic growth in independent India: lumbering elephant or running tiger?', *Economic and Political Weekly*, 15 April: 1451–1458.

NCEUS (National Commission for Enterprises in the Unorganised Sector) (2007) *Report on Conditions of Work and Promotion of Livelihood in the Unorganised Sector*, New Delhi: Government of India.

NSSO (National Sample Survey Organisation) (2006) *Employment and Unemployment Situation in India, 2004–2005 (Part 1)*, New Delhi: Government of India.

NSSO (2011) *Employment and Unemployment Situation in India, 2009–10* (NSS 66th Round), New Delhi: Government of India.

Planning Commission (2001) *Report of the Task Force on Employment and Opportunities*, New Delhi: Academic Foundation, 2002.

Przeworski, A. and Limongi, F. (1993) 'Political regimes and economic growth', *Journal of Economic Perspectives*, 7 (3): 51–69.

Reardon, T. and Gulati, A. (2008) 'The rise of supermarkets and their implications: international experiences relevant for India', February, IFPRI Discussion Paper 00752, New Delhi Office.

Rostow, W. W. (1956) 'The take-off into self-sustained growth', *Economic Journal*, 66 261: 25–48. Reprinted in A. N. Agarwala and S. P. Singh (eds) (1958) *The Economics of Underdevelopment*, London: Oxford University Press.

Rostow, W. W. (1960) *The Stages of Economic Growth: A Non-Communist Manifesto*, Cambridge: Cambridge University Press.

Sen, A. and Himanshu (2004a) 'Poverty and inequality in India – I', *Economic and Political Weekly*, 18 September: 4247–4263.

Sen, A. and Himanshu (2004b) 'Poverty and inequality in India – II: Widening disparities during the 1990s', *Economic and Political Weekly*, 25 September: 4361–4375.

Sen, S. R. (1962) *The Strategy for Agricultural Development and Other Essays on Economic Policy and Planning*, London: Asia Publishing House.

Sengupta, A., Kannan, K. P. and Raveendran, G. (2008) 'India's common people: who are they, how many are they and how do they live?', *Economic and Political Weekly*, 15 March: 49–63.

Sivasubramonian, S. (2000) *The National Income of India in the Twentieth Century*, New Delhi: Oxford University Press.

Tomlinson, B. R. (1998) *The New Cambridge History of India: The Economy of Modern India, 1860–1970*, New Delhi: Foundation Books.

UNDP (United Nations Development Programme) (2002) *Human Development Report 2002: Deepening Democracy in a Fragmented World*, Oxford: Oxford University Press.

Index

Page numbers in *italics* denote tables, those in **bold** denote figures.